D1691420

BAE SYSTEMS
Advanced Technology Centres
Sowerby

CAT:	1016068
CLASS:	658.5 BER
HELD:	Alanbrook Library
Order	Price
Copy No	Date

R&D Management

R&D Management

Managing Projects and New Products
New revised edition

S. A. BERGEN

Basil Blackwell

Copyright © S. A. Bergen 1990

First published 1986

This edition, revised and updated
First published 1990.

Basil Blackwell Ltd
108 Cowley Road, Oxford, OX4 1JF, UK

Basil Blackwell, Inc.
3 Cambridge Center
Cambridge, Massachusetts 02142, USA

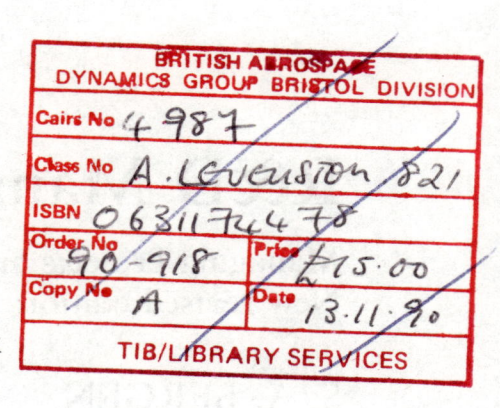

All rights reserved. Except for the quotation of short passages for
the purposes of criticism and review, no part of this publication may
be reproduced, stored in a retrieval system, or transmitted, in any
form or by any means, electronic, mechanical, photocopying, recording or
otherwise, without the prior permission of the publisher.

Except in the United States of America, this book is sold subject to the
condition that it shall not, by way of trade or otherwise, be lent, re-sold,
hired out, or otherwise circulated without the publisher's prior consent
in any form of binding or cover other than that in which it is published
and without a similar condition including this condition being imposed
on the subsequent purchaser.

British Library Cataloguing in Publication Data

A CIP catalogue record for this book is available
from the British Library

Library of Congress Cataloging in Publication Data

Bergen, S A.
R&D management: managing projects and
new products/S. A. Bergen.
—New rev. ed.
   p.   cm.
Includes bibliographical references
ISBN 0–631–17447–8
1. Research, Industrial – Management.   I. R and D management.
II. Title.   III. Title: R&D management.
T175.5.B47   1990
658.5'7–dc 20   90–469 CIP

Typeset in 10½ on 12pt Sabon
by Hope Services (Abingdon) Ltd
Printed in Great Britain by TJ Press Ltd, Padstow, Cornwall

Contents

List of Figures	xi
List of Tables	xiii
Preface	xv
Acknowledgements	xvii

1 Introduction

Functional management	1
Project management	1
The engineer's contribution	2
Engineering and management	4
Company functions	4
Functional interfaces	7
The format of the book	8
References	8
Further reading	8

2 Product strategy

Gap analysis	9
Strategic planning	10
Break-even analysis	12
The marketing function	13
Market/product analysis	14
Multi-dimensional screening	16
R&D resource planning	20
Time and meetings	22
Review	25
References	26
Further reading	26

3 Budgets and accounts

The accounts function	27
Product cash flow	27
What does the accountant do?	29
Company capital	30

Profit and loss account　32
Financial analysis　34
Cash flow analysis　34
Ratio analysis　35
Bookkeeping　38
Marginal costing　39
Standard costing　40
Project budget　42
The R&D budget　42
Review　46
Further reading　46
Appendix 3.1 Double entry bookkeeping　46

4 Project selection

Ranking project proposals　50
Project profile　52
Project merit number　53
Investment analysis　54
Discounted cash flow　56
Review　59
References　59
Further reading　59

5 Uncertainty, risk and decision

Assessment of risk　60
Prior probability　60
Posterior probability　61
Decisions　63
Cumulative density function　64
Decision trees　65
Cost of information　67
Review　69
References　71
Further reading　71

6 Project planning

The product loop　72
Engineering planning　74
Morton's rule　74
The Gantt chart　76
Critical path method　77
Network dummies　78
PERT – Project evaluation and review technique　80

	Research planning diagram	82
	Slip chart	85
	Review	86
	References	86
	Further reading	87
	Appendix 6.1 CPM and PERT exercise	87
7	**The R&D/production interface**	
	The post-development gap	88
	The product structure tree	89
	The 'Gozinto' chart	90
	Operation process chart	92
	Statistical quality control	92
	Design limits	95
	Sample size	96
	Confidence limits	97
	Sampling plan	98
	Maturity of technology	100
	The make or buy decision	101
	Value engineering	104
	Review	111
	References	112
	Further reading	112
	Appendix 7.1 The make or buy decision – worked examples	112
8	**R&D/production relationships**	
	Methodology	116
	Operations by country	117
	Projects by country	123
	Variable correlations within countries	125
	Adherence to programme	129
	Discussion	131
	Review	132
	References	132
	Further reading	132
9	**Contracts**	
	Conditions for successful contracts	133
	Legal definition of contract	134
	Form of contract	134
	The learning curve	135
	Specification	135
	Documentation	136

viii *Contents*

Drafting a contract	137
Incentives	138
The quotation	140
Review	141
References	141
Further reading	141

10 Organization and control

Project life cycle	142
Management by discipline or project	143
Matrix organization	144
Resource allocation	147
The project leader/manager	151
Self-test questionnaire	153
Management relationships	154
Leadership styles	155
Objective setting	156
Review	159
References	160
Further reading	160
Appendix 10.1 Compiling self-test scores	160

11 Communication and structure

Communication exercises	162
Communication structure	164
Feedforward structure	165
Structure development	166
Organizational structure	169
Differentiations	170
First language effect	171
Feedback vesus feedforward in project management	172
Review	176
References	176
Further reading	176

12 Computers in R&D

PC planning systems	180
Review	183
Reference	183
Further reading	184

13 Motivating project teams

Management theory	185
The Hawthorne experiments	185
Transactional analysis	186
Motivation	191
Contingency model	192
Review	193
References	193
Further reading	193

14 Failures and successes

The EMI scanner	194
Discussion	197
Review	198
References	198
Further reading	198

15 Creativity in R&D

Discontinuity	199
Cusp catastrophe	200
Butterfly catastrophe	203
Bias factors	204
Smoothing and splitting factors	205
Discussion	206
Review	207
References	207
Further reading	208

16 Idea generation

Attributes	210
Generic need assessment	211
Differing needs assessment	212
Matrix analysis	213
Scenario analysis	213
Group techniques	215
Miscellaneous techniques	216
Brainstorming	218
Synectics	218
Gordon method	219
Input–output technique	219

	Morphological analysis	220
	Sequence–attribute modifications matrix	221
	Kepner–Tregoe method	221
	Managing group creativity	222
	Review	223
	References	223
	Further reading	223
17	**Synthetic case study**	
	The Pyro Instrument Company Limited	224
	Exhibits in Pyro Instrument Co. Ltd case	226
	Appendix 17.1 The Pyro Instrument Co. Ltd case	229
18	**Project management game**	
	TOWER-8 © S. A. Bergen 1984	233
	The project	234
	TOWER-8 program listing	237
	Appendix 18.1 Contract conditions	241
Glossary		242
Index		247

List of Figures

Figure		Page
1.1	Company functions	5
2.1	Gap analysis	10
2.2	Strategic planning	11
2.3	Break-even analysis	13
2.4	Market analysis	15
2.5	Market/product analysis	16
2.6	Resource planning	21
3.1	Product cash flow	28
3.2	Company financial structure	30
4.1	Project profile	52
5.1	Combined probabilities	62
5.2	Cumulative density function	64
5.3	Project decision tree	65
5.4	Test market influence	69
5.5	Test market proposal	70
6.1	Product loop	73
6.2	Engineering planning	75
6.3	Gantt chart	76
6.4	Critical path method	78
6.5	Dummy activities	79
6.6	Gantt–CPM	80
6.7	PERT symbol	81
6.8	PERT network	81
6.9	Research planning diagram	83
6.10	RPD presentation	84
6.11	Slip chart	85
7.1	Product structure tree	89
7.2	Gozinto chart	91
7.3	Process chart	92
7.4	Frequency distribution	93
7.5	Standard deviation	94
7.6	Sample size and standard deviation	96
7.7	Sampling plan	98

7.8	Process control chart	100
7.9	The make of buy decision	103
7.10	Air control valve	108
7.11	Redesigned air valve	111
9.1	Incentive scheme	139
10.1	Project life cycle	143
10.2	Matrix structure	145
10.3	Leadership styles	156
11.1	Communiction exercise 1	163
11.2	Communiction exercise 2	164
11.3	Structure presentation	167
11.4	Communication exercise 3	169
11.5	Organizational structure	170
11.6	Feedback and feedforward	173
13.1	Parent	187
13.2	Child	188
13.3	Adult	189
13.4	Transactions	190
15.1	The cusp catastrophe	201
15.2	The butterfly catastrophe	203
15.3	Positive cultural bias	205
15.4	Negative cultural bias	205
15.5	Splitting and smoothing factors	206
17.1	Process instrumentation markets	227
17.2	Cost structure of Pyro Co. Ltd	228

List of Tables

Table		Page
2.1	Market and product strategy	17
2.2	An illustration of the multi-dimensional screen	19
3.1	Cash flow budget	35
3.2	Capital and revenue accounts	39
3.3	Marginal costing	40
3.4	Standard cost structure	41
3.5	Project budget	43
3.6	R&D budget	45
4.1	Project checklist	51
4.2	Project merit number	53
4.3	Hypothetical investments	55
4.4	Payback period	55
4.5	Proceeds per unit outlay	56
4.6	Present value at 6%	57
4.7	Present value at 30%	58
4.8	DCF yield	58
4.9	Summary of rankings	59
5.1	Additional information	61
5.2	Test market indication	68
6.1	Critical path method	77
7.1	Maturity of technology	101
7.2	Cost analysis	108
7.3	Function/cost analysis	109
7.4	Function/cost analysis (new design)	110
8.1	Operations management variables	116
8.2	Project management variables	118
8.3	Operations variables – means by country	123
8.4	Project variables – means by country	124
8.5	Correlations between project technical success and the independent variables	127
8.6	Correlations between adherence to programme and the independent variables	128
10.1	New product matrix	148

10.2	Resource allocation	150
10.3	Project leader roles	152
10.4	Project leader ambiguities	153
10.5	Project relationships	155
10.6	Objective setting	157
11.1	Communication structure	166
11.2	Element specification	167
11.3	Structured transmission	168
11.4	Differentiations	171
13.1	Contingency leadership model	192
14.1	Financial analysis	196
14.2	Time lags	197
16.1	Morphological analysis	220
16.2	SAMM technique	221
16.3	Kepner–Tregoe method	222
17.1	Investment in instrumentation (£m)	229
17.2	UK R&D expenditure	229

Preface

Since the first volume of this book was published, undergraduate courses on R&D have built up useful lectures on manufacturing skills and management issues. Companies still do not go far enough in providing young physicists and engineers with insight into the wide range of knowledge required to bring together all functions that together comprise R&D.

This edition retains several chapters dealing with the essential relationships between development, manufacturing and sales. Product strategy and selection compatible with the corporate plan; dealing with uncertainty and risk; organizing and control of projects; team motivation; communication and structure; and quotation and contracts are retained. An aim of the book is to present both formal techniques and principles allied to the human aspects of management.

The additional chapters include a Catastrophe Theory method of understanding the development of new products and accounts from American professors of methods of defining and developing new products. This last chapter summarizes published idea-generation techniques relevant to a wide range of companies and groups them in five classes so that they can be easily considered. There is also a brief chapter on the complex reasons for failures and successes in developing new products.

The book includes a program listing for a microcomputer game simulating many of the real-life aspects of project management.

S. A. Bergen

Acknowledgements

Thanks are due to the following copyright owners who have permitted the use of published material: Engineering Industries Training Board for Figure 7.10, Tables 7.2, 7.3, 7.4 from their booklet *Value Engineering*; John Gooch, Brunel University, for the Self-test Questionnaire in Chapter 10; the Longman Group for Tables 4.1 and 4.2, Figures 2.6 and 4.1 from *Managing Technological Innovation* by Brian Twiss published 1982; The Macmillan Company for Tables 4.3 through 4.9 from *The Capital Budgeting Decision* by H. Bierman and S. Smidt, published 1964; Midlands Consultants Publishers for Figure 3.2 from *Hardy Heating Co.* by Graham Ray published 1968 by the BBC; Professor P. G. Moore for Figures 5.1 through 5.5 and Tables 5.1 and 5.2 from *The Anatomy of Decisions*, Penguin 1976; Prentice-Hall Inc. for Figure 2.2 from *Management* by James A. F. Stoner published 1978 and for Figure 10.3 from *Management of Organisational Behaviour* by Paul Hersey and Keneth Blanchard published 1977; Professor D. S. Pugh for Table 13.1 from *Writers on Organisations*, Penguin 1984; and John Wiley & Sons Inc. for Figures 7.2, 7.3, and 7.7 from *Modern Production Control* by Elwood S. Buffa published 1983.

The author is indebted to Mrs R. Miyajima and Professor C. P. McLaughlin for collecting the raw data on Japan and the USA (Chapter 8).

1 Introduction

Management is the process of planning, organising, leading and controlling the efforts of organisational members and the use of other organisational resources in order to achieve stated organisational goals.

This definition (Stoner, 1978) covers the most important aspects of any field of management, from first line supervision to the top management of a multinational corporation, in any field of endeavour. There are several forms of management at all levels, each with its own characteristics and much has been written about most of them. The broadest practical division is into functional management and project management and this book is about the latter. There are two reasons for this. The first is that the book is written for engineers; project management is for many the first form of management they encounter and the first form to which they are appointed. The second is that teaching on the subject in engineering courses has not always prepared engineers adequately for this progression.

Functional Management

Functional management at any level is concerned with the running of an organization in being, that is charged with providing on-going services of a specified nature in an economic manner for as long as the company is in business. By the nature of his responsibilities and accountability to his superiors, the manager wishes it to operate on a minimum variety basis. This has benefits in reduction of training, creation of competence through experience and reduction of day-to-day supervision. These features represent economic gains.

Project Management

Project management is concerned with achieving a specific goal in a given time using resources available for that period only. A project is a

2 Introduction

bounded, as distinct from an on-going, activity, in terms of time and resources. Since a given project is very rarely repeated, project management is the business of managing variety; benefits tend to flow from the effective exploitation rather than the reduction thereof.

Experience of the realities of management in a specific organization is needed to develop judgement and practice in the relevant skills. What a book can do is to present current thinking on the subject in a logical pattern in language familiar to the reader, so that the concepts of project management are no longer foreign. While unable to solve the reader's specific problems, a book can provide tools and concepts that help the individual to tackle them systematically and with greater insight. The same information will help members of a project team to understand what is going on, and why, strengthening their contribution and going some way to prepare them for the project management role when it comes their way.

The eminent scientist and journalist, Lord Ritchie Calder (1963), defined in another context the added ingredient that distinguishes a good engineer from a good engineering project manager:

> The basic scientists are the 'Makers Possible', the technologists are the 'Makers to Happen', the technicians are the 'Makers to Work' ... the commercial scientists are the 'Makers to Pay'.

It is a reasonable expectation that many more developments and innovations would have achieved commercial as well as technological success if the commercial scientists had a more profound understanding of the problems and achievements of the other three, and vice versa. A question worth asking is whether it will be easier to teach competent makers in the first three categories, in which engineers are well represented, enough about the work of the fourth to understand how a company works, or to teach the fourth about the first three to the same standard.

The Engineer's Contribution

In order to be commercially successful it is not sufficient for a product or a process to be technologically innovative, though this will stimulate interest – from the competition as well as the customer. It must be designed, engineered, produced and marketed to provide the user with the required quality in terms of performance, reliability and appearance, for its design life, at an acceptable price. Less obviously, a good product will be capable of being handled efficiently by every department in the company that makes contact with it, however slightly.

Introduction 3

To make the maximum contribution towards creating the commercially successful product – success in other fields is of trivial interest – engineers must face up to some questions that they may initially feel poorly equipped to answer. Early in a career it may not be the engineer's responsibility to provide the answers to these questions, but inability to discuss them with those who have that responsibility will result in the engineering dimension being omitted from the discussion. For the project this may lead to suboptimal results and for the engineer to suboptimal progress in the company. A first condition for the company to react to the opportunities and constraints offered by the engineering dimension is that the individual engineer should have insight into the responsibilities, problems and attitudes of the other company functions.

What Questions?

How many projects?   The answer to this question is crucial to the efficient utilization of R&D resources, which are always limited. If too many are undertaken the average time to completion will be unacceptably long. If too few, there will not be enough new products.

How much investment?   How is the amount to be spent on R&D decided? Is the case for engineering resources put forward in the right way at the right time?

Which projects?   How are proposals for new products collected and analysed? Does the form of analysis influence the priority they are given?

What resources, when?   How are projects planned and monitored? How are the project plans aligned with the corporate plan?

What design approach?   How is the appropriate quality level established and controlled? How is it decided whether to buy an item or to make it in-house?

What management style?   How does the project manager organize and supervise the people in the team? What problems and what guidelines are there?

What communications?   Is communication difficult? If so, why? What impact do national culture and internal structure have on the problem?

4   *Introduction*

What about people?   Social theories abound. Do any offer help to the project manager in motivating the team? Do any help in choosing project managers?

Engineering and Management

The questions listed above are typical rather than comprehensive. They are nearly all about management, which has much in common with engineering. Both managers and engineers achieve their results through other people. Both are obliged to make decisions on incomplete information. Both have a responsibility for design, the manager, of people systems, and the engineer, of hardware systems. Both have long time constants; what they do may take months or years to show results.

Company Functions

A feature of project management is that it interacts with the company functions managed on the minimum variety basis referred to under 'functional management'. An example is the manufacturing function where product variants are detrimental to productivity. This creates problems of organization and communication. A much simplified model of the main interactions is given in Figure 1.1.

The main functions in an engineering manufacturing company are commercial, R&D, manufacturing, financial control and top management. There are specialist subdivisions of these functions and a number of other departments which have significant contributions to make but are left out to avoid complexity in the diagram.

The first three functions form overlapping segments of the circle representing the company as a whole. Top management is represented by the centre circle and has the responsibility of arriving at and promulgating the corporate plan defining the company objectives. Departmental objectives are required to harmonize with these.

Planning

Planning and plans occupy much of a manager's time at any level in the company, with important consequences. The major difference between levels is the time horizon, or distance ahead that the plans attempt to cover. A first level, supervisor's plans probably concern the next day or the next week while the chief executive officer should be thinking in terms of the next decade in general terms and the next four or five years in more

Introduction 5

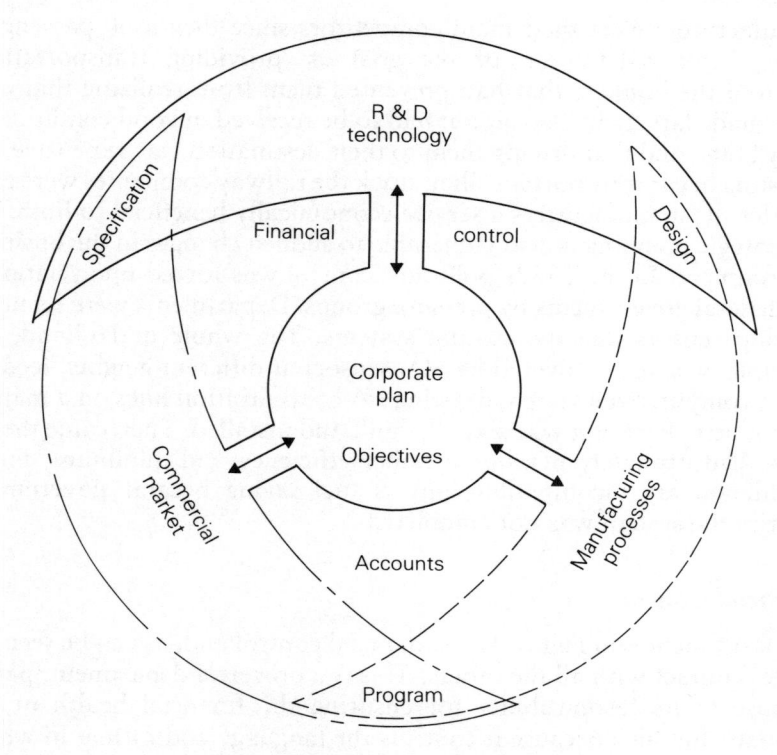

```
                    R & D
                 technology
          Specification
                Financial      control          Design


                          Corporate
                             plan
      Commercial
       market          Objectives                    Manufacturing
                                                      processes

                          Accounts


                          Program
```

Figure 1.1 Company functions

detail. A useful division of plans is between strategic plans and tactical plans. Strategic planning is the business of deciding what the main goals of the organization are and what policies should be adopted in pursuing them. Tactical planning is shorter term and involves deciding how the resources of the organization shall be used to help reach its individual strategic goals.

Goals and objectives are similar in that both provide a direction and a target for company or departmental activities. The terminology of planning is far from standardized. In this book the essential difference is taken to be that an objective must be quantitative in terms of results and time, while a goal may be less rigorously specified.

Strategic planning, because of its greater time horizon, must rely on long term forecasts and is therefore more uncertain. The choice of goals is critical and may demonstrate whether or not the company really understands what business it is in. For many years American railways appear to have assumed that their goal was the building and running of railways. This led them into feeling that airlines and motor car manufacturers were their main competitors since they took passengers away. Later redefinition of the goal as 'providing transportation' removed the blinkers that had prevented them from realizing that cars were made largely in Detroit but had to be received in good condition in every State, and that driving them to their destination was expensive. By investing in car transporter rolling stock the railway companies were able to offer the manufacturers a service economically beneficial to both.

Strategic planning is also vulnerable to sudden changes in the business environment. In the 1970s pollution control was forced upon national and federal governments by pressure groups. Departments were set up to develop sensors and monitoring systems. The whole of Holland, for example, was to be covered by SO_2 sensors at different heights, feeding into a computerized system drawing iso-concentration lines on a map of the country. Part of it was actually built and installed. Then came the oil crisis. Unfortunately maximum boiler efficiency and minimum smoke production are incompatible and as fuel saving became government priority the system was not completed.

Financial Control

The last function in Figure 1.1 is financial control and, as can be seen, it makes contact with all the others. This is a powerful department, partly because of its responsibility for ensuring the financial health of the company but also because it controls the language and format in which the other functions draw up their expenditure plans and report progress against them.

Commercial

An important contribution of the commercial function is to be the main source of information on the market in which the company operates, its needs, preferences, buying patterns and price structure. Some companies have a department labelled 'marketing' to discharge this responsibility. Others take the view that marketing is part of everyone's job and that R&D, in particular, is expected to supplement other inputs by making direct contact with users of company products and with competitive activities. Such companies often adopt a blanket term such as 'commercial' to cover this and other customer-oriented activities.

Research and Development

The contribution of R&D is primarily technology as applied to products and processes. This is particularly true in the specification, design and initial production of a new product. During the last stage it is not uncommon for the project team to spend the majority of its time in production departments.

Manufacturing

The main contribution of manufacturing is the selection and operation of established production processes and the management of an agreed production programme. In the general case manufacturing costs are high compared with those of other functions so the function has a massive influence on company productivity.

Functional Interfaces

The activities described so far have been concerned with periodically recurring factors relating to corporate planning and monitoring of results as part of functional management. The three functions just described also have responsibilities in the field of project management. These come into play after corporate plans have been formulated and are concerned with implementing them. The activity takes place in the overlaps between the three segments of Figure 1.1.

The overlap between commercial and R&D is where the specification of new products is formulated. The rationale for this is clear. There is no point in R&D developing a new product unless commercial thinks it can sell it. While it may not succeed where it thinks it can, if it thinks it can't the probability is that it won't. Conversely there is no point in commercial selling a product that R&D says it can't develop. A practical solution is for the two functions to be jointly responsible, within the constraints of the corporate plan, for product specification, negotiating with each other until an acceptable compromise is reached.

Between R&D and manufacturing the overlap is on the design of the new product. There is no merit in R&D designing something that manufacturing has not the resources to produce efficiently. This is not to say that R&D should not think in terms of processes that do not currently exist, but it emphasizes the need for discussion and agreement on how they shall be provided, in time for them to be in place when they are needed. This involves building any investments required into the company budget as well as providing against project slippage because of any additional prototype stages the new process may make advisable.

The overlap between manufacturing and commercial is the manufacturing programme. Manufacturing fewer units than can be sold either reduces revenue because orders are not accepted or makes for late

8 Introduction

deliveries if they are. Producing more units than are sold builds up surplus stock which is a commitment of working capital. The costs of this are the interest that must be paid on it and the opportunity cost of being unable to undertake some other activity because of lack of funds.

The newcomer to industry should note that the above discussion is not about organization and will not correspond to any official company hierarchical diagram. It attempts to model operational interactions between company functions in one way that is logically sound. There are companies that work in quite different ways; they do, however, have the problems that this model illustrates.

The Format of the Book

Chapters 2 through 16 introduce concepts and techniques found useful in dealing with the questions outlined above and describe some of the relevant aspects of the company functions forming the interfaces. Each chapter begins with a summary of its contents and ends with a review of what the reader should have learned from it. This is followed by references and a short reading list.

Chapter 17 is a synthetic case study of a board meeting in a small engineering company, illustrating some of the pitfalls attending management decisions.

Chapter 18 describes, and provides a program listing for, TOWER-8, a Project Management Game, written for the BBC micro-computer. It simulates a design and build project on a compressed time scale and models the commercial consequences of designing, planning, estimating, tendering for and building to, a contract and specification. It can be played competitively between syndicates or used to experiment with changing parameters as in sensitivity analysis.

A glossary of terms used in the text is given at the end of the book.

References

Ritchie-Calder, Baron 1963: *The Revolution in Science*. UNESCO/Mentor.
Stoner, J. A. F. 1978: *Management*. Prentice-Hall.

Further Reading

Drucker, P. 1969: *The Age of Discontinuity*. Heineman.
Kempner, T. (ed.) 1976: *A Handbook of Management*. Penguin.
MacDonald, S. *et al.* (eds) 1983: *The Trouble with Technology*. Pinter.
Wright, J. F. 1979: *Britain in the Age of Economic Management*. Oxford University Press.

2 Product Strategy

In order to provide maximum benefit to the company, new products must satisfy the requirements of the corporate plan in terms of the market needs they fulfil and their price/performance ratio. The specification of a product and the allocation of resources to develop it are the later stages of a series of planning loops. The starting point of the series is a statement of company objectives as the basis of a company strategy. Strategic planning involves top management and the main company functions in the earlier stages, and departmental management in the later, as they progress from the broadest market and company considerations to the details of specific product launches.

Gap Analysis

As indicated in Chapter 1, top management, led by the chief executive officer – usually the managing director in the UK – has the responsibility for creating the strategic plan for the company. This must include product policy, marketing policy and sales targets as a minimum. In other words it should express, in terms meaningful to all company functions, agreed targets as to what product range(s) are to be sold in which market(s) in what quantities per year over the planning period. It does not at this stage include any specific new products.

What top management needs in order to move towards this plan is an analysis of its present and potential future situation in terms of products and their associated markets. This amounts to a portfolio or collection of possibilities ranked on an agreed basis to enable decisions to be made on allocation of resources. There is no short cut to this goal; it demands systematic collection and analysis of a large amount of quantitative and qualitative data. It also requires presentation in a manner acceptable to both generalist and specialist managers. A first step in the process is to examine the gap between what the company income is likely to be from the products now in production and the income that it wishes to have over the next planning period.

The first step is to take the oldest product and plot the estimated annual revenue from it over the planning period as shown for product A (Figure

10 Product Strategy

2.1). The next oldest product is then plotted in the same way, but using the graph of product A as the base line where both are forecast to be in production together. Other products are treated in the same way, building up a graph of the aggregate sales of existing products. The cumulative revenue from these is represented by the area under the last graph, that of product D. The provision of the data so far is the responsibility of the marketing/sales function.

The next step is to draw, on the same axes, a line representing the target income for the planning period as proposed by top management as part of the corporate plan. Between this line and that representing the sales of existing products there is now a gap. The strategic planning goal is to produce plans that will present a credible set of proposals for filling this gap with sales of new products or services.

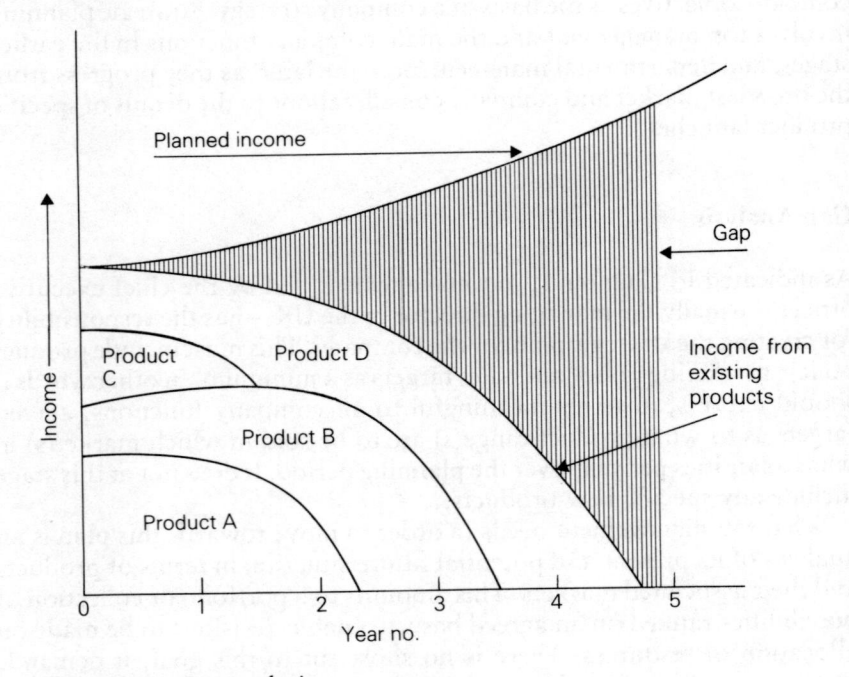

Figure 2.1 Gap analysis

Strategic Planning

Strategic planning is, like all planning, an iterative process. It is, like politics, the art of the possible. It is concerned with what is possible in the context of the strengths and weaknesses of the company and the threats and opportunities it perceives in the world outside the company, the environment in which it operates. From the analysis of these factors tentative goals are selected. These are broad descriptions of how the company wishes to see itself developing over the planning period. Further discussion and analysis refines these descriptions until they can be converted into company objectives.

The essence of an objective is that it is specific, quantitative, on a time base and measurable. Thus the statement that the company needs a new product in the X range is not an objective but may be a goal. As an objective it must also cover the market it will sell in, a sales estimate and a target date for launching, whether it replaces or supplements other products in the range and any other relevant information defining the nature of the product. The stages of strategic planning are shown in Figure 2.2.

The triangle formed by nodes 1, 2 and 3 is iterated until there is agreement between marketing and R&D that such a product has a high probability of being (a) feasible and (b) viable and that measurable objectives have been unambiguously recorded. This is part of the activity in the overlap between commercial and R&D in Figure 1.1.

The next loop to be tackled is 3, 4, 5. The departments involved must now look closely at the stated objectives and work out how they will discharge their responsibilities, going round the loop until there is agreement that this can be done. Alternatively, if this agreement is not reached, the objectives reached in node 3 must be reconsidered. A compromise on objectives may be needed to allow the process to proceed.

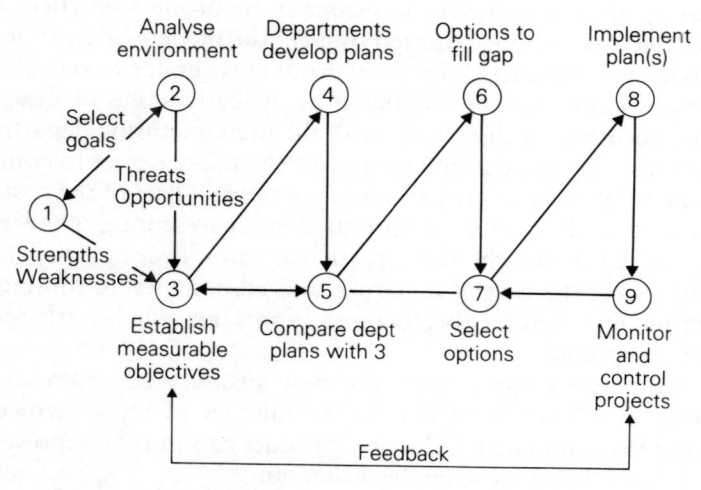

Figure 2.2 Strategic planning

12 Product Strategy

When the departmental plans and the (if necessary) revised objectives are compatible the triangle 5, 6, 7 can be discussed.

The objectives thus agreed can probably be achieved in more than one way. The purpose of the loop 5, 6, 7 is to focus the attention of the department on the problem of optimizing the solution from all points of view. In the case of R&D or engineering this will amount to looking in more detail at the possible design approaches to the new product and selecting the most promising for development. Rigorous analysis at this stage is needed to ensure that the optimum option is found. Unfortunately there is always great pressure on the designer at this stage, however long the preceding stages have taken. The danger is that the designer will accept the first feasible design solution found, rather than systematically search for the optimum. The benefits to productivity and profitability of really good design are such, however, that such pressure should be resisted. The company memory of the late launch of a profitable product will convey more merit than the prompt launch of a failure, whatever the arguments put up at the time.

The progress of the design chosen – as with that of the marketing activities in support of the launch – at node 8 is monitored at node 9 and control actions decided by comparison with the objectives established at node 3.

Break-Even Analysis

In the course of departmental planning to meet the demands of the corporate plan it is necessary to estimate the production costs and the sales volume that will be required to meet the income and profit targets for a given new product. If the new product is similar to one already in production, costs may be estimated at an early stage of design with adequate accuracy by discussion with the manufacturing department. If this is not the case the design may have to be taken nearer to completion before an estimator can provide tentative figures. Part of the cost will be independent of the volume of production, representing a share of the fixed costs of running the factory, such as rates, heating, etc. The other part will reflect the cost of materials and labour used in producing the product and will therefore be, to a first approximation, linearly related to production volume.

The estimated income from the new product is, again to a first approximation, linearly related to the number of units invoiced. The profit and loss estimate for the new product can thus be represented by Figure 2.3, the break-even analysis diagram.

The fixed costs of manufacturing the new product are represented by

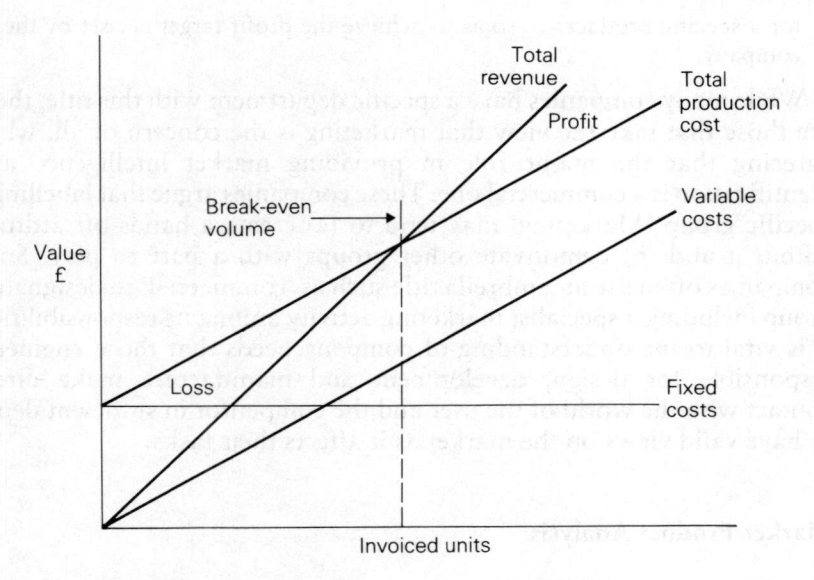

Figure 2.3 Break-even analysis

the horizontal line since they are not influenced by the volume produced. The variable costs start from zero, since labour and material are not consumed until production starts, and in the simple model rise linearly with volume. The total production cost is the sum of these two quantities, giving the line so marked. The revenue from the product also starts from zero when none are sold and rises proportionately to invoiced sales. For the product to be viable this line must have a steeper slope than the total cost line and intersect it at some point. This is the break-even point where total cost equals total revenue. At sales levels above this volume the product is profitable, the profit being the area between the revenue and cost lines. Below this volume the product makes a loss.

The viability of the new product at various sales and production levels can thus be visualized and its contribution to the planned income gap assessed by drawing its graph on top of the existing product income line in Figure 2.1.

The Marketing Function

Marketing is defined by the Institute of Marketing as:

> The organisation and direction of all those business activities involved in assessing and converting customer purchasing power into effective demand

14   Product Strategy

for a specific product ... so as to achieve the profit target ... set by the company.

While many companies have a specific department with this title, there are those that take the view that marketing is the concern of all, while agreeing that the major role in providing market intelligence and identification is a commercial one. These companies argue that labelling a specific group 'Marketing' may tend to (a) create a hands-off attitude within it and (b) demotivate other groups with a part to play. Such companies often use an umbrella title such as 'commercial' to designate a group including a specialist marketing activity among its responsibilities. It is vital to the understanding of company needs that those engineers responsible for design, development and manufacture make direct contact with the world of the user and the competitor in sufficient depth to have valid views on the market as it affects their tasks.

Market/Product Analysis

The analysis of markets and products as they relate to the customer is a prime marketing task. It often takes the form of a matrix representing the business on two axes, 'market attractiveness' and 'business strength'. In one form – the earliest is usually attributed to the Boston Consulting Group, USA – a 3 × 3 matrix is set up on the two axes as in Figure 2.4. Business strength increases vertically and market attractiveness increases from right to left. Business strength is a measure of the proficiency with which the firm deals with all aspects of the specific product/market complex in question at the present time. It does not necessarily reflect the trading position of the company as a whole. Market attractiveness is a measure of the estimated potential benefits to the company from entering the market/product complex proposed. It does not necessarily describe any intrinsic quality of the market itself. The nine squares are viewed as three groups of three.

Products which fall in the top left-hand group are those which are in attractive markets and which the company handles well. In some of these cases the company may be the market leader, that is to say it has the largest single share of the market and because of this has a major influence on market prices and product design. They represent present success and future expansion.

Products forming the bottom right-hand group are in a market that does not offer future prospects of expansion and profit to the company. Further, they are not dealt with very successfully by the company from one or more aspects such as technology or sales or servicing. They

Product Strategy 15

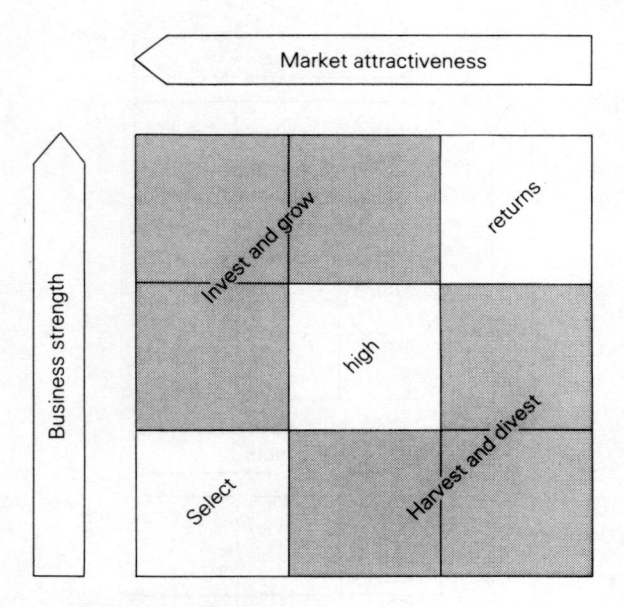

Figure 2.4 Market analysis

represent an area of the business whose prospects are so poor that they do not justify any further investment.

The group of products falling into the three diagonal squares are between these two extremes on one or both axes. They may be in attractive markets but poorly handled by the company or vice versa. They may be less than satisfactory on both counts.

The position in the matrix indicates strategy to be adopted. Those in the top left-hand group represent the present and future of the company and should be invested in to push them further into the corner. Those in the bottom right-hand group should probably be got rid of by withdrawing all investment and selling everything that can be made. This strategy is capable of converting them from the least profitable product group to the most profitable – for a time. If all investment and most resources are withdrawn, whatever is sold has a high profitability and generates cash which is available to invest in the top left-hand group. The diagonal group is treated as individual cases.

Figure 2.5(a) illustrates the analysis of a product in four markets and Figure 2.5(b) the analysis of a group of products in one market. The size of the circles indicates the estimated market size in both cases.

A merit of this approach is that the variables are visually presented in a style that can be understood by generalists and specialists alike. The clear indications of the appropriate direction in which to move any product or

16 Product Strategy

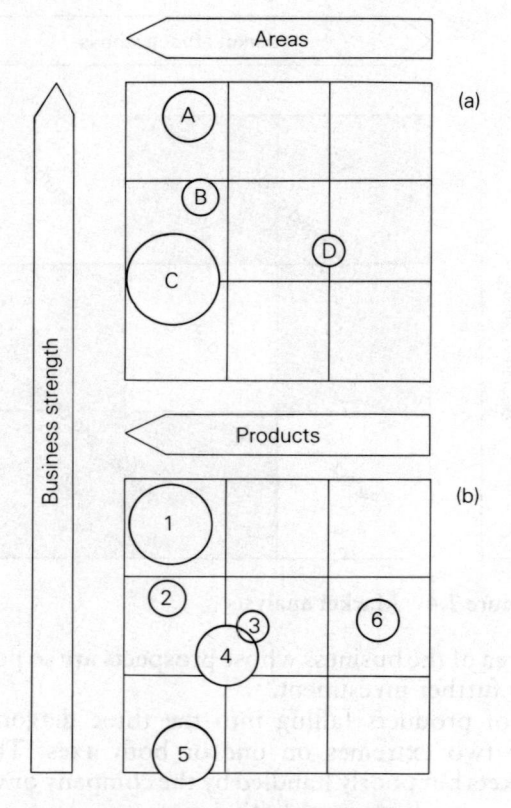

Figure 2.5 Market/product analysis

market for the benefit of the company makes for good communication and useful discussion. Table 2.1 shows the resulting policy indications for the more important business aspects.

The method of scoring products on the two axes in order to fit them into the matrix is that of multi-dimensional screening, taking into account the attributes of the competition as well as the two dimensions already mentioned. It involves detailed examination of commercial records and discussion with virtually all company functions that come in contact with the products and markets to be analysed.

Multi-Dimensional Screening

The method of positioning a product in the matrix is by marking each axis with a scale, typically 1–10, and scoring the products in terms of their

Product Strategy

Table 2.1 Market and product strategy

	Top left	Diagonal	Bottom right
Investment	Maximum digestible	Select high return segments	Maximize income
Risk	Accept contain	Limit	Avoid
Price	Lead, exploit cost/value effects	Maximize contribution	Lag – even if volume reduced
Products	Lead, diversity	Specialize	Reduce range
Costs	Go for scale	Reduce variable, optimize fixed	Cut
Marketing	Creative	Focus on range coverage	Cut
Management	Entrepreneurial	Balanced	Cost control
Strategic focus	Long term profit	Short term earnings	Maximum cash generation

market attractiveness and business strength. In order to do this the factors influencing the scores must be chosen, identified with one of the two axes and judgements made on their order of importance. These judgements are interpreted as a weighting number for each factor. A scale of 1–5 is a good compromise between difficulty in making judgements and failing to differentiate between the importance of factors.

Each of the factors to be taken into account is then scored, for the product being examined, in relation to the other products on the list. The scale is not very important provided it is chosen at the start and not changed throughout the exercise. This provides a large number of scores for each product, one for each factor, which is then multiplied by the appropriate weighting, giving a weighted score. The sum of the weighted scores for each axis is a measure of the product ranking on that axis and the set of scores is normalized to a scale of 1–10. By superimposing the same scale on the two axes of the matrix, the product can then be positioned, represented by a circle of which the area is proportional to the forecast market size, possibly with another inside it representing the estimated market share.

18 Product Strategy

The screening can usefully be carried out under three headings:

(1) Market attractiveness
(2) Business strength
(3) Competitive activity

The following factors are typical of those included but are neither comprehensive nor universally relevant. The factors chosen must relate to the company, its products and its market position.

(1) Market attractiveness

   Market segmentation (what part of the market does it fit into?)
   Sales territories
   Sales organization
   Type of market; risk involved
   Market size – growth forecast, total and accessible
   Market sensitivity
   Who benefits?
   Selling price brackets
   Purchasing influences
   Position in life cycle
   Political factors
   Social factors

(2) Company strengths

   Policy
   Philosophy
   Technology
   Resources
   Competence
   Training
   Management
   Collaborators needed?
   Probability of success
   Costs
   Coverage of problem areas

(3) Competitive analysis

   Alternative products
   Conflict of programmes
   Funding of programmes
   Other countries' activities
   Market cover
   Market segmentation

Table 2.2 gives an illustration of the use of the multi-dimensional screen; the first three elements are applied to the proposed new radiation pyrometer, data on which is given in the Pyro Instrument Company case in Chapter 17. The weighting for each element of the screen is on a scale 1–3 and the score on a scale 1–5.

Table 2.2 An illustration of the multi-dimensional screen

		Weight	Score	Total
Market attractiveness				
Segmentation	Clearly defined. Non-contact temperature measure over range giving technical advantage	3	1	3
Sales Territories	Existing territories satisfactory	2	3	6
Type of market risk	Industrial, probably more spot measurements than fixed installations	2	1	2
Business strength				
Policy	Extends existing product/market application range	3	4	12
Philosophy	Increases revenue without competing with existing products	2	4	8
Technology	No experience in company	3	1	3
Competitive analysis				
Alternative products	Tempo Ltd very strong	2	1	2
Conflict of programmes	None known	2	2	4
Funding of programmes	As for Pyro Co. Ltd	2	2	4

Some factors in the competitive analysis will relate to market attractiveness. If the competition offered no alternative to the proposed new product it would score highly. Since the competition is the market leader in radiation pyrometers it attracts a low score.

20 Product Strategy

The other two factors in the competitive analysis relate to business strength. The scores are fairly neutral.

The last two sets of totals are added to the market or business total as appropriate and the new totals normalized, that is, presented as totals out of ten. For market attractiveness the possible total is 45 + 15 from competitive analysis, that is 60. The actual total is 11 + 2 from competitive analysis, that is 13. The normalized score is therefore 2. For business strength the normalized score is 4. The positioning of this proposal in the matrix, due to the elements listed above, is therefore 2 for the market attractiveness and 4 for business strength. The size of the circle can be obtained from the Pyro Case exhibits.

R&D Resource Planning

The planning so far has taken into account the needs of the strategic company plan and the opportunities for achieving it in terms of products and markets. Some of the company strengths and weaknesses emerging in discussion with marketing and other functions will have already acted to restrict these opportunities. A further restriction directly influencing the capacity to undertake projects is the availability of R&D resources.

The company strategic plan will always include a budget allocating resources to each function, including R&D, in terms of staff and funds. The amount actually available for the generation of new products is, however, much less than this figure. This is because of the many other commitments of R&D, a fact not always grasped by top management. Figure 2.6 shows the pattern of original R&D resources allocation from the strategic plan and the internal allocation of those resources within the function.

It will be seen that the top line of activities repeats the first stage of the company strategic plan as it affects R&D. Consideration of threats — what is the competition doing, are some markets closing? — and opportunities — are new components now available, can a new product create its own market? — together with company capabilities, result in an R&D strategy and plan which corresponds to the 3, 4, 5 loop in the company strategic plan.

Before the resources for the R&D plan can be allocated, however, other factors have to be taken into account. There will be a number of on-going projects in the department and the resources for these must be maintained or the projects cancelled. A second reduction of available resources is due to short term problems in other company functions. Particularly in manufacturing, R&D is never quite free from its past projects and a substantial proportion of its resources must be earmarked for trouble-

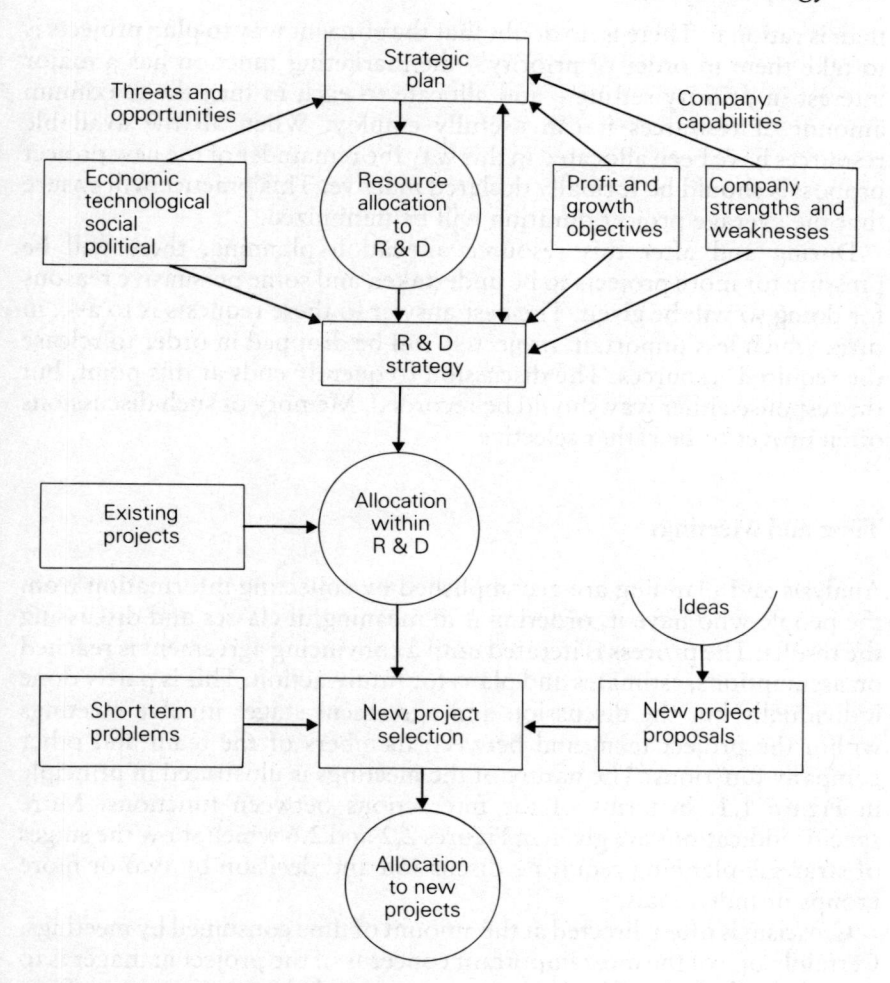

Figure 2.6 Resource planning

shooting arising from, for instance, the need to find a substitute for an obsolescent component before it is in short supply. Some resource will also be needed to deal with technical problems and enquiries from sales and commercial departments. In a company involved in a fast moving technology and consequently a continuous output of new products, this commitment can amount to 30 per cent of total R&D resources.

Only then can the resources available for new projects be quantified and decisions made on how many and which to undertake. At this point there is apt to be pressure on R&D to agree to undertake more projects than is rational. There is no doubt that the efficient way to plan projects is to take them in order of priority – the marketing function has a major interest in priority setting – and allocate to each in turn the maximum amount of resources it can usefully employ. When all the available resources have been allocated in this way the remainder of the new project proposals should be formally declared inactive. This practice will ensure that the average project duration will be minimized.

During and after this resource allocation planning, there will be pressure for more projects to be undertaken and some persuasive reasons for doing so will be given. The best answer to these requests is to ask, in turn, which less important project(s) will be dropped in order to release the required resources. The discussion frequently ends at this point, but the response either way should be recorded. Memory of such discussions often proves to be rather selective.

Time and Meetings

Analysis and planning are accomplished by collecting information from the people who have it, ordering it in meaningful classes and discussing the results. The process is iterated until a convincing agreement is reached on assumptions, estimates and plans for future action. This is partly done individually but the discussion and agreement stages involve meetings within the project team and between members of the team and other company functions. The nature of the meetings is illustrated in principle in Figure 1.1, in terms of the interactions between functions. More specific indications are given in Figures 2.2 and 2.6 which show the stages of strategic planning requiring discussion and decision by two or more groups or individuals.

Criticism is often directed at the amount of time consumed by meetings. Certainly one of the most important concerns of the project manager is to know how the time of his team, and particularly his own, is spent. Time spent is not recoverable, while improved performance will often enable recovery of money in the medium term; thus time is the most scarce resource at the project manager's disposal.

Control of Time

Some of the project manager's time will be committed in advance to systematic management of the project. The system should not in any way restrict the contribution of any of the members of the team; it should enhance their efforts by providing routine channels for the routine aspects of their activities, so that they are not obliged to devote intellectual effort to them. It should focus attention on the key results areas of the project and on the contributions of individuals towards achieving them. It is the project manager's task to define the key results areas, to set priorities for the contributions and to ensure that they are adhered to. The system must ensure that all involved are kept aware of progress, decisions and changes concerning them. It must emphasize results rather than the work content.

The time not spent on this type of activity may be regarded as the project manager's discretionary time. The efficient use of discretionary time is a decisive factor in a manager's effectiveness. Time is wasted in a number of ways. Bad organization is responsible for an excess of meetings because decisions that should be routine become unclear and demand further discussion, sometimes as a matter of urgency. Bad information has the same effect. These aspects of time control start from the communications problem, discussed in Chapter 11.

Most project managers, like most other managers, will offer an estimate of how much of their time is discretionary and how they allocate it. In general they overestimate the amount available and underestimate the time wasted by being fragmented in small amounts on rather trivial matters. The best way of establishing the facts is for project managers to keep a detailed log of their daily activities on, say, a half-hourly basis, for a week. At the end of that time the conscientious manager may well find it difficult to credit the evidence. Analysis of the record will throw light on the state of the project organization, the external influences on it and the manager's own working habits. Once analysis of the log makes obvious any deficiencies in time allocation to specific areas, as it will, correction is simple and straightforward. It is frequently not permanent, however, and the exercise can usefully be repeated at intervals, say twice a year.

It is essential that the project manager organizes the project so that he can give uninterrupted thought for adequate periods to the key results areas. The human span of attention is limited; for most people an hour is a long time for concentrated thought on one topic. Periods of this order should be allocated to the major problems and decisions, protected from disturbance. Very few crises elsewhere are so disastrous that they cannot wait an average of 30 minutes.

Meetings

Meetings are, nevertheless, necessary. The stage-by-stage process of strategic planning, illustrated in Figure 2.2, demands a series of meetings to assemble and discuss the relevant information, formulate opinions and arrive at decisions. Meetings are also part of the communication system. Some subjects are best discussed on a one-to-one basis; this requirement is treated in Chapter 10 under Objective Setting. Others lend themselves to

24 Product Strategy

group discussion where the moral support of peers encourages individuals to put forward their views in the presence of management.

Whatever the purpose of the meeting, it should be stated at the outset and adhered to. The chairman must not allow the discussion to wander into other subjects unless there is a direct relevance. The purpose should have been notified in advance so that those attending are able to assemble any information they need. It should only be changed at the start of the meeting in the case of a genuine crisis. An efficient procedure, essential if more than one subject is to be discussed, is to circulate an agenda giving the date, time, venue, subjects and a list of those attending.

The question of the size of meetings is important. Large meetings are notoriously less productive and more difficult to handle, so the numbers should be restricted to those with a contribution to make. A perception can arise, particularly in those organizations not accustomed to regular meetings, of personal status being reduced by not being invited to certain meetings. This can often be dealt with by notifying the individual of the meeting and its purpose and saying that he will be welcome to attend if he feels that he has a specific interest in the proceedings. The decision now being his, no status problems arise. Unless he has a part to play he is unlikely to attend after the first appearance.

The purpose of a meeting can be whatever the project manager decides would be useful. Typical purposes are:

(1) To define a problem
(2) To list alternative solutions
(3) To decide on the best alternative
(4) To plan future activities
(5) To inform those present
(6) To collect views
(7) To discuss and clarify
(8) To review progress

The location, starting time and duration should be included in the notice of the meeting to allow those attending to plan their time; also the agenda should be included in sufficient detail to indicate what preparation they need to do. This information should be presented in a standard form, as should the minutes of the meeting, recording the essentials of discussions and the decisions made. Wide margins should be left on either side of the minutes. That on one side can be used to record the names of the individuals responsible for taking any actions that have been decided on. The other margin is for notes by the person receiving the minutes after the meeting. For routine meetings with fixed agenda, such as project review meetings, it is often possible for the agenda and the minutes to be the same standard form, one part of which records the information to be considered (the agenda) and the other the decisions taken (the minutes). The project review and resource allocation meeting described in Chapter 10 under 'Matrix Organization' is an example of this approach. It should be remembered that in meetings of this type the minutes act as the authority for implementing the decisions. The action, the person responsible and possibly the resources to be used, must be stated clearly and the chairman's signature appended with the date.

In project work there are a minimum number of formal meetings of the type described above necessary to monitor the progress of the project and authorize use of resources when needed. There are a larger number of informal meetings not preceded by any significant preparation to deal with the day-to-day problems of keeping the project moving. These are often *ad hoc* verbal discussions between the individuals directly affected, sometimes requiring official blessing, sometimes requiring no further action. If any decisions are taken at either type of meeting they should be recorded. In the formal case the record will be in the minutes; in the informal case a dated note should be inserted in the minute file giving the time, place and people present when the decision was taken and a brief statement of the decision.

Review

This chapter has:

(1) Explained how the required company revenue from new products is estimated.
(2) Described the sequence of stages of strategic planning.
(3) Explained break-even analysis.
(4) Defined the marketing function.
(5) Described a technique of market/product analysis.
(6) Described the process of resource planning.
(7) Explained the importance of controlling the use of time and how to analyse it.
(8) Described the part played by meetings in reaching planning agreements.

The next chapter explains the preparation of project and departmental budgets and the nature of accounts. It provides insights into the purposes of balance sheets, profit and loss accounts and methods of costing projects and production.

References

Drucker, P. 1967: *Managing for Results*. Pan Piper.
Law, P., Weinberg, C., Doyle, P. and Simmonds, K. 1974: *Product Management*. Harper & Row.
Twiss, B. 1974: *Managing Technological Innovation*. Longman.

Further Reading

Archibald, G. (ed.) 1973: *The Theory of the Firm*. Penguin.
Argenti, J. 1968: *Corporate Planning*. Allen & Unwin.
Bolton, W. K. 1980: Industrial Product Strategy, *R&D Man.*, 10.
Ryan, C. G. 1984: *The Marketing of Technology*. Peregrinus.
Wright, W. 1971: *Direct Standard Costs*. Macdonald.

3 Budgets and Accounts

When product strategy has been established, planning of the R&D programme can proceed. In order to deal with the problems of budgeting for this it is necessary to know something of company financial and cost accounting. Two common forms of costing are discussed together with the make-up of project and departmental budgets. A simplified model of financial structure is presented.

The Accounts Function

The envelope of project work has now emerged from the planning described in Chapter 2. One of the resources involved is, of course, money. All resources used must be monitored so that project progress can be compared with plan, and the monitoring of expenditure brings R&D into contact with the accounts department which exercises surveillance on all company financial transactions. It is essential, but not always obvious, that R&D workers should understand what accountants do sufficiently to be able to communicate with them and on occasion to negotiate change in the detail of how they do it.

An individual accountant will often be charged with the task of recording project expenditure so that, as at node 9 of Figure 2.2, it can be fed back and compared with the project plan. In order to do this it will be necessary to have records of expenditure on materials and weekly time sheets recording time spent on individual projects by each worker. The accountant can be of great help in a staff relationship to the project leader in keeping the project expenditure under control. While the responsibility for doing so remains with the project leader, the accountant should be accepted as a part time member of the project team and encouraged to contribute ideas.

Product Cash Flow

The importance of project control can be illustrated by means of the product cash flow diagram (Figure 3.1).

28 Budgets and Accounts

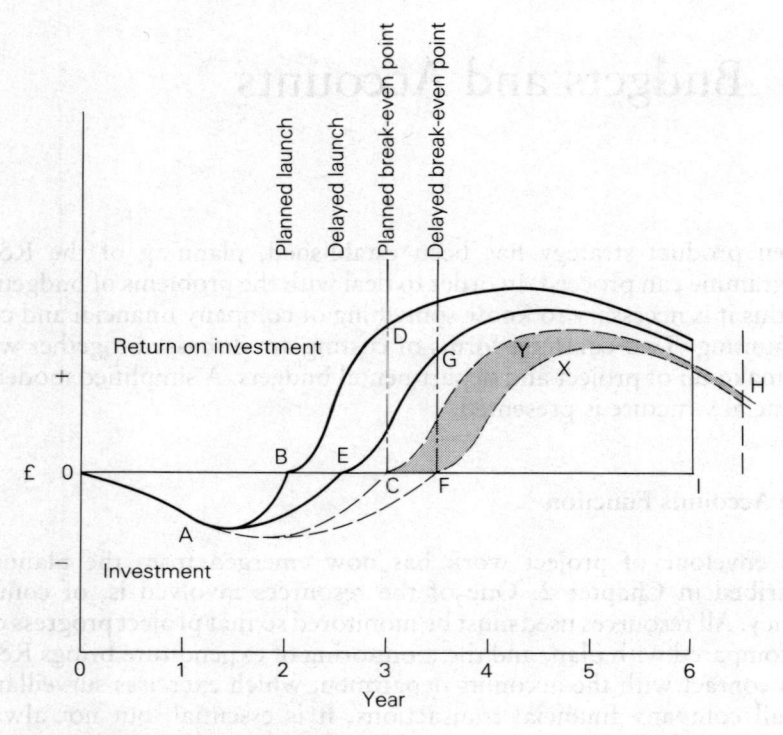

Figure 3.1 Product cash flow

The horizontal axis is a time base and the vertical axis displays positive and negative cash flow. Negative cash flow is the expenditure incurred in designing, developing and making the new product, that is cash flowing out of the company. Positive cash flow is that coming into the company, the revenue from the sale of the product.

Initially the cash flow will be negative, rising from a low figure due to the relatively small resources needed for selecting and planning the project, increasing steeply as investment in production plant and methods begins then returning in a curve to zero as development is completed and production begins. As planned, it might follow the solid line OAB. The last point is the launch date from which sales and shipments take place along the line BD, rising to a peak, then falling to a point I where the product is withdrawn. The reason for the fall in later years is that costs tend to increase as the product ages – apart from production costs there may be increased costs in selling against more up-to-date competition – and sales tend to decrease.

Budgets and Accounts 29

The investment in the new product, the area under the line OAB, is not recovered until an equal area, represented by the space BCD appears under the revenue line. It is not until point C on the time base that net positive cash flow begins. The broken line CYH is therefore the planned revenue from the new product.

If expenditure on the project goes over budget, or the launch is delayed – perhaps because resources are not available as planned – the second sales line EG results from the delayed launch. This, in turn, means that the start of net positive cash flow is delayed until point F and proceeds along the curve FXH. Because of normal time delays, revenue continues for a while after sales cease. Note that the product is withdrawn on the same date in both cases. This event is determined by the market and the competition. The fact that it was launched later will have minimal effect on the withdrawal date. The consequence is that the revenue represented by the shaded area between curves CYH and FXH has been lost. Not only is it not recoverable but it has taken place at the most profitable period in the product life, before the adverse effects of ageing have affected its sales and costs.

Not all the losses resulting from a delayed product launch are concerned with that product. The fact that resources which should have been released at point B are not available to work on the next planned project until point C is an 'opportunity cost' and will quite possibly result in that project being delayed too.

Monitoring of project progress and expenditure, to enable prompt corrective measures to be taken when needed, is essential if project plans are to be achieved and planned return on investment in new products realized.

What Does the Accountant Do?

The accounts department is responsible for ensuring that top management is aware of the financial state of the company and for advising it on appropriate actions to ensure that it remains sound. The financial director is usually a member of top management and, in UK industry, many chief executive officers have come up through financial functions.

The main documents that are used to convey the financial information are the balance sheet, which lists the sources of the company's capital and how it is used in the company, and the profit and loss account, which quantifies the aggregate expenditure and income of the company. It also shows how the company profits are distributed. Figure 3.2 is a much simplified model of a company financial system showing how the two documents interact.

30 Budgets and Accounts

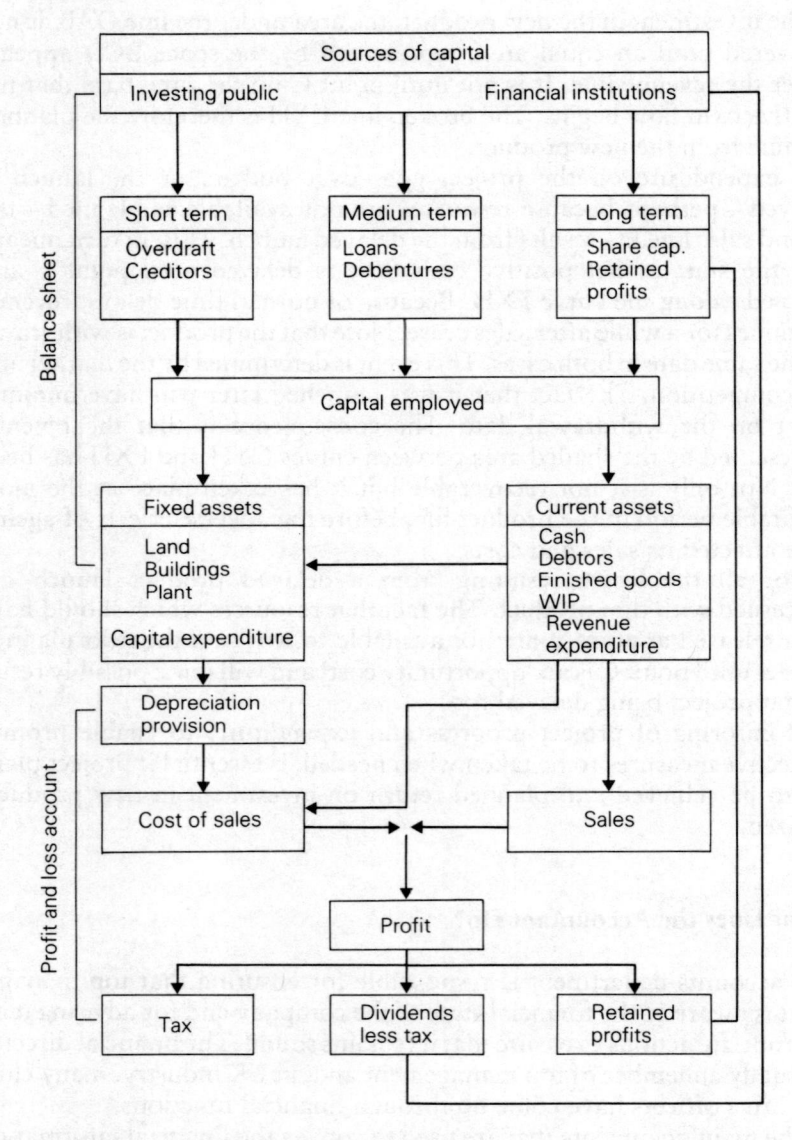

```
                    Sources of capital
        Investing public    Financial institutions

  ┌──────────────┬──────────────┬──────────────┐
  │  Short term  │ Medium term  │  Long term   │
  │   Overdraft  │    Loans     │  Share cap.  │
  │   Creditors  │  Debentures  │   Retained   │
  │              │              │    profits   │
  └──────────────┴──────┬───────┴──────────────┘
                  Capital employed

        Fixed assets              Current assets
          Land                      Cash
          Buildings                 Debtors
          Plant                     Finished goods
                                    WIP
      Capital expenditure         Revenue
                                  expenditure

        Depreciation
         provision

        Cost of sales  ←———————→   Sales

                        Profit

          Tax       Dividends      Retained
                    less tax       profits
```

(Balance sheet brackets top portion; Profit and loss account brackets bottom portion.)

Figure 3.2 Company financial structure

Company Capital

The sources of capital for most private sector companies are the investing public, that is, people who have bought shares either in an individual company or in a unit trust holding such shares in its portfolio, and the financial institutions. The latter are banks, insurance companies, pension funds and the like, and they have, of course, much bigger shareholdings and consequently more influence. Legally, the shareholders are the owners of the company and the directors are elected to run it on their behalf.

Company capital may be viewed as being of three types, short term, medium term and long term. The first is in part provided by banks in the form of overdrafts, that is, the company may, by agreement, write cheques for larger sums than it has on deposit. Interest is payed to the bank on the difference at a rate which reflects the bank's view of the soundness of the company and the prevailing rates in the money market; these rates will vary from time to time. A less obvious source is the company's creditors. If a company does not pay a supplier's bill on time it has the use of that money until it does so. Many companies delay payment as long as they can while maintaining an accounts section charged with chasing their own debtors for early settlement of accounts.

A medium-term loan at a fixed, but higher, rate of interest may be provided by banks and financial institutions such as Finance for Industry. Large loans are often provided by syndicates of such bodies. A debenture is a type of loan in which a fixed interest security, dated for redemption at its nominal value, is issued in return for a term loan.

Long-term capital is mainly that provided by selling shares as described above and by retaining profits within the company. The major difference in practice between share (equity) and loan capital is that the interest on the latter must always be paid whether the company makes a profit or not. Dividends, which are what the shareholder is paid for the use of his money, are recommended by the directors and authorized by the annual general meeting of shareholders. When profits are low they will be reduced or 'passed'. Since shareholders thus take greater risks than banks, their return in good times is higher.

The sum of all these classes of funds is the capital employed in the company. It is used to acquire fixed assets such as buildings and plant and to provide working capital. This is the money required to make up the difference between what the company can pay and what it owes at any one time or, in accounts department terms, net current assets minus current liabilities. The essence of the balance sheet is that the sum of the fixed and current assets shall equal the capital employed, thus explaining its use in the company.

The ratio of fixed interest debt to shareholder's capital plus the debt is known as gearing, or leverage or debt ratio. High gearing increases the shareholder's risk. Conservative financial management in the UK usually recommends a level of about 30 per cent. Lower ratios do not make proper use of cheaper capital; higher ratios risk an unacceptably high fixed-interest burden in bad times.

Profit and Loss Account

As seen in Figure 3.2, capital employed divides between fixed assets and current assets. The former represent buildings and plant. Their replacement when worn out is provided for by depreciation.

Current assets are those that can be turned into cash at short notice, in addition to cash in hand or at the bank. The difference between sales and cost of sales is the gross profit which is distributed as tax and dividends. The remainder is retained as addition to capital.

Depreciation

Provision for depreciation of a company's assets is always made before calculating profit. The rationale for doing so is that consumption of capital assets is one of the costs of earning the revenues of the business and as such is paid from untaxed income under the tax authority's rules. Since the actual amount needed can only be known accurately at the end of the life of the asset, which in turn may not be known in advance of the event, it is necessary to estimate both. Company financial policy will contain guidelines for doing this, based on past experience.

Care should be taken to ensure that such guidelines are used only in appropriate cases. At a time when computer technology was advancing rapidly and any given computer-based business management system tended to be technically obsolescent in a short time, a company made a reasonable decision that all such computers would be depreciated at 50 per cent per annum, making prudent financial provision against their short useful lives. When the company began to embody computers in its products, the engineers responsible were dismayed when they found that a 50 per cent overhead on the purchase price of the hardware had been charged by the estimators. This was, of course, a misinterpretation of the accounting rules, since the two cases are not comparable. If not detected and corrected this error would have priced the said products out of the market.

There are a number of methods of calculation of annual depreciation. Of these the two most generally used are the 'straight line method' and the 'reducing balance method'. In the first method the scrap value of the asset at the end of its life is estimated and deducted from its original cost to the

Budgets and Accounts 33

company. The difference is divided by the number of years of estimated life and the resulting figure deducted from revenue as an annual expense. In the second method the expense charge is set at a constant percentage of the written down value (WDV) of the asset — the original cost less the cumulative depreciation charge — resulting in a diminishing absolute amount to be set against revenue. The percentage is calculated to reduce the WDV to the scrap value over the estimated life of the asset. This means that the charges are much higher in the early years, resulting in both profit and asset value being shown as artificially low. This makes capital employed difficult to estimate for purposes of financial ratio analysis. The written down value has no relation to the market value of an asset and thus there can be a profit or loss in the accounts when it is sold.

In times of inflation the replacement cost of an asset may be much greater than its original cost. This can be dealt with by revaluing the asset annually using special indices of cost of capital and adjusting depreciation provisions accordingly. This is known as replacement cost accounting as opposed to historic cost accounting when the original cost is retained. Annual revaluations of assets is not the practice in all countries. Where it is not done, sale of the asset after some time has elapsed can generate substantial revenue at the cost of a relatively small disposal of asset value.

A major reason for depreciation charges in the accounts is to ensure that the costs of services provided by capital assets are included in the selling price of the company's products. This is in fact more important from the company management point of view than the notion of building up funds to replace assets at a given date. The amounts charged are treated as part of the net cash flow of the business and are available for use as transfers from fixed assets to current assets and possibly back again, in whatever way is most beneficial to the business. What has actually happened to them is not always clear from the balance sheet.

The calculation of depreciation for tax purposes is governed by the tax authority's rules and is not necessarily related to the amounts actually charged in the business accounts.

In bookkeeping terms the depreciation amounts are regarded as debit entries in an intermediate account which is then transferred to the profit and loss account at the end of the accounting period. The corresponding credit entries go to the asset account concerned, reducing the written down value, and to a depreciation reserve account. Balances of both depreciation reserve and asset accounts are carried forward to the end of the useful life of the asset. At this point any scrap value received is credited to the asset account and any additional money needed for replacement is transferred from the P&L account. Any excess over cost of replacement is credited to capital reserve or a specific asset replacement account.

Financial Analysis

The balance sheet and P&L account provide quite a lot of information on the financial health of the company but it is in the nature of a snapshot of conditions at a particular moment in time. One can tell whether a profit has been made in the period in question but it is necessary to have the results of several years trading, ideally together with several years forecasts, to form a judgement on the operating conditions, that is whether results are improving, stable or deteriorating.

It is quite possible for a company to show a trading profit on its normal operations over a year and to cap this by receiving an enquiry for its most profitable product many times greater than any previous order. This will no doubt be welcome, but before accepting it the company should be sure that it is aware of all the consequences of doing so and can handle them. An order of this nature will demand purchases of materials greater than before and probably take longer to fulfil. There will consequently be a longer gap than usual between buying the material and receiving payment for the delivered order. In this gap the outgoings of the company for its normal operations carry on. Has it enough working capital to enable it to wait out this period without becoming insolvent? Many companies have been obliged to cease trading while under the impression that they were doing well; the press tends to report that they were 'overstretched'.

Cash Flow Analysis

A cash flow forecast, showing the sources and uses of money for the period in question is as important as the balance sheet in this situation. It consists of a table, as typically shown in Table 3.1, setting out, period by period, the forecast flows of money into and out of the company. The inflows would typically be revenues from sales of products, sales of fixed assets, issues of shares and loans. Outflows would be costs incurred requiring payments to creditors – therefore not including depreciation – and purchases of fixed assets or investments for either credit or cash. Another column – budget – records the forecasts for the year and for each period and a third – variance – the difference between budget and actual for each period. The cumulative totals for each column are also entered. Analysis of the period and cumulative variances provide a control mechanism helping to ensure that each expenditure and commitments are not allowed to rise above the company's ability to provide the funds from its operations.

Table 3.1 Cash flow budget

Receipts	Jan.			Feb.			March			Totals		
	B	A	V	B	A	V	B	A	V	B	A	V
Balance at 1st of month												
Cash sales assets sold												
Receipts from creditors												
Total receipts												
Payments												
Cash purchases												
Payment to creditors												
Wages & salaries												
Rent & rates												
Heat & light												
Assets bought												
VAT												
Balance												
Overdraft												

Ratio Analysis

Liquidity

Liquidity is the degree to which the company assets are in the form of cash or can readily be converted into cash. As seen in the example given in 'Financial Analysis' this is not the same as profitability. A company showing a profit in the accounts may suddenly be unable to meet its current obligations. In extreme cases its creditors may then petition for it to be put into liquidation, that is convert all its assets into cash, usually on the unfavourable terms of a forced sale, in order to recover the sums owed to them. A measure of the company's ability to meet its obligations is the current ratio:

$$\frac{\text{current assets}}{\text{current liabilities}}$$

Currents assets are typically finished goods, work in progress, raw materials, cash and debtors. Current liabilities are trade creditors, tax and any other creditors. Suppliers extending credit to the company expect to see a substantial buffer of current assets to protect their claims and the ratio should not normally be allowed to fall below a given point. What point this is will depend on the nature of the company's operations. In batch manufacturing industry a figure of 2 : 1 is regarded as satisfactory.

Some current assets are by nature needed to maintain the company operations and would not normally be available to meet short-term obligations. The ratio measuring this ability, often called the 'acid test' is

$$\frac{\text{cash + debtors (quick assets)}}{\text{current liabilities}}$$

A manufacturing company would be expected to maintain a 1 : 1 ratio to be credit worthy. A company buying on credit and selling for cash with a rapid stock turnover, such as a supermarket, might have no financial problems with a ratio of less than 1 : 1. As with nearly all financial data, changes in the ratios may be more significant than their absolute values.

Profitability

High liquidity ratios indicate short-term financial strength but do not measure efficiency of utilization of resources. If this is poor, medium-term profitability will also be poor. Three factors are involved:

(1) Capital employed
(2) Profit
(3) Sales

The relationships between these three can be expressed as

$$\frac{\text{profit}}{\text{capital employed}} = \frac{\text{sales}}{\text{capital employed}} \times \frac{\text{profit}}{\text{sales}}$$

The return on capital employed, which is the long-term measure of the financial health of the company, is affected by both the other ratios. Anything done to increase either will benefit the company. Turnover of assets, the second ratio, is a direct measure of efficiency of utilization of resources.

These ratios are most helpful when income is constant. Unfortunately this is not always the case and gross fluctuations bring the risk of being unable to meet interest payments on borrowings. A ratio measuring this risk is

$$\frac{\text{income before interest and tax}}{\text{annual interest charges}}$$

Evaluating this ratio for the extremes of fluctuation experienced gives an indication of the cover against the risk. The greater the fluctuations the higher should be the ratio.

Stock turnover, as well as capital turnover, is an important ratio, reflecting both profitability and liquidity, as does the ratio of sales to debtors

$$\frac{\text{sales}}{\text{stock}} \qquad \frac{\text{sales}}{\text{debtors}}$$

These ratios indicate the speed with which stock and debtors are converted into cash, to the benefit of liquidity. The interrelationship of the factors involved is manifest in the ratios. It is important to look at ratio trends over extended periods in order to judge the progress of the company. It may be helpful to management to express both stock level and debtors in terms of weeks of sales, giving figures more easily related to company day-to-day operations.

Investors

The above ratios are useful in managing the company. Potential investors use others, some of which are published in the national press. They will be interested in the return on investment and the risk involved.

The ratios relating to return on investment are

$$\text{Earnings per share} \quad \frac{\text{profit after tax and preference dividend}}{\text{no. of ordinary shares issued}}$$

$$\text{Dividend yield} \quad \frac{\text{dividend per share}}{\text{market price}}$$

$$\text{Price/earnings ratio} \quad \frac{\text{market price of shares}}{\text{earnings per share}}$$

Some estimate of the risk taken by the investor can be derived from the ratios

$$\text{Times interest earned} = \frac{\text{profit before interest and tax}}{\text{debenture interest}}$$

$$\text{Times dividend covered} = \frac{\text{profit after tax and preference dividend}}{\text{dividend}}$$

Creditors

The risk to the creditor, as distinct from the investor is indicated by the gearing of the company. A high proportion of equity capital is a safeguard for creditors since they are entitled to be paid in full before the owners receive anything on liquidation.

Limitations

It should be borne in mind that these ratios are based on financial statements which only report on those 'facts' that can be expressed in money terms. The inverted commas are used to emphasize that such statements contain estimates and personal decisions that are sometimes arbitrary and refer to specific accounting periods which may not be representative of the operational situation.

Those aspects of the business not capable of being expressed in financial terms may have an important effect on its success. Use of the ratios as measures of the efficiency of individual managers should be treated with great caution unless they are part of a well-thought-out scheme of key results and objectives for individuals.

Ratios cannot usefully be compared between companies unless their sizes, product, processes and markets are closely similar. Even then, differences in the format of their respective accounts may render comparison meaningless without a great deal of investigation. They give managers additional information on which to base their judgements, but they do not provide a company control system.

Bookkeeping

Initial records of expenditure and income are kept in day books. The entries are periodically posted to accounts held in ledgers, usually in an integrated accounting system which is the responsibility of the accounts department. The standard system for doing this is double entry bookkeeping, invented in the fifteenth century by an Italian monk.

All changes of value are recorded in accounts. These are sheets of paper divided vertically into two, one side forming a list of value moving in and the other list of value moving out. The principle is that all movements are entered twice, once in the 'in' or credit side of one account and once in the 'out' or debit side of a different account. The debit totals will, if there are no bookkeeping errors, always equal the credit totals when all transactions are complete. If positive and negative errors of the same amounts occur these will not, of course, be detected.

Accounts are of two types, capital and revenue. The former record what a company owns and what it owes, while the latter record the income and expenditure of the company in the course of its day-to-day operations. For accounting purposes 'income' includes payments due from customers, so it is not the same as 'receipts' which is cash actually received. Expenditure and payments differ in the same way.

One difficulty for non-accountants is in deciding on which side of an account to enter a given sum. Table 3.2 shows the principle involved. A starting point is that there is always a cash account. Since the company owns the cash, it is an asset and therefore a capital account. Cash coming into the company is entered on the left and that going out on the right.

Table 3.2 Capital and revenue accounts

	Left	Right
Capital	Assets	Liabilities
Revenue	Expenditure	Income

At the end of the accounting period the revenue accounts are totalled and the balance, positive or negative, transferred to the profit and loss account. The company profit (loss) is the difference between the two sides after any capital reduction has been made good. Profit retained is an addition to capital; loss is always a loss of capital.

An exercise in double entry bookkeeping is given in Appendix 3.1.

Marginal Costing

Another duty of the accounts department is that of recording the costs incurred in company activities such as manufacturing. One method of doing this is the system of marginal costing. Marginal cost is defined as 'prime cost plus variable overheads' and is explained by the example in Table 3.3.

40 Budgets and Accounts

Table 3.3 Marginal costing

A factory produces 20 000 units and sells them all at £2.00 each

Materials consumed	20 000	
Direct wages	10 000	
Factory expenses	6 000	of which 3600 is fixed
Office expenses	1 800	all fixed
Selling expenses	1 200	of which 600 is fixed

Find the marginal cost of sales and the break-even point in terms of units sold

Materials consumed	20 000
Direct wages	10 000
Factory variable expenses	2 400
Selling variable expenses	600
Total variable expenses	33 000

Marginal cost per unit = 33 000/20 000 = £1.65

Recovery of fixed expenses = 2 − 1.65 = £0.35 per unit (contribution)

Factory fixed expenses	3600
Office fixed expenses	1800
Selling fixed expenses	600
Total fixed expenses	6 000

Sales required to recover the fixed expenses (breakeven)
6000/0.35 = 17 143 units

This method of cost accounting gives an overall picture of the profit or loss situation and in many cases is adequate for controlling operations. It does not lend itself to detailed cost investigation of departments and activities because it does not indicate where the overheads are actually consumed. This information can be obtained if needed, at the penalty of a more complex and expensive system.

Standard Costing

In this system, which is sometimes known as absorption costing, a budget is produced in which all overheads are allocated to the activities associated with them. 'Standard rates' for each activity are calculated from the direct expenditure plus the allocated overheads. The 'standard cost' per unit is then calculated from these rates. This becomes the target cost which the actual cost as recorded is compared. The performance of each department or activity can thus be judged as well as the overall profitability of the product. Table 3.4 illustrates such a cost structure.

Table 3.4 Standard cost structure

	Budgeted profit	Average SP
FSP	Selling expenses	Gross margin
	Admin.	
LMO	Start-up	Initial costs
	Tools, test equipment	
	Development	
L + O	Material	Manufacturing costs
	Material handling	
	Subcontract	
	Dept 1	
	Dept 2	
	Dept 3	
	Dept 4	
	Other	
	Establishment overheads	Allocated overheads

42 Budgets and Accounts

Establishment overheads are those costs which cannot easily or economically be charged directly to an activity, that is, without creating an unreasonably complex and expensive system. They are therefore allocated to the departments on a commonsense basis so that they are all 'absorbed' in the various departmental rates. The rates themselves can usefully be regarded as percentages of either factory standard price per unit or average selling price per unit. Care should be taken in any discussion to establish unambiguously which convention is to be used; failure to do so leads to much confusion later.

A limitation of standard costing is that, since all the overheads must be absorbed by the products to which the associated activities ultimately contribute, the redesign of a product, so that its production no longer needs a certain activity, may not result immediately in a reduced cost. This is because a cost reduction in one product for this reason would demand the recalculation of all the other allocations of overheads to ensure that the total is still absorbed. When a large number of products are involved this considerable effort may not be worthwhile until all overhead allocations are routinely reviewed.

It is probably best for engineers to avoid words like 'real' and 'true' in discussing costs and to regard accounting as a convention that, if adhered to, can with experience be a valuable means of monitoring the use of company resources.

Project Budget

The standard costing system is helpful in creating a budget for an R&D project to specify, design, develop and manufacture a new product, since the standard rates for all the activities planned, multiplied by the time estimate for each phase of the project, give the estimated investment in the new product in a form lending itself to detailed discussion. Table 3.5 is a typical form of project budget.

There is merit in confining the project budget to a single sheet of paper displaying the names of the people concerned, the estimates on which the decision to go ahead is based, and the authority for doing so. By providing several columns for the estimates, the stages in arriving at the final budget and any changes of mind during the working stages of the project, can be recorded. This is another area where human memory tends to be selective in the absence of such records.

The R&D Budget

The project budget can be seen to be a result of the strategic planning (Figure 2.2) loop 5, 6, 7. As many good projects – those with a high

Table 3.5 Project budget

Commercial auth.	Project no.
Development auth.	Model part no.
Project leader	Product group
Description	

Date			
1 Laboratory 2 DO 3 Model shop 4 Electronics 5 Material 6 Mods to 1st WO			
7 Total dev. cost			
8 Jigs and fixtures 9 Test equipt 10 Start-up costs			
11 Total prod. prep.			
12 Contingency 13 Tools			
14 Total prod. costs			
15 Total initial costs			
17 Previously auth'd 18 This request			
19 Project start 20 Release to production 21 Release to sales			
22 No. off per year 23 FSP per unit 24 Average SP			
25 Total revenue			
26 Comments			
Approvals 27 Project leader 28 R&D manager 29 Manufacturing 30 Marketing 31 Cost accountant			

probability of being profitable – as possible should be estimated. The most beneficial projects should then be selected until the aggregate resources estimated equal those allocated to new projects in Figure 2.6. This group of projects, together with the resources allocated for other purposes in Figure 2.6 and any recovery amounts, form the R&D budget. Recovery is the term used to describe the result of charging work done for other departments to their respective budgets and crediting the R&D budget with the same amount. A typical format is illustrated in Table 3.6.

The budget is divided into planning periods to suit the nature of the company's business and each period is represented by three columns. These are headed budget, actual and variance. The last term is the difference between the first two columns, not the more complex statistical measure. The budget figures for the selected projects and the other resource-consuming activities are entered into the budget column and subtotals calculated. The budgeted total outflow of funds per period is entered on the second last line with the cumulative total to date below it.

At the review dates the expenditure per planning period is entered in the actual column opposite the relevant activity. An important aspect of monitoring the progress of a project is to examine the variances and observe whether they are positive or negative. The trend of variances is a useful indicator of the likely degree of achievement of the R&D budget.

Table 3.6 R&D budget

R&D Budget £1000s

Allocated	Period 1			Period 2			Period 3			Period 4			Total
	Budget	Actual	Variance	Budget	Actual	Variance	Budget	Actual	Variance	Budget	Actual	Variance	
Project 100	4	3	1	4	3	1	4			3			5
101	6	6		3	6	(3)							9
102				8	8		7			7			22
103							5			5			10
Marketing assist.	2	4	(2)	2	2		2			2			8
Production assist.	2		2	2	2		2			2			8
Subtotal	14	13	1	19	21	(2)	20			19			72
Less recoveries	4	4		4	4		4			4			16
Net	10	9	1	15	17	(2)	16			15			56
Overheads admin.	3	3		3	3		3			3			12
travel	1	1		1	2	(1)	1			1			4
library	1	1											1
other	2	2		2	2		2			2			8
Subtotal	7	7		6	7	(1)	6			6			25
Capital exp.				10	10					3			13
Total exp.	17	16	1	31	34	(3)	22			24			94
Cumulative	17	16		48	50	(2)	70			94			

46 Budgets and Accounts

Review

This chapter has:

(1) Explained the need for project management.
(2) Presented a simplified model of company financial structure.
(3) Described the purpose of the balance sheet and the profit and loss account.
(4) Explained the purposes of depreciation provisions and financial ratio analysis.
(5) Described forms of project budget and departmental budget.

The next chapter will discuss financial techniques used in setting criteria for the selection of project proposals to maximize profitability. Non-financial criteria will be used to ensure that the potential new products are such as to contribute to the corporate plan.

Further Reading

Batty, J. 1976: *Accounting for R&D*. Business Books Ltd.
Wright, W. 1971: *Direct Standard Costs*. Macdonald.

Appendix 3.1   Double Entry Bookkeeping

Joe Bloggs decides to start a small import–export business. His financial transactions during the start-up period are listed below in the first column and are identified by capital letters. Place a sheet of paper across the page under row A and post the transaction in the second column as described in Chapter 3. Move the paper down to row B and check your answer against the correct one now exposed in the third column. Repeat through to transaction E then see if you can list the balances to agree with those shown.

Budgets and Accounts 47

Joe Bloggs Import/Export plc

	Transaction	Your entry		The answer	
A	His aunt lends him £1500 to start business	Cash		Auntie	
B	He buys an old van for cash	Cash	Transport	Cash A1500	Auntie A1500
C	Buys typewriter and filing cabinet £60 the lot	Cash	Office eq.	Cash B240	Transport B240
D	Bank lends him £500 for 6 months	Cash	Bank	Cash C60	Office eq. C60
E	Joe subscribes £1000 as capital	Cash	Owner's cap.	Cash D500	Bank D500
				Cash E1000	Owner's cap. E1000

Listing all the entries in the table above, the balances left on the accounts are as follows:

Cash		Auntie	Transport	Office eq.	Bank	Owner's cap.
1500	240	1500	240	60	500	1000
1000	60					
500						

Listing the balances on these accounts:

Cash	2700	
Auntie		1500
Transport	240	
Office eq.	60	
Bank		500
Owner's cap.		1000
Totals	3000	3000

48 Budgets and Accounts

Joe then begins active trading and his first period transactions are listed below. Post his figures on a copy of the table below. They follow on from the first set and the opening balances are already entered.

- F He purchases goods for £200 cash.
- G He pays £12 sundry expenses such as stationery.
- H He pays £50 cash for the first month's rent.
- I He sells all the goods he bought (F) for £240 cash.
- J He pays a further £6 sundry expenses.
- K He pays £14 wages to a temp for some typing.
- L He purchases goods for £600 cash.
- M He sells the goods (L) for £700 cash.
- N He purchases £300 worth of goods from Smith on credit.
- O He sells the goods (N) to Jones for £350 on monthly account terms.
- P He repays the bank loan of £500.

Joe decides to draw up a profit and loss account for this initial period.

All the postings you have made of the above list are P&L transactions and now need to be transferred to the P&L account. Do this and see what the balance on the P&L comes to. Has he made a profit? List the balance left on the accounts.

Budgets and Accounts 49

Joe Bloggs Import/Export plc

Cash	Capital	Auntie
2700	1000	1500

Office eq.	Bank	Transport
60	500	240

Purchases	Sundry exps	Office rent

Sales	Wages	P&L account

Smith	Revenue reserve	Jones

4 Project Selection

The selection of projects from the list of proposals for inclusion in the R&D programme is a matter of ranking them in order of benefit to the company. The criteria for doing so will be specific to the company but will always include a minimum return on investment in addition to non-financial criteria. Typical criteria, methods of applying them and the influence of financial analysis methods on ranking order are discussed.

Ranking Project Proposals

Previous chapters have indicated how to establish the number of new products needed by the company, the funds available to R&D for development and design and how these funds are accounted for. The next stage is to decide which of the potential projects to work on. This is a complex question. A good new product must meet some specific market need, be capable of being handled efficiently by every department in the company, be a good fit with the company objectives and optimize the use of company resources.

The first requirement is to have a large number of potential projects from which to select and then to select those which will produce the best returns on the resources available. The most efficient way of loading R&D resources is to place the proposals in order of priority and then to allocate to them, in that order, all the resources they can usefully employ until all allocated resources are committed. There will always be pressure to take on more projects than this; it should be resisted. This procedure ensures the minimum average project duration, gets the product on the market as early as possible, minimizes development costs and opportunity costs. Not least, it reduces the time in which the specification can be changed.

To establish the merit of project proposals without overlooking any significant factor, it is highly desirable to have a selection system that is applied to all cases. A good starting point is a check list with sections covering criteria for acceptance by all the main company functions. Of necessity this will be specific to a company in terms of its markets and capabilities and a comprehensive universal list is not practical. The type of checklist shown in Table 4.1 (Twiss, 1982) provides a reasonable starting point for creating such a list, adding and subtracting elements as required.

Table 4.1 Project checklist

A *Corporate objectives, strategy and values*
  1   Is it compatible with current strategy & long range plan?
  2   Does its potential warrant a change in strategy?
  3   Is it consistent with company image?
  4   Is it consistent with company attitude to risk?
  5   Is it consistent with company attitude to innovation?
  6   Does estimated timing fit company needs?

B *Marketing criteria*
  1   Does it meet clearly understood and defined market need?
  2   Estimated total market size
  3   Estimated market share
  4   Estimated life in market
  5   Probability of commercial success
  6   Likely sales volume
  7   Time relationship to market plan
  8   Effect on current products
  9   Pricing policy and customer acceptance
  10 Competitive position
  11 Distribution channels
  12 Estimated launching costs

C *R&D criteria*
  1   Is it consistent with R&D strategy?
  2   Does potential warrant change in R&D strategy?
  3   Probability of technical success
  4   Development cost and time
  5   Patent position
  6   Potential future extensions of product and technology
  7   Availability of R&D resources
  8   Effect on other projects
  9   Environmental effects

D *Financial criteria*
  1   R&D costs: capital and revenue
  2   Manufacturing investment
  3   Marketing investment
  4   Availability of finance on time scale
  5   Effect on other project funding
  6   Time to break even and maximum negative cash flow

52 Project Selection

Table 4.1 *(continued)*

7	Potential annual benefit and time scale
8	Expected profit margin and ROI
9	Does it meet company investment criteria?

E   *Production criteria*
  1   Are new processes required?
  2   Availability of personnel with necessary skills
  3   Compatibility with existing capability
  4   Cost and availability of raw material
  5   Cost of manufacture
  6   Engineering investment
  7   Additional facilities required
  8   Manufacturing safety
  9   Subcontract content
  10 Value added in production

Project Profile

The criteria listed in Table 4.1 present some problems in their present form in assessing the order of priority of projects. One method of displaying the data in a more usable form is the project profile, illustrated in Figure 4.1. The merit of the project in relation to each criterion is assessed in terms of the five classes, ranging from very good to very poor. A dot is placed in the appropriate column opposite each criterion and the dots are joined up by a line. The pattern formed by the line is an indication

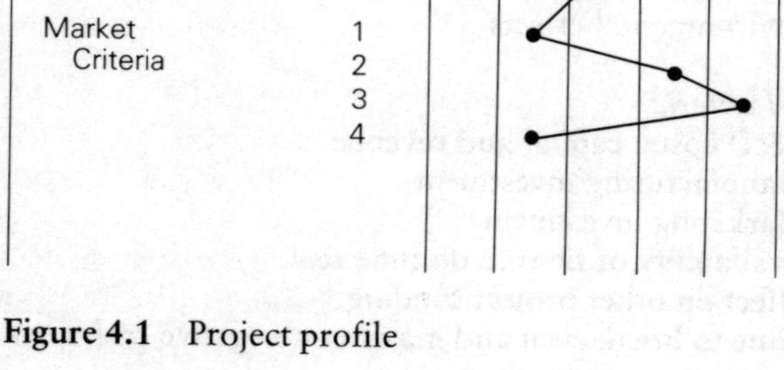

Factor	Evaluation	VG	G	AV	P	VP
Corporate Objectives	1	•				
	2		•			
	3	•				
	4			•		
Market Criteria	1			•		
	2				•	
	3					•
	4			•		

Figure 4.1 Project profile

of the overall merit of the project: the more the line conforms to the VG column and the less it wanders towards the VP column the better the project in terms of the criteria.

Project Merit Number

A slightly more refined method of handling the data is shown in Table 4.2. In this case the merit of the project in terms of each criterion is scored on a 1 to 5 scale. In addition, to allow for the fact that some criteria will be more important to the company than some others, each criterion is given a weighting on a scale of 1 to 10. This number is entered into the appropriate column. The third column contains the product of the first two, providing a merit number for each criterion and the sum of these is the overall merit number for the project. The projects may then be ranked numerically by merit number.

Table 4.2 Project merit number

Factor		Weighting 1–10	Evaluation 1–5	Merit number
Corporate objectives	1	10	5	50
	2	8	4	32
	3	8	5	40
	4	9	3	27
			Total	149
Market criteria	1	10	4	40
	2	6	2	12
	3	8	1	8
	4	7	4	28
			Total	88
			Overall merit number	237

Having ranked the proposals in order of compatibility with company objectives it remains to establish the order of priority in terms of return on investment. The data for this analysis is the set of project budgets as shown in Table 3.5.

This groups the estimated costs under appropriate headings with subtotals. By breaking the activities under each heading into relatively small parts, which are fairly easy to estimate, the overall estimate can be made more reliable. As in the case of the checklist the detail of the format must be specific to the company using it. A section of the form records the estimates for sales and production volumes. Production costs are estimated by using the cost structure in Figure 3.4. Other costs are usually obtained as standard company percentages of those estimated so far, arriving at labour, materials and overhead or the LMO level. Adding the standard uplift for development and initial production costs produces the factory standard price (FSP) against which manufacturing performance will be judged. Above this line standard uplifts for selling expenses and budgeted profit are added to arrive at average selling price. This procedure assumes the use of a standard costing system in an established product line. If such a system is not used, or a completely new and different production process is to be used, it may be necessary to estimate and allocate overheads from scratch. This will often be done by estimators, but engineers involved in the project should ensure that the results make sense from their own viewpoint.

The average selling price, together with the estimates of sales volume, provides the total estimated income from the project. This, with the total cost estimate, is the basis for estimating the return on investment of the project.

There is merit in confining all this data to one sheet of paper. Since it may be appropriate to vote funds piecemeal to a project in order to control the financial risk involved, several columns for estimates should be provided. A small feasibility study may be an economical way of reducing the uncertainty – see Chapter 5 – in a specific aspect before authorizing the funding of the whole project. This should be viewed as an investment in risk reduction and the cost regarded as an insurance premium. Overruns on the original budget should result in that budget being closed and a new one authorized to cover the estimated additional requirement in the next column. Initials in the appropriate approvals section ensure that such additions have been properly authorized and advised to the cost accountant.

Investment Analysis

The funding of a project is no different in financial terms from any other company investment. Management must make a judgement, based on estimates of cost and benefit, as to which of the competing project proposals they will accept. The degree of risk will vary between proposals, but some risk will always be present and the information will seldom be complete. A number of techniques of investment analysis are commonly in use, each with merit in some cases. The method used can have a decisive influence on the ranking of the proposals. This effect is illustrated in the hypothetical set of proposals given in Table 4.3 (Bierman and Smidt, 1964).

Table 4.3 Hypothetical investments

Case	Initial cost	Net cash proceeds per year		
		Year 1	Year 2	Year 3
A	10 000	10 000		
B	10 000	5 000	5 000	5 000
C	10 000	2 000	4 000	12 000
D	10 000	10 000	3 000	3 000
E	10 000	6 000	4 000	5 000
F	10 000	8 000	8 000	2 000

In some cases inspection of such a table is all that is needed to decide which investment to accept. If the choice were between cases A and D there would be no problem. In other cases a criterion may be needed, and one frequently used is the payback period. This selects the case which takes the shortest time to generate the income needed to pay back the total investment in the project. Such a technique ranks the above investments as in Table 4.4.

Table 4.4 Payback period

Case	Payback period (years)	Ranking
A	1	1
B	2	4
C	2.33	6
D	1	1
E	2	4
F	1.25	3

The weakness of this method is that it takes no account of what happens after the payback date is reached. Case A ranks equally with case D which produces a further 6000 after payback, while case A produces nothing. One method of taking this into account is by using the proceeds per unit outlay as the ranking criterion, as seen in Table 4.5.

56 Project Selection

Table 4.5 Proceeds per unit outlay

Case	Total proceeds	Investment outlay	Proceeds per unit outlay	Ranking
A	10 000	10 000	1.0	6
B	15 000	10 000	1.5	4
C	18 000	10 000	1.8	1
D	16 000	10 000	1.6	3
E	15 000	10 000	1.5	4
F	18 000	10 000	1.8	1

It will be seen that this technique has the effect of interchanging the rankings of the best and worst cases in Table 4.4, emphasizing the importance of sticking to one method of analysis. There is still a deficiency in the method. It does not take account of the timing of the outlays and proceeds. Case D, although ranked 3, earns 7000 more in the first 2 years than case C, which is ranked 1. This could be decisive if the company objectives stressed the need for income over that period.

Discounted Cash Flow

If there were a choice between receiving £100 now and the same amount a year hence there would be no doubt as to which would be preferred. This subjective preference is quite rational. If one has to pay a creditor £100 in one years time, it is not necessary to have £100 today. What is needed today is that sum which, invested, will with interest amount to £100 in one year. If the rate of interest in, say a Building Society, is 8 per cent, what is needed today is £92.60. This is known as the present value of £100 in one years time at a discount rate of 8 per cent, or the DCF PV at 8 per cent.

DCF Net Present Value

The DCF PV of any sum can be calculated from the expression:

$$\text{NPV} = I(1+r)^{-n}$$

where I = investment
r = rate of interest
n = number of years

There is seldom any need to apply the formula as tables of both present values of future sums and present values of sums received per period are to be found in most books dealing with investment and financial decisions. The procedure is to obtain from the tables the PV values of both outlays and proceeds for each year. The total PV of outlays is subtracted from the total PV of proceeds giving the net PV of the investment. Since in all the investments considered the entire outlay is in the first year, it is already a present value. Any proceeds in year 1 are also present values, but those in succeeding years are discounted by multiplying them by the fraction given at the appropriate year in the chosen rate of interest column in the tables. Table 4.6 gives the results of NPV analysis at 6 per cent applied to the investments listed in Table 4.3.

Table 4.6 Present value at 6%

Case	Present value of proceeds	Present value of outlay	Net present value	Ranking
A	9 430	10 000	−570	6
B	13 365	10 000	+3 365	5
C	15 526	10 000	+5 526	2
D	14 620	10 000	+4 620	3
E	13 418	10 000	+3 418	4
F	16 344	10 000	+6 344	1

The NPV of an investment, at the interest rate at which the firm can borrow capital, may be regarded as the profit on the investment when all costs, including interest payments, have been met. Alternatively it can be seen as the maximum amount the firm can pay for the opportunity of making the investment, without being worse off financially. The preferred investment is that with the highest NPV. If there is no competition for funding then all investments with a positive NPV can be accepted. Table 4.7 shows that the discounting rate used is significant in ranking investments.

Another use of the DCF method is to establish the maximum rate of interest a company can afford to pay to borrow the capital needed for the investment.

The DCF Yield of an Investment

The DCF yield, or rate of return, uses the same concepts as NPV and consists in finding by trial and error the interest rate that makes the discounted outlays and proceeds equal. The NPV is then, of course, zero.

58 Project Selection

Table 4.7 Present value at 30%

Case	Present value of proceeds	Present value of outlay	Net present value	Ranking
A	7 690	10 000	−2 300	6
B	9 080	10 000	−920	5
C	9 366	10 000	−634	3
D	10 831	10 000	+831	2
E	9 257	10 000	−743	4
F	11 789	10 000	+1 789	1

This permits the direct comparison of the rates of return of any number of competing investments. If it is proposed to borrow the money for the investment, the DCF yield is the highest interest rate the company can pay without making an overall loss. No investment having a DCF yield lower than the company's cost of capital would normally be accepted. Table 4.8 shows the result of ranking the hypothetical investments on this basis.

Table 4.8 DCF yield

Case	Yield %	Ranking
A	0	6
B	23	5
C	27	3
D	37	2
E	24	4
F	44	1

The effect of analysis techniques on the ranking of investments is shown in Table 4.9 where it can be seen that each method produces a different ranking. The ranking produced by the NPV 30 per cent and the yield tables are the same since the rates found in the latter are of the order of the 30 per cent applied in the former.

No single method supplies all the answers to investment decisions. An NPV result of £100 000 may look attractive. If the investment involved is £100 million, however, it is not so good. In the same way a DCF yield of 500 per cent looks good at first sight, but if the investment is 6p it is not worth considering. The method used must relate to the type of decision to be made. Particularly if dissimilar investments with different time scales

Table 4.9 Summary of rankings

Measure of worth	A	B	C	D	E	F
Payback period	1	4	6	1	4	3
Proceeds per unit outlay	6	4	1	3	4	1
DCF yield of investment	6	5	3	2	4	1
Net present value at 6%	6	5	2	3	4	1
Net present value at 30%	6	5	3	2	4	1

are in competition for funds, the NPV method has merit in the general case, because it takes these factors into account. If the competing investments are similar, say a choice has to be made between proposals for new products in the same product range, the complexity of DCF methods may not be justified. A simple comparison of total estimated income from the competing products may provide as good a guide to decision making.

Review

This chapter has:

(1) Described a project selection check list.
(2) Described methods of ranking project proposals.
(3) Described methods of investment analysis.
(4) Explained the concept of discounted cash flow.
(5) Demonstrated the influence of analysis methods on ranking.

The estimates on which ranking decisions are taken involve uncertainties. The next chapter puts forward a method of making best use of such information and a general method of taking decisions under uncertainty.

References

Bierman, H. and Smidt, S. 1964: *The Capital Budgeting Decision*. Macmillan.
Twiss, B. 1982: *Management of Technology Innovation*. Longman.

Further Reading

Basilio, A. and Gastwirt, L. 1979: *Turning R&D into Profits*. Amacom.
Garbutt, D. 1967: *Introduction to Capital Expenditure Decisions*. Pitman.

5 Uncertainty, Risk and Decision

Most decisions in industry are taken in conditions of some degree of uncertainty. Design, development and management have in common the absolute necessity of taking action based on incomplete information. The practical implication is that the outcome of any action, unless it has been previously proven, cannot be predicted accurately. The best that can be done is to convert the uncertainty, which is not quantifiable, into risk, which is. This permits the use of probability theory to compare the nature and range of outcomes of activities and help to form judgements as to the best course of action in given circumstances.

Assessment of Risk

A risk is an uncertainty to which a probability can be assigned. Probability is measured on a scale from 0 to 1. The chance of flying to the moon under one's own power has a probability of 0. The probability of dying is 1. In the final analysis assessment of risk is subjective, but there are techniques for aiding the assessor and the fact of subjectivity does not render the assessment useless. It is additional information that should not be neglected but used in a valid manner in the process of reducing overall risk.

Some people find it difficult to judge the probability of a given outcome, say the success of a specific development job, directly. It can often be brought into areas where they feel more willing to express an opinion by putting the problem in terms of comparative bets, using the notion of the equivalent urn.

Prior Probability

As an example of one technique, assume that a project leader is told that his current project, if successful, will earn the company £1000 profit, if a failure, nothing. That is one bet. Assume next that an urn has been filled with 1000 identical marbles. Of these 500 have been coloured red and the remainder blue. They have been well mixed and cannot be seen. The second bet is that drawing a red marble wins £1000, drawing a blue marble wins nothing. Clearly the chance of winning this bet is 0.5 since one of the two colours must be drawn, there being no other possibilities.

The project leader is now asked which of the two bets he prefers. If he says the second it means that there is a better chance of winning £1000 by drawing a red marble from the urn. This in turn means that the probability of project success is less than 0.5, in his judgement. By changing the proportion of red to blue marbles progressively, there comes a point where the project leader has no preference between the two bets. The chances of winning the two bets are at that point judged to have the same probability, given by the ratio of red to blue marbles. Such an initial assessment, based on the information available at the time, is the prior probability of success.

Posterior Probability

In a development project there are usually prospects of increasing the information available as time goes on. This may be by consulting a specialist in the field or by doing some research to fill in the gaps in knowledge, as part of the project. This additional information can be used to reduce the level of uncertainty in the project, producing the posterior probability of the same outcome.

One would like the additional information to be conclusive so that the success or failure of the project could be predicted with certainty. This will rarely be the case. The new information will indicate that the project will succeed or fail but the information itself will have only a probability of being correct. The consultant or the additional research will express a view on project success or failure and the probability of this view being correct is assessed in each of the two cases. Assume that this is represented by Table 5.1.

Table 5.1 Additional information

Project outcome	Additional Research		Totals
	Favourable	Unfavourable	
Succeed	0.9	0.1	1.0
Fail	0.2	0.8	1.0

This means that, should the project have a successful outcome, there is a 0.9 chance that the additional research supported this outcome and 0.1 chance that it did not. Conversely, if the project fails there is a 0.2 chance that the additional research supported it and a 0.8 chance that it did not. These additional probabilities must sum to 1. The assessments of these probabilities are made on the basis of what is known about the additional research, or the consultant, in relation to the unknowns in the project (Moore and Thomas, 1979).

The two sets of probabilities can now be combined as in Figure 5.1. In the figure ABCD, the base line DC is divided into the chances of success and failure. Assume that these have been assessed at 0.6 and 0.4. The vertical AD is divided into the probabilities of the additional information being correct or false in the case of project success, assessed at 0.9 and 0.1 respectively. The vertical BC is divided into the probabilities in the case of project failure, 0.2 and 0.8. The figure therefore gives the possible combinations of project outcome and additional information. Assume that the additional information predicted project success. The part of Figure 5.1 to be considered is therefore the area EFGHCD. The proportion of this corresponding to project success is

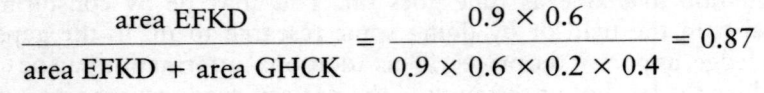

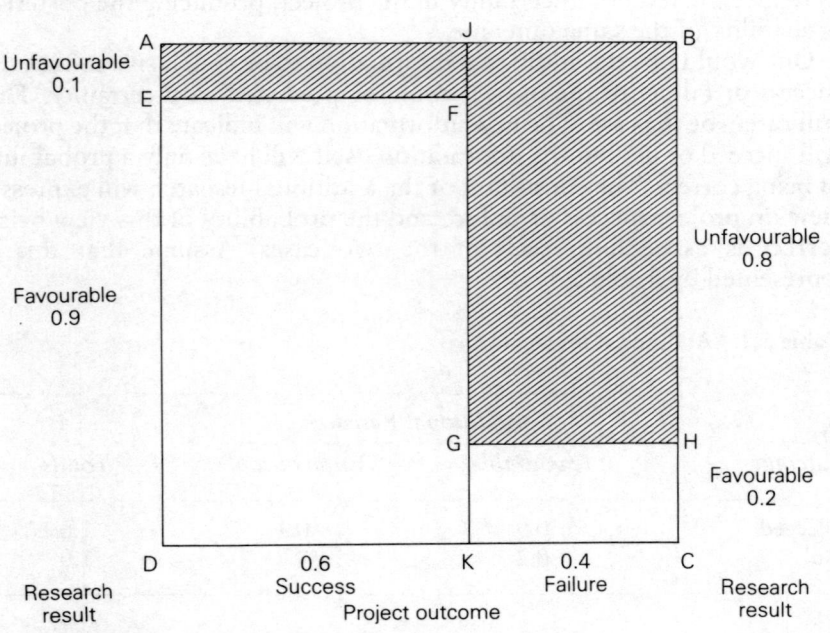

$$\frac{\text{area EFKD}}{\text{area EFKD} + \text{area GHCK}} = \frac{0.9 \times 0.6}{0.9 \times 0.6 \times 0.2 \times 0.4} = 0.87$$

Figure 5.1 Combined probabilities

The knowledge that the additional information was favourable has lifted the probability of project success from a prior probability of 0.6 to a posterior probability of 0.87. The posterior probability of project failure, calculated in the same way, would be 0.13. They add up to 1 as would be expected. There is now a much greater difference between the probabilities of success and failure on which to base a decision.

The above approach is an application of a theorem formulated in 1760 by the Reverend Thomas Bayes FRS and named after him. A set of mutually exclusive events B_1, B_2, B_3 has associated probabilities p (B_1), etc. If any of these events occur, event A can occur, but with a different probability for each B. Assume A to have occurred. p (B_1), etc., are the prior probabilities. The probability of B_1 occurring, given that A has occurred, written p $(B_1|A)$, is the posterior probability. The probability $p(A|B_1)$ is called the likelihood. The theorem states that the posterior probability is proportional to the prior probability multiplied by the likelihood.

The use of the Bayes theorem assumes knowledge of prior probabilities. Bayes' postulate is that, when nothing to the contrary is known, the probabilities should be assumed to be equal.

Decisions

Decisions in project management start with the choice of project and spread throughout its duration. These decisions will have a profound bearing on the future viability of the resulting product or process and should therefore take into account the most likely consequences. The decision to terminate a project can only be made rationally if the consequences of doing so can be compared with the consequences of carrying on. These cannot be known at the time the decision is to be made and a means of stating what is known and what is assessed of the influence of future events on the commercial performance of the product, permitting comparisons between options, is needed. Such means have been developed, under the general heading of 'utility theory', with a specific unit of measurement, the utile. For the purposes of this chapter the monetary 'expected value' concept will be used. This is the estimated pay-off in money terms of a given event multiplied by the probability of that event occurring. When only one of events A, B and C can occur and there are no other possible events, the sum of the probabilities of A, B and C must be 1. The expected value at this point is the sum of the possible pay-offs multiplied by their respective probabilities (Dewhurst, 1972).

Cumulative Density Function

By definition, an uncertain quantity is one whose value can lie anywhere along a specified range. It is often easier to assess a continuous probability distribution than a set of specific values. In many contexts, such as the RPD project planning technique described in Chapter 6, it is also more useful in decision making, in that the decision maker knows what risk he is taking, and in lending itself to sensitivity testing of possible decisions. In Chapter 6 the cumulative density function (CDF) is arrived at by calculating probabilities for all possible paths through a network after the probabilities of individual outcomes of activities have been assessed subjectively. It is also possible to assess a CDF as a series of step-by-step subjective judgements of the overall outcome.

The form of the CDF is shown in Figure 5.2 where the horizontal axis is a scale of all possible values of the uncertain quantity X and the vertical axis is the probability that the true value is equal to or less than X. In the case described in Chapter 6, X is the date of completion of the project.

To assess the distribution, the project leader is first asked to give a date such that the true date is as likely to be after it as before it. He should be as prepared to place a bet on completion before this date as on completion after it. As a 50/50 bet, this date corresponds to 0.5 on the probability scale. It is the project leader's indifference value for the true date.

He is then asked to assume that the true date will be before the p0.5 date and asked to nominate an earlier date that would again divide the range into two 50/50 bets. This is the p0.25 point. Another such procedure gives the p0.125 point. The p0.75 and p0.875 points are arrived at in the same

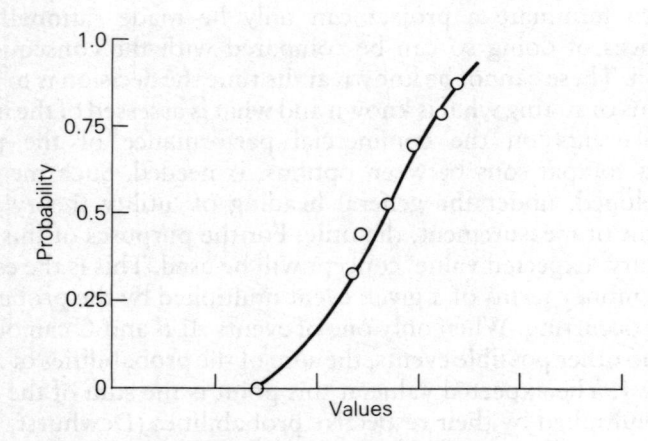

Figure 5.2 Cumulative density function

Uncertainty, Risk and Decision

way. These points are plotted and joined by a smooth curve which is the cumulative density function (CDF).

Decision Trees

Decisions in project management are frequently sequential. Decision B can only be taken after the result of action consequent upon decision A is known. Looking ahead from the starting point of a project the possible actions spread out like the branches of a tree. This analogy leads to the 'decision tree', a useful way of structuring the multiple problems associated with development projects so that the expected value (EV) criterion can be used to help decide which branch to follow. Figure 5.3 is a decision tree for a hypothetical development project to develop and market a new product.

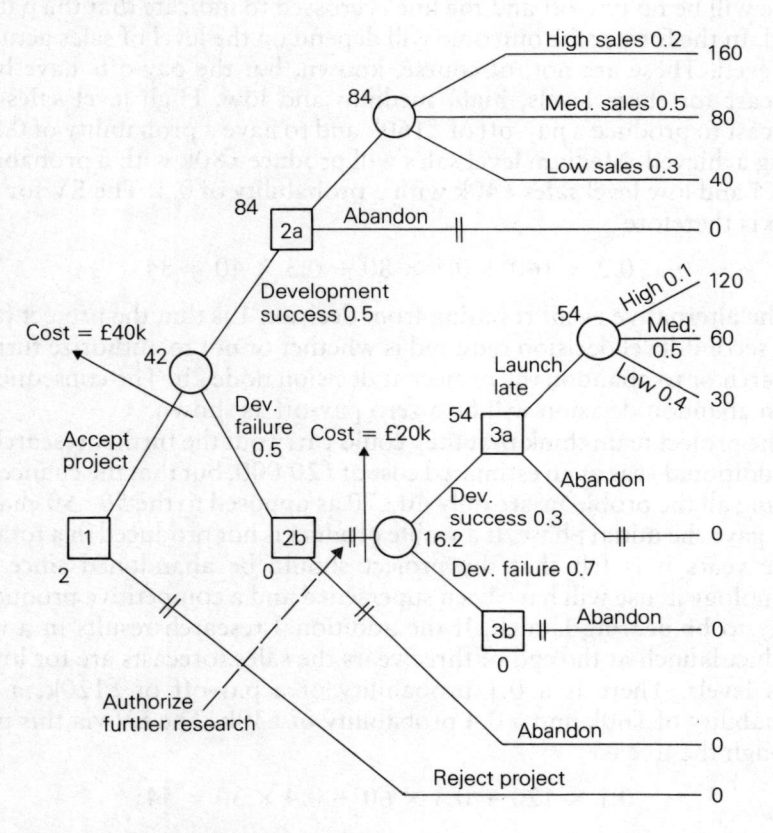

Figure 5.3 Project decision tree

66 Uncertainty, Risk and Decision

The basic tree consists of a network branching out from an initial decision of whether or not to undertake the project. The symbol for a decision node is a rectangle with a number in it indicating the decision level, in this case level 1. At the far right of the figure the net present values of the possible pay-offs from the various courses of action are listed. The decision not to start the project obviously has a pay-off of 0.

A line emerging from a decision node is a consequent action leading to an event node, indicated by a circle. There will be one or more events resulting from this decision, over which the project leader has no control but for which probability assessments can be made. In this case the probabilities of success and failure are assessed at 0.5. The cost of the project has been estimated at £40 000.

The second level of decisions is now reached and all the feasible possibilities are entered. If the project succeeds, the choice is between making and marketing the product or abandoning it. In the latter case there will be no pay-off and the line is crossed to indicate that the path is dead. In the former the outcome will depend on the level of sales actually achieved. These are not, of course, known, but the pay-offs have been forecast for three levels, high, medium and low. High level sales are forecast to produce a pay-off of £160k and to have a probability of 0.2 of being achieved. Medium level sales will produce £80k with a probability of 0.5 and low level sales £40k with a probability of 0.3. The EV for this path is therefore

$$0.2 \times 160 + 0.5 \times 80 + 0.3 \times 40 = 84$$

The alternative event resulting from decision 1 is that the project fails. The second-level decision required is whether or not to authorize further research or to abandon the project at decision node 2b. The consequence of an abandon decision will be a zero pay-off as shown.

The project team think that they could carry out the further research in an additional year at an estimated cost of £20 000, but that the chances of solving all the problems are only 30 : 70 as opposed to the 50 : 50 chance they gave the initial phase. If a viable product is not produced in a total of three years it is felt that the project should be abandoned since the technology in use will have been superseded and a competitive product is likely to be nearing launch. If the additional research results in a new product launch at the end of three years the sales forecasts are for lower sales levels. There is a 0.1 probability of a pay-off of £120k, a 0.5 probability of £60k and a 0.4 probability of £30k. The EV via this path through the tree is

$$0.1 \times 120 + 0.5 \times 60 + 0.4 \times 30 = 54$$

The remainder of the analysis is carried out by 'rolling back' the decision tree, that is by moving back from the final pay-off figures, node by node, multiplying each pay-off by the probability of each event passed through in the network. Thus the net present values of the EVs at the events consequent upon decision 2b would be either zero or £16.2k. Since the cost of the research is estimated at £20k this would result in a loss to the company in either case. The decision line to authorize further research is therefore broken.

Rolling back the pay-off via decision 2a, the EV following the initial development project is £42k. Since the cost of the project is estimated at £40k the expected profit is £2k.

The best strategy with this project is to carry out the initial development and, if it is successful within 2 years, launch the project. If the project fails within the two-year period it should be abandoned. Other projects competing for company resources should be analysed in the same way and ranked according to the levels of pay-off for each. This provides a priority list, in terms of EVs, as one factor in the decision making process of arriving at a portfolio of R&D projects. While the EV figures will only be guidelines for any individual project, the expected and actual cumulative figures will converge in the long run if the method is consistently applied, maximizing the productivity of the R&D function.

Cost of Information

Additional information can lead to better odds and bigger returns but if the information costs more to obtain than the increase in returns the result is a net loss. Perfect information is usually not practicable but the concept is useful in establishing how much can be paid for whatever additional information is available.

As an example take the case of a new product that has been developed and is ready for launch. Costs of development are history and do not enter into the next set of decisions. The cost of an abandon decision is therefore zero. The pay-offs have been estimated for market penetrations of 10 per cent and 2 per cent. In the first case the pay-off is £500k with a probability of 0.7 and in the second −£250k with a probability of 0.3. The prior EV of the launch is therefore

$$500 \times 0.7 - 250 \times 0.3 = 275$$

That of abandon launch is

$$0 \times 0.3 = 0$$

If the information were perfect the launch would take place in the 70 per cent of cases where a 10 per cent share was forecast and not in the others. The EV under these conditions would therefore be

$$500 \times 0.7 + 0 \times 0.3 = 350$$

The EV of perfect information in this case is the difference

$$350 - 275 = 75$$

Clearly even information that would predict the market share perfectly must not cost more than £75k or an overall reduction in pay-off will result. As already seen in this chapter, such perfection is not to be expected and the probability of the additional information being accurate must be taken into account. Assume that a test marketing exercise can be carried out, at a cost of £10k, to establish whether the higher or lower market share is the more likely. The results confirm or reject the sales estimates with the probabilities shown in Table 5.2.

Table 5.2 Test market indication

Sales level	Confirm	Reject	Totals
High (10%)	0.85	0.15	1.00
Low (2%)	0.25	0.75	1.00

The probabilities displayed in Table 5.2 can be combined as shown in Figure 5.4. If the test result confirms the 10 per cent forecast the shaded portion of Figure 5.4 is relevant and the combined probabilities are

$$\frac{0.7 \times 0.85}{0.7 \times 0.8 + 0.25 \times 0.3} = 0.89$$

If the 2 per cent level is confirmed the combined probabilities are

$$\frac{0.25 \times 0.3}{0.7 \times 0.85 + 0.25 \times 0.3} = 0.11$$

For the reject results the same calculations are done on the unshaded area giving revised probabilities of 0.32 for the 10 per cent and 0.68 for the 2 per cent levels. A decision tree can now be drawn as in Figure 5.5, the above probabilities entered on the appropriate branches and the pay-offs rolled back.

The EVs of the two main branches are 278.5 for the path including the test marketing program and 275 for that without it, a difference of 3.5 in favour of the first. Since, however, the cost of the program is 10 this means a reduction in pay-off of 6.5, so it is not worth doing. In this case

Uncertainty, Risk and Decision 69

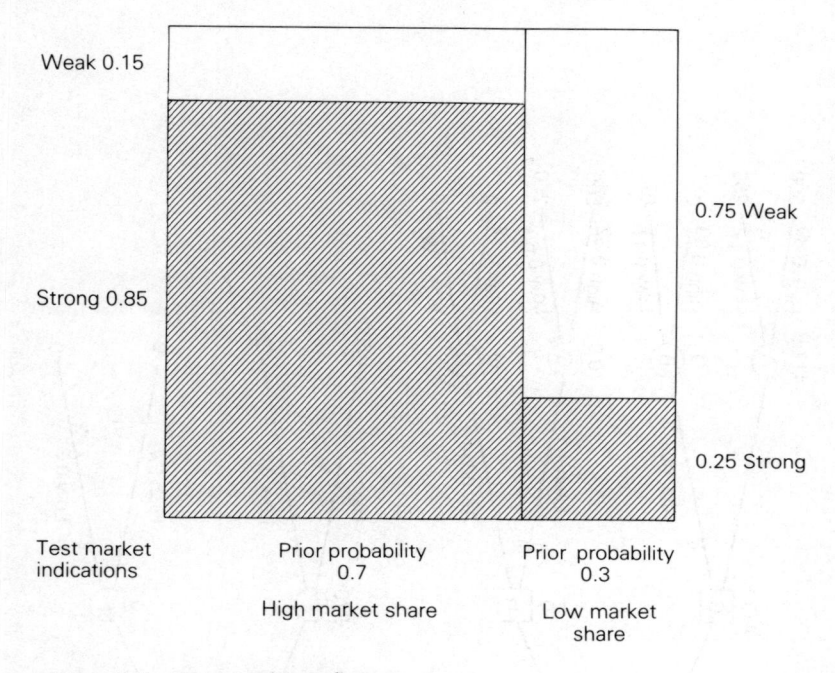

Figure 5.4 Test market influence

the benefit from the additional information is less than the cost of obtaining it. This is a consequence of the quality of the information as well as of the cost.

Review

This chapter has:

(1) Defined uncertainty, risk and probability.
(2) Described techniques for assessing probability.
(3) Defined prior and posterior probability.
(4) Explained how to combine probabilities.
(5) Explained how to use decision trees.
(6) Explained the cost of information concept.

Techniques for detailed planning and monitoring of projects are described in the next chapter.

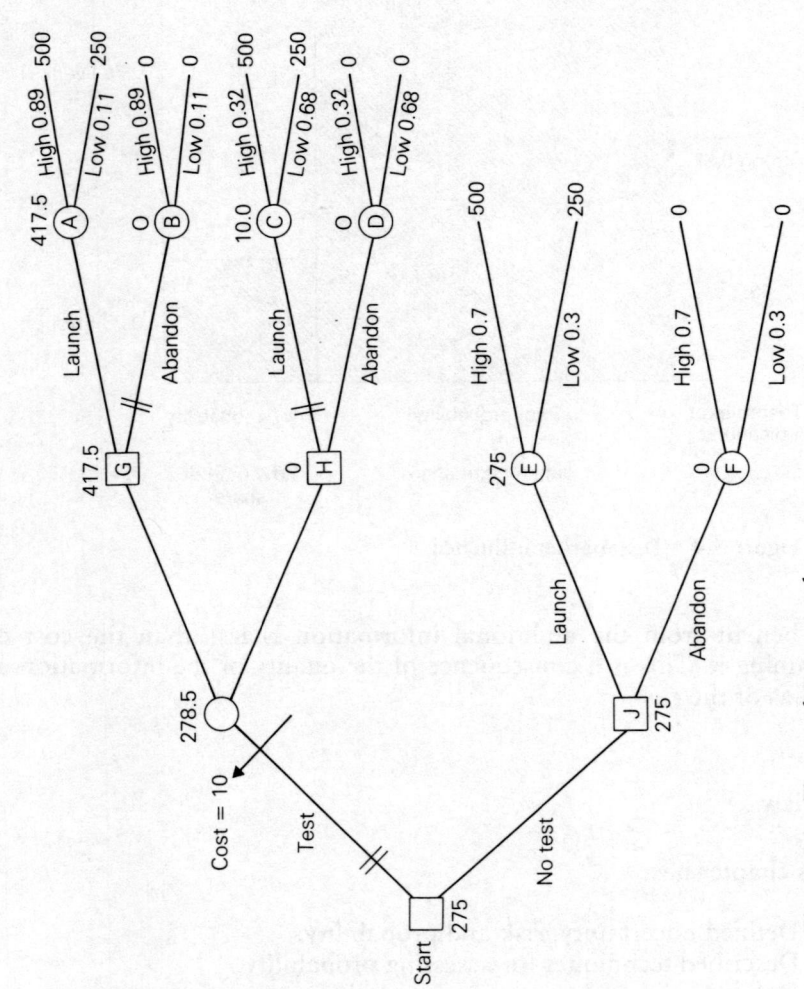

Figure 5.5 Test market proposal

References

Dewhurst, J. 1972: *Business Cost-benefit Analysis*. McGraw-Hill.
Moore, P. G. and Thomas, H. 1979: *The Anatomy of Decisions*. Penguin.

Further Reading

Dewhurst, J. 1968: *Maths for Accountants and Managers*. Heinemann.
Moroney, M. J. 1976: *Facts from Figures*. Pelican.

6 Project Planning

Ranking project proposals in terms of fit with company objectives, then creating a ranking list from the best of these on agreed financial criteria provides the basis for choosing the projects to which available R&D resources will be allocated. The next task is to take the projects in order of ranking and plan them. Since people are not necessarily interchangeable it may be necessary on occasion to depart from the priority order. Resource limitations may make it impossible to follow one project with the next one on the list, and projects must then be resourced in an order that makes efficient use of the resources available.

The Product Loop

The relationship between the company and the market place is in the form of a loop as shown in Figure 6.1. The three main company functions described in Chapter 1 are elements in this loop, sometimes as individuals and sometimes in collaboration. The potential new product may start anywhere in this loop depending on the origin of the proposal. If a new market need is identified the starting point would be at stage 1. The form of the diagram amplifies Figure 1.1. If the project is to develop and install a new process, the parts of the loop dealing with series production will not be included. If it is for the modification of an in-house process only those parts up to the pilot plant stage are relevant. In all cases the customer or user is a critical element in the loop.

Each function embraces three vertical columns, the centre one on its own and the other two shared with the other functions. Thus in stage 1 the task of analysing the market and answering the question 'what business are we in?' is seen to be mainly the province of the marketing function. In stage 3 the responsibility for deciding how to fill the market need thus established is jointly that of marketing and R&D. In the same way R&D has the main task of carrying out the feasibility study and the development but shares with manufacturing the responsibility for ensuring that the production design is efficient from the latter's point of view.

If the proposal is for a change to an existing product rather than

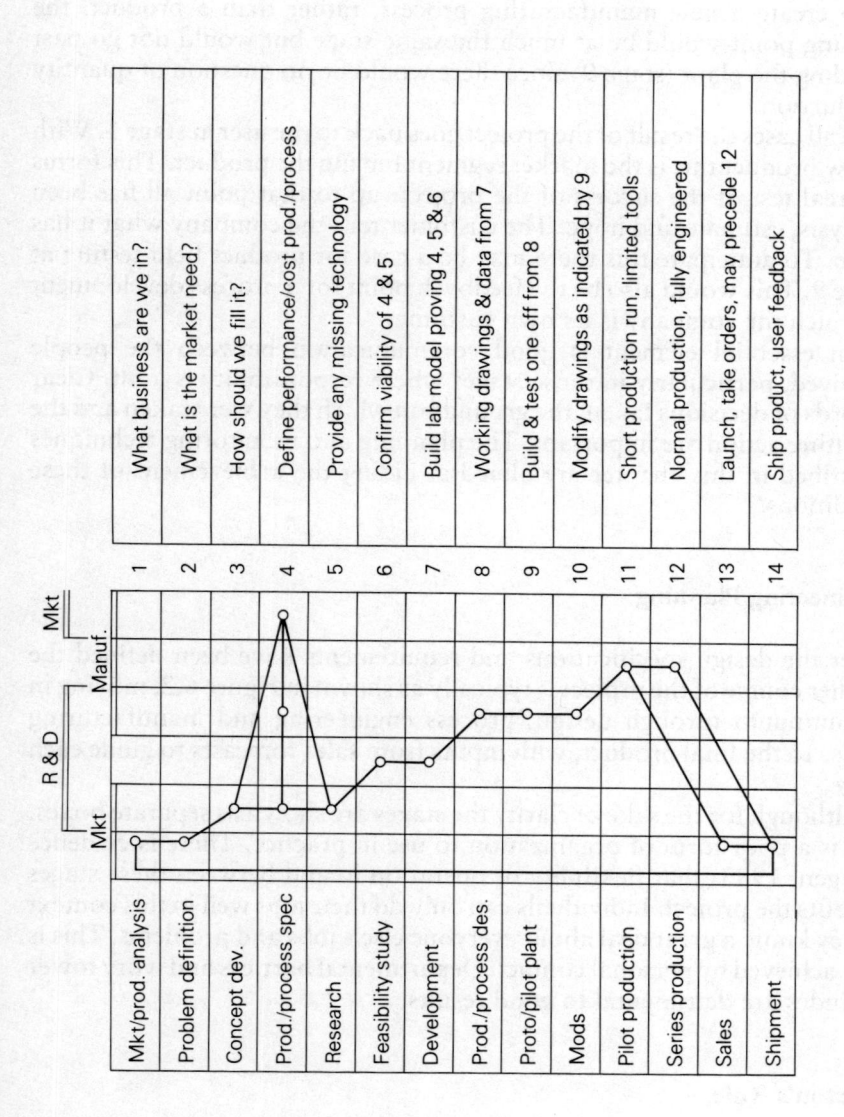

Mkt/prod. analysis	1	What business are we in?	
Problem definition	2	What is the market need?	
Concept dev.	3	How should we fill it?	
Prod./process spec	4	Define performance/cost prod./process	
Research	5	Provide any missing technology	
Feasibility study	6	Confirm viability of 4 & 5	
Development	7	Build lab model proving 4, 5 & 6	
Prod./process des.	8	Working drawings & data from 7	
Proto/pilot plant	9	Build & test one off from 8	
Mods	10	Modify drawings as indicated by 9	
Pilot production	11	Short production run, limited tools	
Series production	12	Normal production, fully engineered	
Sales	13	Launch, take orders, may precede 12	
Shipment	14	Ship product, user feedback	

Figure 6.1 Product loop

creating a new one, the starting point might be at stages 6, 7 or 8 depending on the level of technical risk in the modification. If the project is to create a new manufacturing process, rather than a product, the starting point would be at much the same stage but would not go past building the plant (stage 9) since there would be no question of quantity production.

In all cases the result of the project goes back to the user at stage 1. With a new product this is the market segment buying the product. This forms the real test of the success of the project: up to that point all has been analysis, estimate and hope. The customer tells the company what it has done. To anticipate this there may be a case for product field testing at stage 9. This would also be the feedback point for a process development in which the company is its own customer.

An essential element is good communication between the people involved, particularly in those stages where responsibility is joint. Clear records of decisions taken, the grounds on which they were taken and the resulting action are important. The planning and monitoring techniques described in this chapter are aimed at aiding the achievement of these conditions.

Engineering Planning

After the design specifications and requirements have been defined the further course of the project is typically as shown in Figure 6.2, moving in a continuum through design, process engineering and manufacturing stages to the final product, with inputs from sales forecasts to guide each stage.

Although for the sake of clarity the stages are shown as separate boxes, this is a poor form of organization to use in practice. There is evidence (Bergen, 1983) that flexibility of operation in and between these stages benefits the project. Individuals can only do their jobs well in this context if they know a great deal about everyone else's jobs and problems. This is best achieved by personal contact. Departmental barriers and ivory tower attitudes are detrimental to good results.

Morton's Rule

A useful rule to apply is that of Jack Morton (1964), a past Head of Components Laboratory at Bell Telephones, New Jersey. He postulated that any two people who have to collaborate to produce a result can have between them bonds and barriers of two types, spatial and organiza-

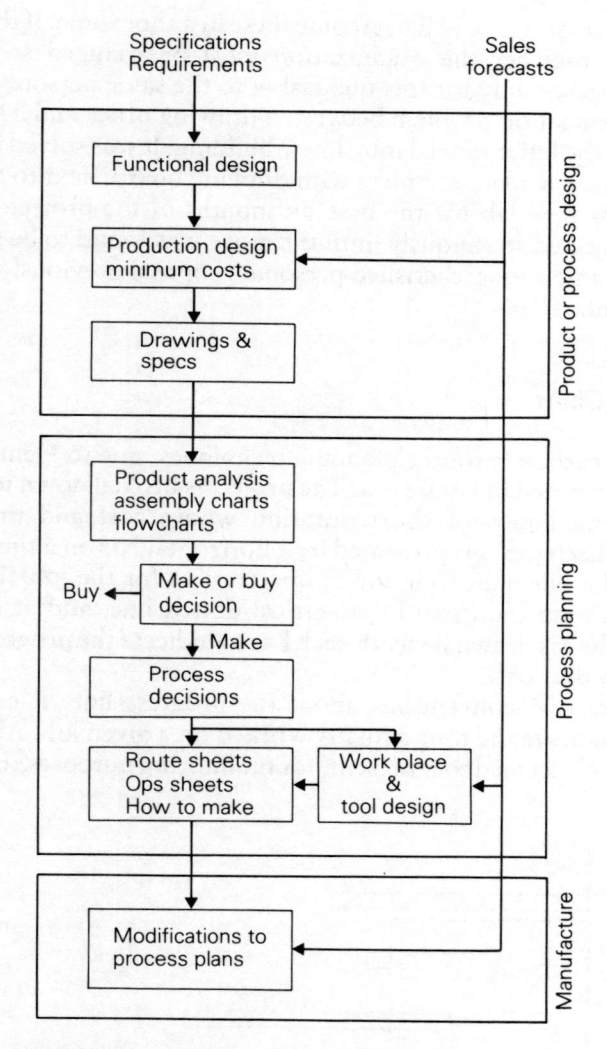

Figure 6.2 Engineering planning

tional. If they sit at the same or adjacent desks they have a spatial bond. If they are in different rooms they have a spatial barrier. If they report to the same boss they have an organizational bond; if they are in different departments they have an organizational barrier. Morton's rule is that a double bond is advantageous and that a double barrier must never be permitted. If they are in different departments they must be brought together physically, whatever departmental objections are raised at first.

Improved performance will overcome these in a short time. If they cannot be brought together the organization must be changed so that they report — possibly only for this one task — to the same person.

A communication problem between a drawing office and a laboratory arose when the latter moved into a new building. It was solved by moving the DO section leader, complete with drawing board, next to the project leader in the new lab for the first six months of the project. The chief designer objected strenuously until the move was found to be successful, when it became a long-cherished personal proposal previously vetoed by management.

The Gantt Chart

One of the earliest resource planning techniques, due to Henry Gantt in 1903, is illustrated in Figure 6.3. The project is broken down into a series of well-defined jobs of short duration whose cost and time can be estimated. Each job is represented by a horizontal bar on a time base, the length of the bar indicating the estimated time for the job. The project review dates are indicated by a vertical dotted line, and at this time a horizontal line is drawn beneath each bar to indicate the progress actually made up to that date.

There are two conventions about the progress line. It can be used simply to indicate the time actually worked on a given job. Alternatively the bar can be deemed to represent, for monitoring purposes, 100 per cent

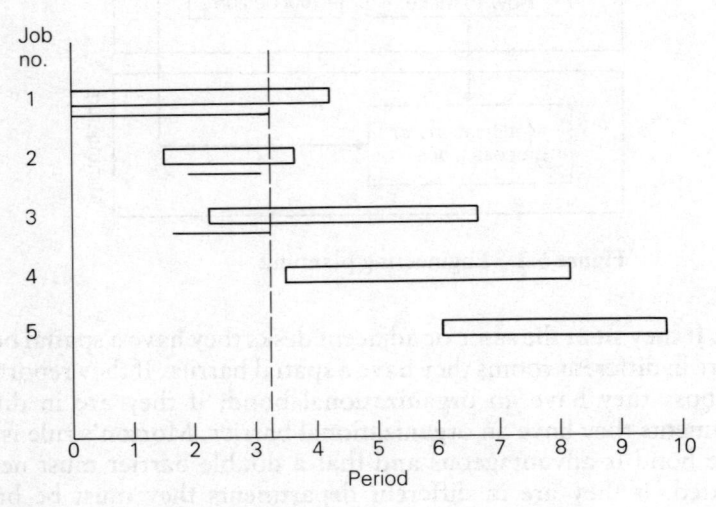

Figure 6.3 Gantt chart

of the job. The length of the progress line is then drawn to represent the percentage of the job that has been completed at the review date. The difficulties of estimating percentage completion of R&D jobs is such that the former method is preferred for this type of project. The latter is valid for projects of low uncertainty capable of accurate estimating.

Critical Path Method

Critical path method (CPM) is a network planning system developed by Dupont in the 1940s and provides more information on the progress of the project than does the basic Gantt chart. The jobs are defined and estimated as before but in this case two columns headed 'precede by' and 'follow by' define the sequence of events to be followed in the project as illustrated in Table 6.1.

Table 6.1 Critical path method
Project: To move machine tool from factory to new site and install.

Job		Est. time days	Precede by	Follow by
A	Prepare plans of site	4	—	B,C,G
B	Clear site	3	A	D
C	Dismantle m/c tool	2	A	E
D	Prepare foundations	4	B	F
E	Move tool to site	1	C	F
F	Install m/c tool	4	D,E	H
G	Run services	5	A	H
H	Connect services	1	F,G	J
I	Test	1	H	—

Following the logic of the last two columns of Table 6.1, a network diagram is drawn (Figure 6.4) in which the lines between the nodes represent the jobs, the nodes being numbered to identify the jobs for the benefit of a computer, if used. The skill in planning consists in the decisions taken in completing the two columns so that the overall network time is minimized without contradicting the logical sequence in which the jobs must be done. In any such network there will be one or more paths which are longer than any other. Slippage on any job on this path will entail slippage on the overall project. This path is indicated by a double line through the network, drawing the project leaders attention to

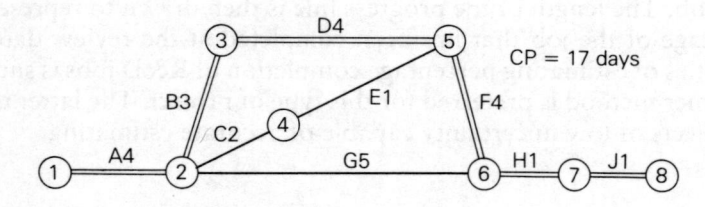

Figure 6.4 Critical path method

the need to take emergency action when such slippage appears. The other paths have, by definition, some slack in them and some slippage can be tolerated as the end date will not be affected until the slippage results in the job becoming part of a new critical path.

Network Dummies

One of the conventions of network diagrams is the dummy job. This is necessary to avoid ambiguity, unnecessary constraints in the plan and to avoid forming loops from which the computer cannot escape. A dummy has all the restrictive properties of a real job but no time content. Figure 6.5 illustrates the more usual cases.

Advantages

Network planning of this type has a number of advantages:

(1) It forces the project leader to think clearly and rigorously about all the activities in the project in the planning phase.
(2) It focuses attention on the critical path, where any slippage will delay completion of the project.
(3) It promotes awareness of the integrative aspects of the project.
(4) Reviewing the progress of the project in terms of the network provides feedback to the project control system.
(5) By displaying both critical path and slack it stops crash programs being set up for every activity.
(6) It can be used as a simulation for test and planning.

There are also some disadvantages:

(1) Analysing the network can be expensive.
(2) The preparation time is significant.
(3) Like a computer, it may lend credence to false data.

Project Planning 79

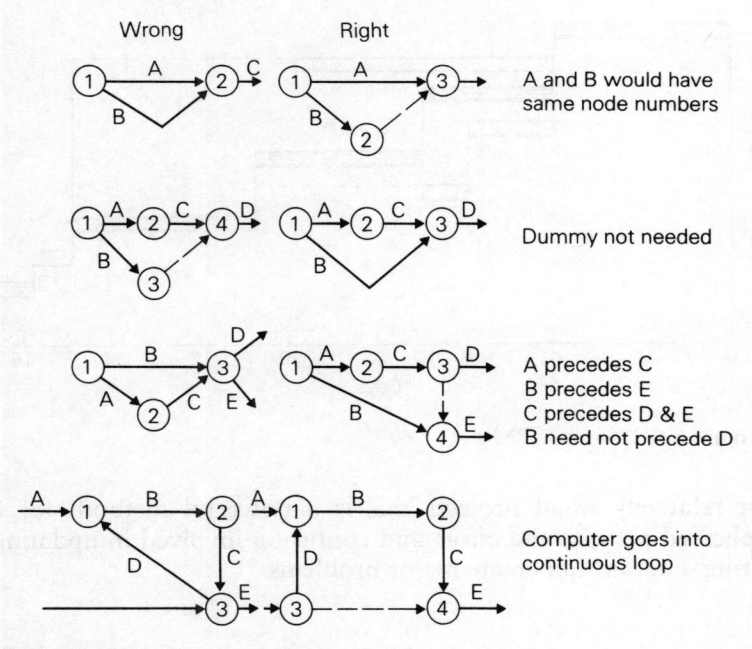

Figure 6.5 Dummy activities

(4) It may consequently give a false sense of security.
(5) If the network contains activities in other departments local supervision may resent this.
(6) It is difficult to handle overlapping activities.
(7) It does not display work load.
(8) The amount of detail displayed may be confusing.
(9) After the first 20 per cent of the project, revisions become difficult to carry out if done manually or expensive if computerized, for major projects.

Gantt–CPM

It is possible to combine the simplicity of the Gantt chart with the logic of the CPM method to display both the critical path and the slack in a very accessible manner. The bars representing the jobs are rearranged in order so that they do not overlap each other when the logic is represented by vertical lines connecting job starts with the finish of a job that must precede them. The bars are on a time base as in the Gantt chart and slack is indicated by horizontal dotted lines connecting finishes to starts. Figure 6.6 displays the same project as Figure 6.4.

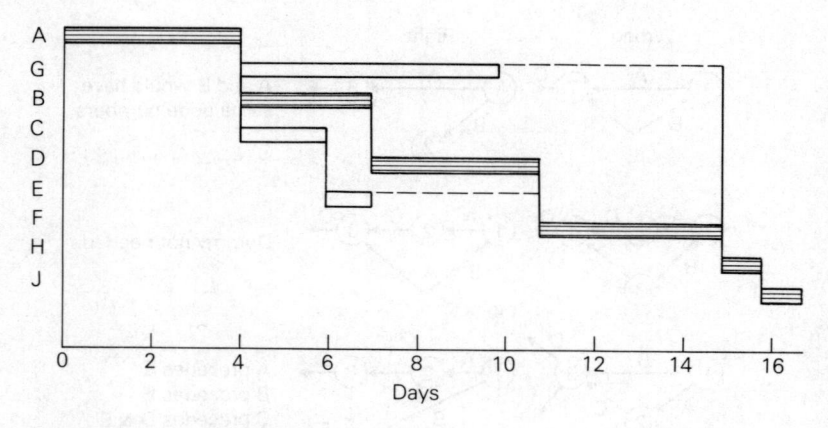

Figure 6.6   Gantt–CPM

For relatively small projects this is a powerful method: for large complicated projects the effort and confusion involved in updating the resulting diagram can create major problems.

PERT – Project Evaluation and Review Technique

An alternative technique, first used to control the Polaris project in 1958, reverses the convention of CPM. The job content is in the node, in the form of a PERT symbol, rather than in the network line. The symbol is illustrated in Figure 6.7 and contains more information on the provisions of the plan than does CPM. The form illustrated is one of several in use. The centre circle of the symbol contains the job identification code, in this case X, and the time estimate for the job. The left wing of the symbol contains two figures, the early start time on the left and the late start time on the right. The right wing carries the early finish time on the left and the late finish time on the right. At any job symbol both the free float and the total slack, as defined in Figure 6.7, can be calculated.

Figure 6.8 shows the PERT network for the same project as Figures 6.5 and 6.6. Early starts and early finishes are arrived at by a forward pass through the network. If the project starts at time zero and job A is estimated at 4 time units, the early start for jobs B, C and G, which follow it, are all 4. Job B has an estimated time of 3 units, so the early finish of B is $4 + 3 = 7$. Since job D has to wait for completion of B, and only B, before it can start, the early start for D is 7. The job time of D is 4, so the early finish is $7 + 4 = 11$. The forward pass through the network consists of repeating this procedure by adding the job time to the early start time and

Project Planning   81

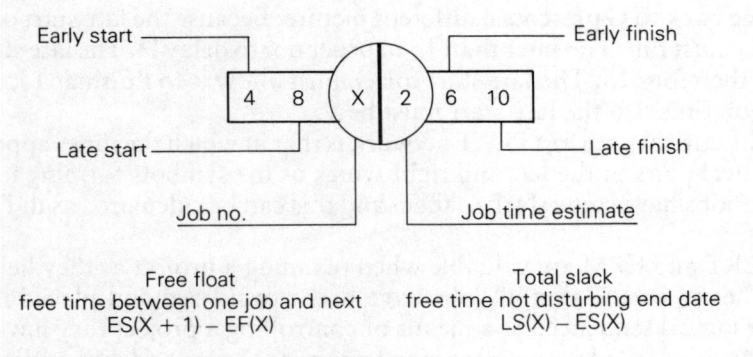

Figure 6.7   PERT symbol

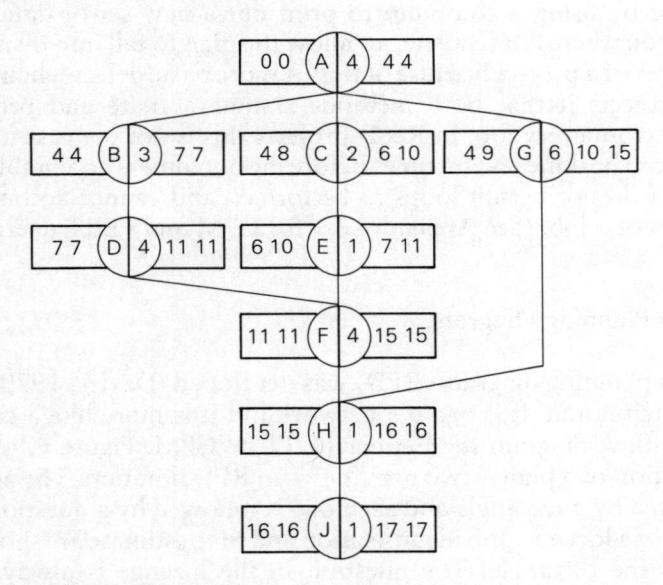

- Early start / Early finish
- Late start / Late finish
- Job no. / Job time estimate
- Free float: free time between one job and next ES(X + 1) − EF(X)
- Total slack: free time not disturbing end date LS(X) − ES(X)

Symbol example: 4 8 (X) 2 6 10

Figure 6.8   PERT network

Network values:
- 0 0 (A) 4 4 4
- 4 4 (B) 3 7 7
- 4 8 (C) 2 6 10
- 4 9 (G) 6 10 15
- 7 7 (D) 4 11 11
- 6 10 (E) 1 7 11
- 11 11 (F) 4 15 15
- 15 15 (H) 1 16 16
- 16 16 (J) 1 17 17

making this the early start time of the next job in sequence if no other preceding job has a later early finish. Thus in the case of job H the early start time is not 10, which is the early finish time of preceding job G, but 15 which is the early finish of F and is on the critical path.

The late starts and late finishes for the jobs are obtained by a backward pass through the network. In Figure 6.8 the project end date is 17 units, obtained by adding the job time of J to its early start time. Subtracting the job time from the end time gives a late start time of 16, the same as the early start. H is treated in the same way and this repeats for F, D, B, and A.

82 Project Planning

Going back to G presents a different picture. Because the late start of H is 15, G must finish no later than 15 in order not to delay H. The late start of G is therefore 15. The late start for G must allow it to finish at 15. Since the job time is 6 the late start must be 9.

The critical path in a PERT network is that in which the times appear in identical pairs in the left and right wings of the symbols forming it. The other jobs have some slack in them and this can be calculated as in Figure 6.7.

PERT and CPM are valuable when planning a project as they help the planner to ensure that all jobs have been considered and placed in the right logical sequence. As a means of controlling a project they have two weaknesses. All plans need revision from time to time and difficulties arise in reading the networks after several such changes. This is largely overcome by using a computer to print out a new set of data at each revision, but there is a tendency to allow the plan to fall into disuse in the later stages of a project because of this. A more basic defect when used for R&D projects it that both methods assume a finite and predictable outcome from every job. In R&D projects this is not the case and a job may have to be done several times before the outcome is acceptable. PERT and CPM do not permit loops to be formed and cannot accommodate repetition of a job. (See Appendix 6.1 for CPM and PERT exercise.)

Research Planning Diagram

Research planning diagram (RPD) was developed (Davies, 1970) to deal with this situation. It is again a network but it is more like a computer program flow diagram than either PERT or CPM. Figure 6.9 shows a small section of a plan – two activities – in RPD notation. The activity is represented by a rectangle and each one is followed by a question box in the form of a lozenge. Job identification and time estimate are shown as in PERT in the rectangle. The question in the lozenge is always 'is the outcome of the activity acceptable?'. If the answer is 'Yes' the exit is from the bottom of the lozenge to the next job rectangle in the network. If 'No' the exit is from the side of the lozenge, looping back to the input side of the job rectangle to repeat it. In planning the project, subjective judgements – see Chapter 5 – are made as to the probability of having to repeat each job one or more times. These probabilities are noted alongside the exit from the lozenge. In Figure 6.9 the planner has expressed the view that there is a 0.5 probability that job X will be repeated once and a 0.2 probability that it will then be necessary to repeat it once more.

The analysis of the RPD is best carried out by computer since it involves tracing every possible path through the network and calculating the

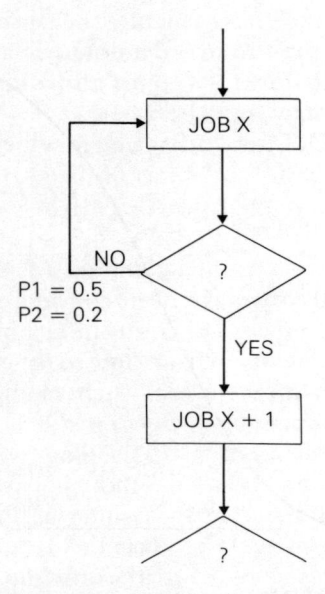

Figure 6.9 Research planning diagram

cumulative probability for each path. The presentation of this information is shown in Figure 6.10 and is in the form of an 'S' curve of probability of completion against time. This is more representative of the nature of R&D projects than is the single date often given as the result of a PERT plan. PERT was originally developed on a probability basis but is not much used in this way now because of the amount of work involved.

RPD has important attributes for the company as a whole as well as for the project team. All R&D projects involve an element of risk as described in Chapter 5. This is largely in the accuracy of the estimated completion date. There is evidence (Norris, 1971) that cost estimate overruns are significantly lower than time estimate overruns. The evaluation of investment risks is generally accepted to be a corporate responsibility. If top management is presented with a finite completion date, the risk in R&D project investments is being evaluated by the project leader. If the nature of the risk is displayed as in Figure 6.10, corporate management is explicitly given the data it needs for evaluation. It could be argued that in agreeing to a single date the project leader is taking decisions more properly the province of higher management.

A further merit of the presentation is the help it offers to those company functions whose responsibilities involve risks contingent upon the completion date of an R&D project. The materials manager does not purchase all the material he could possibly need in a given period. He

84   Project Planning

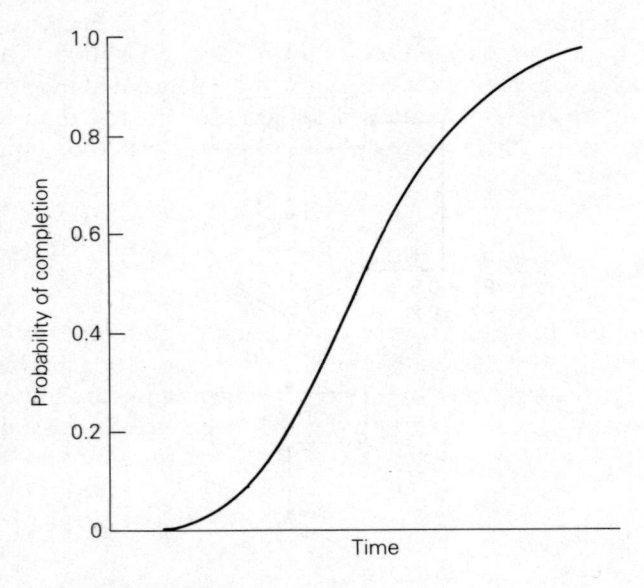

Figure 6.10   RPD presentation

accepts an agreed risk – there should be a company policy to guide him – of running out of stock as a means of optimizing the amount of company capital tied up on his shelves. The RPD presentation allows him to use his normal criteria in relation to R&D projects which result in new products. He will probably set his purchasing date near, but not at, the bottom of the 'S' curve. He will thus avoid buying material before it can be used by accepting a small and defined risk of delaying production.

In the same way the sales manager can optimize his launch date to ensure earliest returns on the new product by accepting a small risk that he will not be able to deliver on the promised date. He will work near, but not at, the top of the 'S' curve.

The descriptions above have been based on estimating and planning the use of time on the project. Equally the costs of the project can be dealt with in the same way.

Current Status of PERT

Of the several planning techniques described, PERT is the one most discussed, though not necessarily most used, in industry. The current status of the method in the USA was surveyed by Dougherty and Stephenson (1984) in firms in the Fortune 500 (most commercially successful of the year) class. They found that it was used in 40 per cent of development projects but only 16 per cent of research projects, and then mainly in large, complex projects costing over $500 000. The cost of running PERT varied between 3 per cent and 9 per cent of the project cost, the latter figure applying mainly to projects costing less than $100 000. The opponents of PERT were convinced that it was too sophisticated, inflexible and expensive.

Slip Chart

Monitoring the progress of projects is often done by means of project review meetings of which the minutes form a record of achievement and decisions. Particularly in terms of slippage the minutes are sometimes less than satisfactory, recording only the slippage since the last meeting. It may be necessary to go through the whole file in order to find how much the project has slipped altogether. The slip chart, due to Brooke (1973), presents the complete history of the project on one sheet of paper by continuously comparing planned time with elapsed time, as shown in Figure 6.11.

The project is first laid out on a time base and the job completion dates

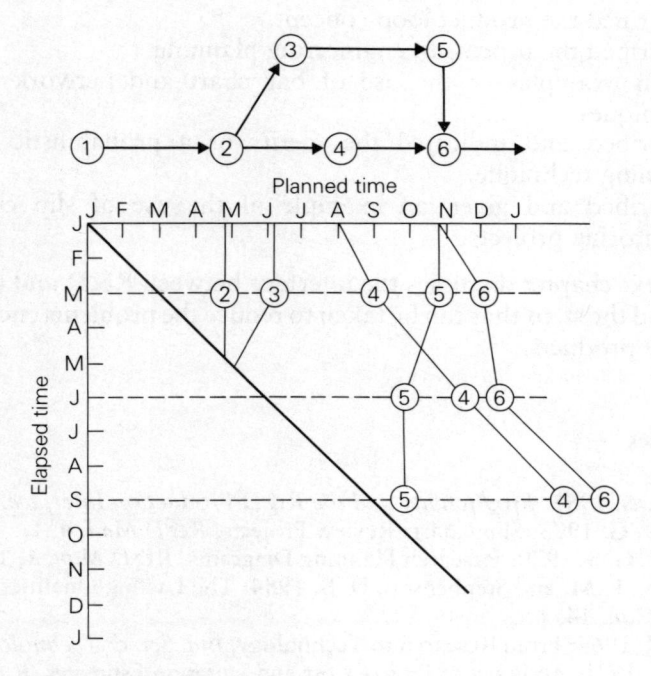

Figure 6.11 Slip chart

transferred to the horizontal scale representing planned time. The vertical axis to the same scale represents elapsed time and the diagonal is drawn in as shown. At the first review date the completion dates are re-estimated and the new dates entered on the planned time axis in line with the review date on the elapsed time axis. The original estimates are joined to the new ones by lines. Since any point on the diagonal makes the same intercepts on both scales any job whose line hits the diagonal has been completed. A line moving vertically downwards indicates a job that is on schedule. If the line is sloping to the left the job is in advance of the schedule and if to the right it is slipping behind schedule. If it is sloping to the right so much that it is nearly parallel with the diagonal it will never be completed unless drastic action is taken.

The same procedure is repeated at each review date. The diagram provides a complete and updated history of the progress of the project on a single sheet of paper.

Review

This chapter has:

(1) Described the product loop concept.
(2) Described the process of engineering planning.
(3) Given examples of the use of bar chart and network planning techniques.
(4) Described and indicated the merits of a probabilistic network planning technique.
(5) Described and given an example of the use of slip charts for monitoring projects.

The next chapter discusses the interface between R&D and manufacturing and the steps that can be taken to reduce the problems encountered with new products.

References

Bergen, S. A. 1983: *Productivity and the R&D/Production Interface*. Gower.
Brooke, D. G. 1973: Slip Charts Review Projects, *R&D Man.* **4**, 1.
Davies, D. G. S. 1970: Research Planning Diagrams, *R&D Man.* **1**, 1.
Dougherty, P. M. and Stephenson, D. B. 1984: The Lasting Qualities of PERT, *R&D Man.* **14**, 1.
Morton, J. 1964: From Research to Technology, *Ind. Sci. & Technology* (May).
Norris, K. 1971: Accuracy of Project Cost and Duration Estimates, *R & D Man.* **2**, 1.

Further Reading

Pearson, A. W. 1983: Planning and Monitoring in R&D – A 12 Year Review. *R&D Man.* **13**, 2.
Schliep, W. and Schliep, R. 1972: *Planning and Control in Management – The German System.* P. Peregrinus.

Appendix 6.1 CPM and PERT Exercise

The data from the CPM example in Chapter 6, for moving a machine tool from a factory to a new site, is repeated below. The overall length of the project was given in the example as 17 days. How much can you reduce the time? What assumptions did you make to achieve the improvement?

Project: To move m/c tool from factory to new site and install.

Job		Est. time (days)	Precede by	Follow by
A	Prepare plans	4		
B	Clear site	3		
C	Dismantle m/c tool	2		
D	Prepare foundations	4		
E	Move m/c to site	1		
F	Install m/c tool	4		
G	Run services	6		
H	Connect services	1		
J	Test	1		

7 The R&D/Production Interface

While new and innovative technology is exciting to work with and highly regarded, it is not in itself a guarantee of a profitable product. The treatment of the new product in all departments must be such as to ensure a product with a price/performance ratio and a quality – that is, fitness for purpose – which matches the market need. This calls for high levels of skill in design and production and the necessity for the two functions to co-operate to produce an optimum result.

The Post-development Gap

A phenomenon that has been called 'the post development gap' (Davies, 1980) has produced severe losses in a number of innovative companies.

The pattern is that an innovative company, after spending much time and money on a technically successful development embodying new technology, puts a first generation product on the market. For a few years it has a monopoly in world markets and a good order book. Then, if the product appears to be commercially successful, as well as a technological *tour de force*, suddenly competitors are marketing what amounts to a second generation product. They have taken the technology as they found it, at relatively low cost, and invested in re-engineering the product for efficient production, quality and reliability and a better price/performance ratio.

The hypothetical company has now lost its market. It may be tempted to re-invest in more R&D to gain another technological lead. The chances are that the same cycle will repeat even if it is successful in doing so; success in innovative technology cannot be guaranteed.

Some countries place less importance on innovation and more on sound conventional engineering. Professor Hutton's massive study of engineering in Germany (Hutton *et al.*, 1977) found that the average West German engineer values the ability to apply well-proven engineering solutions to problems, in a professional manner, above original thought. This cultural factor has been to the commercial benefit of West Germany since the 'economic miracle' of the 1950s.

It must never be lost sight of that the objective of an R&D project is not

The R&D/Production Interface 89

only to meet the target performance specification but, equally importantly, to produce and prove a design that can be manufactured efficiently and exploited profitably. This is true whether the end product is a manufactured item for sale or a production process for producing it. The project team cannot guarantee that the product will be so exploited, it can only make it possible. It can, however, make it impossible if it does not attack the problem with sufficient energy and insight.

The Product Structure Tree

At some stage of manufacture the new product must be assembled from its components. This must condition the designer in all that he does. The early creation of a product structure tree, along the lines of Figure 7.1, is the starting point and is the minimum he needs to produce. By ensuring that each component of the design has, at the time he is working on it, a rational and logical position on the tree, assembly interferences and later modifications to the design can be minimized if not avoided entirely.

The product structure tree deals with materials, processes and

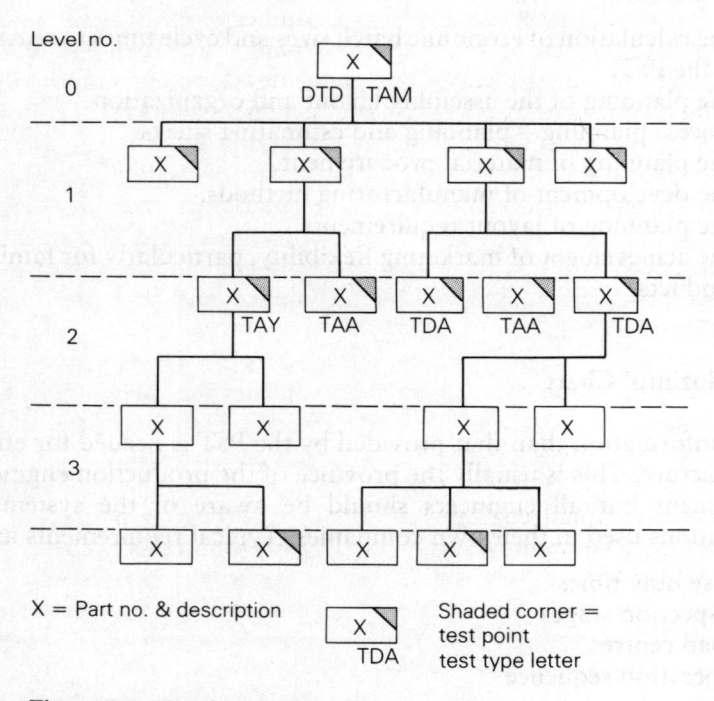

Figure 7.1 Product structure tree

organization. It identifies each component by its part number and displays the assembly sequence in a series of levels. These start with the raw material and smallest components, at the highest levels, and display the order of assembly stages into larger and larger subassemblies as the level numbers decrease, the lowest level being the complete product. At each stage relevant information such as test points and test types are indicated together with special notes on the assembly process. This information, together with the associated parts lists, is the information needed first in manufacturing departments to allow them to plan their contribution to the project. They should not be officially released until they are in their final form. By working on the design and the product structure tree (PST) in parallel the designer goes some way towards ensuring that there is a logical manufacturing sequence that does not require, for example, partial disassembly at some stage. Wherever possible assemblies and subassemblies must be specified and designed so that they can be inspected and tested as separate items independently of the remainder of the product.

The purpose of the PST is to provide a basis from which calculations, plans and actions can be generated to aid manufacture of a product. These would include:

(1) The calculation of economic batch sizes and cycle times for each level of the PST.
(2) The planning of the assembly layout and organization.
(3) Process planning – planning and estimating sheets.
(4) The planning of material procurement.
(5) The development of manufacturing methods.
(6) The planning of layout requirements.
(7) The achievement of marketing flexibility, particularly for families of products.

The 'Gozinto' Chart

More information than that provided by the PST is needed for efficient manufacture. This is usually the province of the production engineering department but all engineers should be aware of the systems and conventions used in their own companies. Typical requirements are:

(1) Assembly times
(2) Inspection stages
(3) Load centres
(4) Operation sequence

(5) FSP of assemblies
(6) Set-up times
(7) Parts lists

This information is conveyed on planning sheets and calculation sheets such as the assembly or 'Gozinto' chart, Figure 7.2, and the operation process chart (Stoner, 1978). The Gozinto chart does exactly what its name implies. It shows what goes into what to create a subassembly and identifies by coding and symbols the processes involved. In Figure 7.2 operations are indicated by circles containing code numbers referring to company standards or special instructions and identifying the sequence in which they are to be performed. Inspection and test stages are indicated by rectangles also with identifying codes. It is useful in making preliminary plans showing the relationship of the parts, the sequence of assembly and which groups of parts make up subassemblies. It is a schematic diagram of the manufacturing process at that level of detail for a simple capacitor.

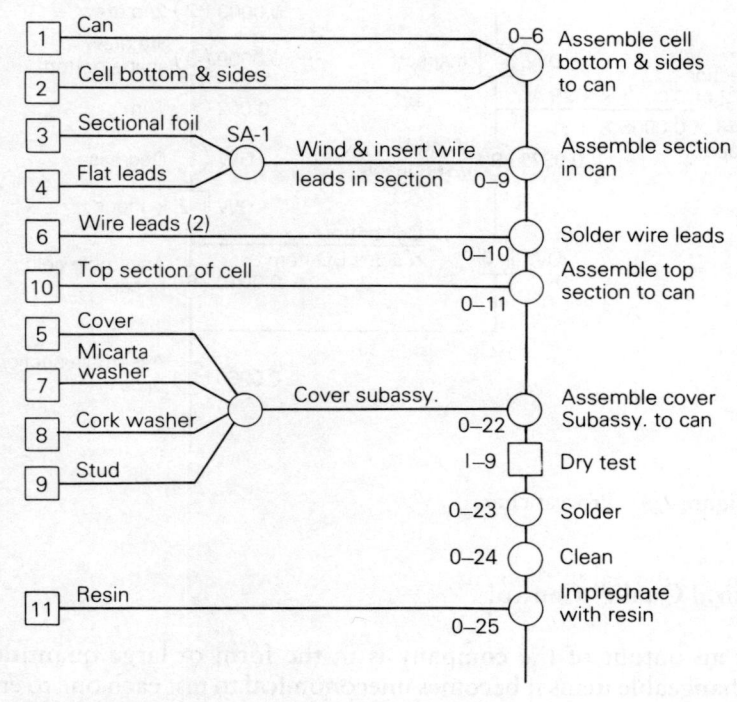

Figure 7.2 Gozinto chart

Operation Process Chart

The engineering drawings of the product define dimensions, tolerances and materials to be used. They specify locations and sizes of holes, with their respective tolerances and the finishes required. From this data the most economical processes, equipment and sequences can be planned. Figure 7.3 illustrates this for the same capacitor as that in Figure 7.2. The operation process chart is a summary of all required operations and inspections: it is a general plan for manufacture.

There are significant differences in the approach to these tasks depending on whether the manufacturing system of the company is product-focused or process-focused.

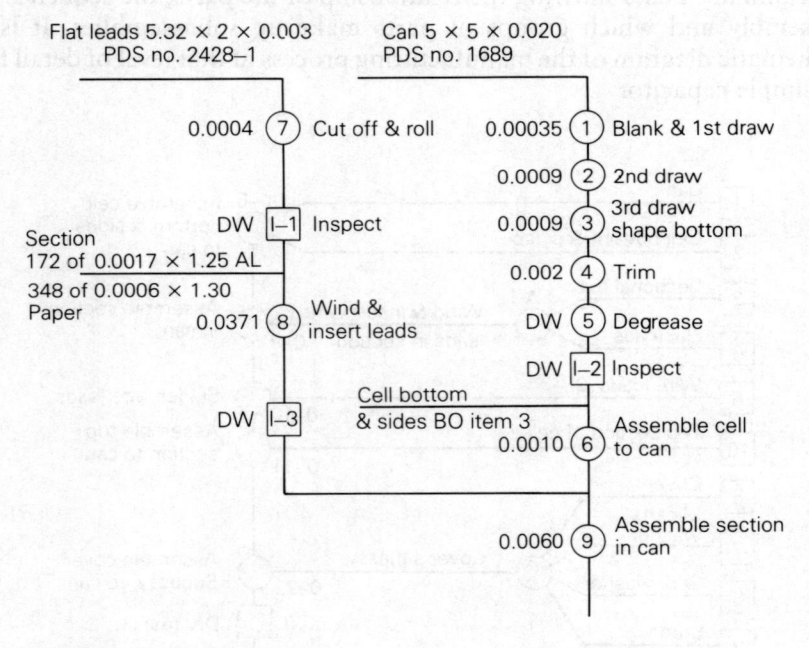

```
Flat leads 5.32 × 2 × 0.003           Can 5 × 5 × 0.020
   PDS no. 2428–1                        PDS no. 1689

              0.0004  (7)  Cut off & roll      0.00035  (1)  Blank & 1st draw
                                                0.0009  (2)  2nd draw
                                                             3rd draw
                      DW  I–1  Inspect          0.0009  (3)  shape bottom
Section
172 of 0.0017 × 1.25 AL                          0.002  (4)  Trim
348 of 0.0006 × 1.30
Paper                      Wind &               DW  (5)  Degrease
              0.0371  (8)  insert leads
                                                DW  I–2  Inspect
                           Cell bottom
                      DW I–3   & sides BO item 3         Assemble cell
                                                0.0010  (6)  to can

                                                             Assemble section
                                                0.0060  (9)  in can
```

Figure 7.3 Process chart

Statistical Quality Control

When an output of the company is in the form of large quantities of interchangeable items it becomes uneconomical to test each one to ensure that it conforms to specification, so tests are carried out on samples. Some means of relating the results of the sample tests to the batches they are

The R&D/Production Interface 93

taken from is needed. Statistical approaches to this problem are widely used and some of the basic ideas are introduced below.

Frequency Distribution

In practice the items referred to above will not be identical and the departure from the nominal dimensions will determine the degree of interchangeability and hence the quality of the batch. This will, in turn, influence the value to the customer and the price he will be willing to pay.

If the same dimension of each item is measured and a graph drawn of the number of times each value of that dimension appears, as in Figure 7.4, the result is called the frequency distribution of the variable or just the distribution. The dimension measured is called the variate and may be any physical quantity. The method applies to electrical and chemical quantities as well as mechanical dimensions. The batch from which the sample is drawn is referred to as the population.

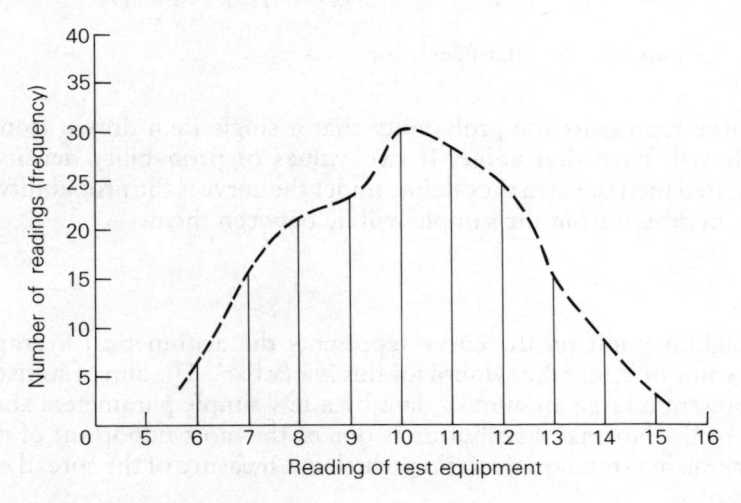

Figure 7.4 Frequency distribution

If the jumps in the dimension measured are small, the curve will be smooth, symmetrical and bell-shaped as shown in Figure 7.5. This is the Normal or Gaussian curve and represents the distribution of events due to chance. Because its characteristics can be treated mathematically it is central to quality control via samples. The height of the curve at any point on the dimension axis x is called the probability density of that particular value. When the distribution is normalized, that is the area under the curve is converted to unity, representing total probability, the height of

94 The R&D/Production Interface

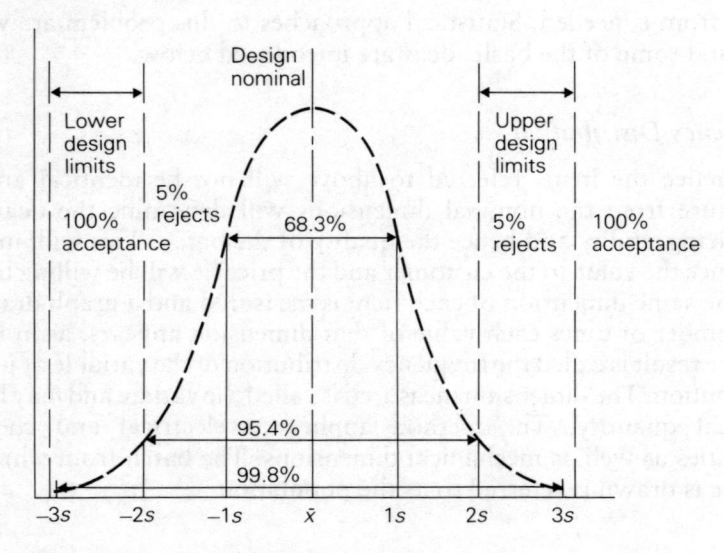

Figure 7.5 Standard deviation

the curve represents the probability that a single item drawn from the sample will have that value. If two values of probability density are nominated then the area they define under the curve is the probability that any item drawn from the sample will lie between them.

Mean

The highest point on the curve represents the arithmetical average or mean value of x, and the symbol for this is $\bar{x}$ (x bar). The aim of statistics is to represent a large amount of data by a few simple parameters and the mean of the Normal distribution is one of the most important of these. Another is the standard deviation which is a measure of the spread of the values of x.

Standard Deviation

The deviation of a value of x is the difference between it and the mean of the sample. The mean deviation is the sum of the deviations of a sample, treating them all as positive, divided by the number of items in the sample. The standard deviation is the most important measure of the spread or dispersion of x. It is analogous to the 'root-mean-square deviation' in electrical engineering and to the 'radius of gyration' in moments of inertia in mechanical engineering. It is arrived at by calculating the mean of a set of values and measuring the deviation between this and each value. Each deviation is then squared; the sum of these values is called the sample sum of the squares and is divided by the number n of items in the sample giving a quantity called the sample variance. The square root of this number is the standard deviation for which the formula is

$$s = \left(\frac{\Sigma(x - \bar{x})^2}{n}\right)^{\frac{1}{2}}$$

From the values of the mean and standard deviation a useful picture of the distribution of the sample values can be formed. The standard deviation can usefully be visualized as the distance from the mean to the point of inflection of the bell-shaped curve. Figure 7.5 illustrates the information available when these two parameters are known.

No matter what the proportions of the normal curve are, 99.8 per cent of all values will lie within 3 standard deviations of the mean, 95.4 per cent within 2 standard deviations and 68.3 per cent within 1 standard deviation. Another way of stating the information, since the area under the curve represents probability, is any item taken from the sample at random will have a 68.3 per cent probability of lying between -1 and $+1$ standard deviations of the mean and a 95.4 per cent probability of lying between -2 and $+2$ standard deviations of the mean.

Design Limits

From this information the design limits for any manufactured item can be set to the economic optimum. The outer limits shown in Figure 7.5 will allow all but 0.2 per cent of the items produced to be used in the finished product. This will in many cases create a problem. Either the physical limits of the item are wide, so that the design and production of the mating parts become difficult and expensive, or they are narrow so that they can only be produced by expensive processes. In the first case the item in question is cheap to produce but the parts to which it assembles are difficult to design and the assembly process demanding. In the second the assembly process is easy and the overall design simple but the items themselves are expensive and difficult to produce.

By judicious choice of the design limits in relation to the curve of Figure 7.5 a compromise may be possible at say, 2 standard deviations either side of the mean at which 4.6 per cent of the items will be rejected as unusable. The remainder of the assembly will not now be required to tolerate as much dimensional variation in the first item, reducing the design difficulty and assembly costs. If the saving in this direction is greater than

Sample Size

The information obtainable on the quality of a batch of items, intended to be as near identical as is economically achievable, is related only to the number in the sample. The size of the batch from which it is taken makes no difference. It is therefore most economical, from the quality control point of view, to produce large batches. If sets of samples are taken and averaged, these averages will form a tighter cluster around the average of the population than will individual samples. The larger the sample the more closely will its average agree with the population average, as seen in Figure 7.6 where the population average is represented by the central zero. The distribution remains normal but the standard deviation decreases as the square root of n, the sample size. The quantity $s/\sqrt{n}$ is known as the standard error of the mean and the degree of uncertainty in estimating the standard deviation of the population from a sample is given by $s/\sqrt{(2n)^{\frac{1}{2}}}$, the standard error of the standard deviation. The symbol for the standard deviation of the population is σ to distinguish it from that of the sample, s.

Standard deviation $\propto \dfrac{1}{\sqrt{n}}$

— Averages of 25 items

The normal curve is specified by
$\bar{x}$ the mean
σ the standard deviation

— Averages of 9 items

The larger the sample size n the smaller is σ

— Averages of 4 items

— Individual items

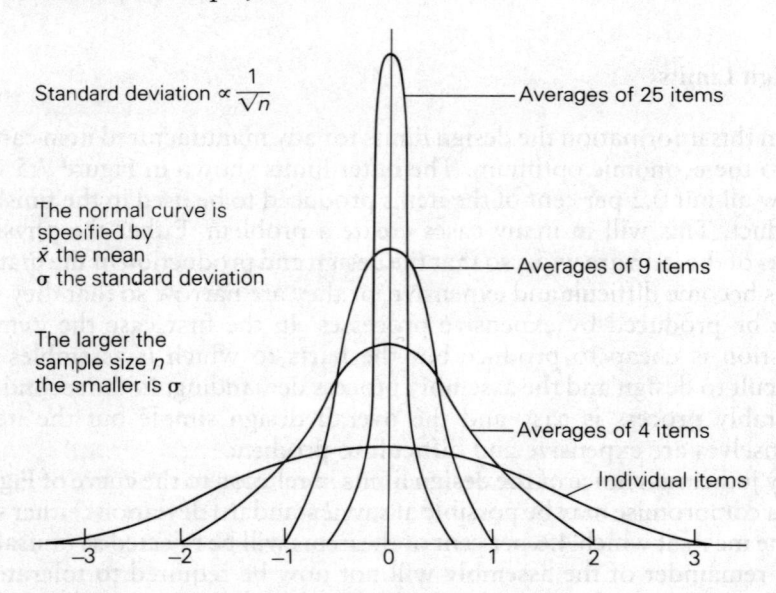

Figure 7.6 Sample size and standard deviation

Before this text: "the cost of the difference between 4.6 per cent and 0.2 per cent rejects, which are still cheap to produce, the compromise is worth adopting."

Confidence Limits

A confidence limit is the interval within which we can say that the true value of the quantity we are estimating will lie with a specified probability. When the sample size is large, say 100, the standard error of the mean can be taken as the standard error of the estimate. It can therefore be said that in a long series of estimates under the same conditions the population mean would lie within one standard error of the mean 68 per cent of the time, or within two standard errors 95.4 per cent of the time. The confidence limits for estimates of the standard deviation of the population can be treated in the same way when the estimate is based on large samples, using the standard error of the standard deviation as the standard error of estimate.

For small samples, say below 50, the normal distribution cannot be used and it is necessary to use the Student's t distribution. When small samples are used to estimate population standard deviations, the results are biased in the direction of underestimation. In terms of variance, that is the standard deviation squared, the relationship is

$$\hat{\sigma}^2 = \left(\frac{n}{n-1}\right) s^2$$

where the population variance is σ^2 and the sample variance is s^2, the circumflex accent indicating 'best estimate'. The expression in brackets is known as Bessel's correction. It will be seen that as n increases the expression approaches unity; when the sample size is 50 the correction is 0.98. Student's t is calculated as

$$t = \frac{|\bar{X} - \bar{x}| \, (n-1)^{\frac{1}{2}}}{s}$$

where $|\bar{X} - \bar{x}|$ is the absolute value of the difference between the means of the sample and the population. It can be seen from this that the larger the error between the sample and population means the greater is the value of t. Tables are available in statistical texts showing the values of t for given probability levels, relating any given error of estimate to the probability of it being present.

Sampling Plan

The areas under the normal curve outside the upper and lower design limits shown in Figure 7.5 represent the probability of items in that batch being unusable. A complete sampling plan for quality control can be constructed on this basis (Buffa, 1983). In Figure 7.7 half of the normal distribution is drawn. The vertical axis is a measure of the probability of acceptance of an item by the user. The horizontal axis is a measure of the actual percentage of defective items in the lot being offered to the user, that is the quality of the lot. Two quality levels are decided, the acceptable quality level (AQL) and the lot tolerance percentage defective (LTPD). Items at AQL have a high, but not unity, probability of acceptance. The LTPD is the dividing line between good and bad quality and has a low, but not zero, probability of acceptance. There is therefore a risk that good items will not be accepted and a risk that bad quality items will be accepted.

The risk that good quality items will not be accepted is the producer's risk and is commonly set at about 5 per cent. The risk that bad quality items will be accepted is the user's risk and is commonly set at about 10

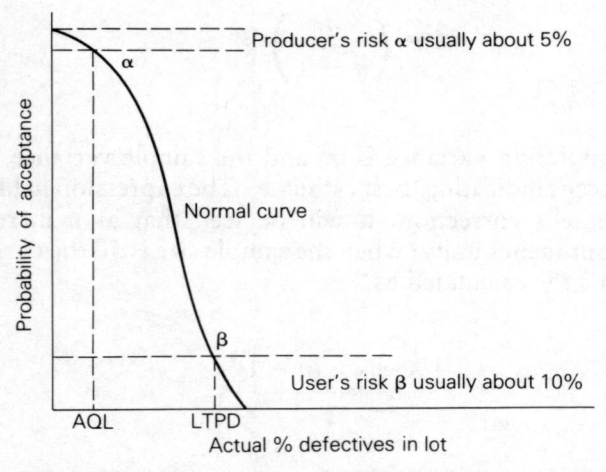

AQL	Acceptable quality level – high probability of acceptance
α	Producer's risk – probability that lots at AQL will not be accepted
LTPD	Lot tolerance % defective – selected dividing line between good and bad quality, low probability of acceptance
β	User's risk – probability that lots at LTPD will be accepted

Figure 7.7 Sampling plan

per cent. The pricing of the items to the user reflects the settings of these two parameters, which are specified in the contract of procurement.

Process Drift

Patrol inspectors move around the factory in a systematic manner making spot checks during production runs and stopping the process when readjustment is necessary. A better arrangement is to detect the process drift before that point is reached and rejects are actually produced. The problem is that the inspector only inspects a small sample at intervals and this can be misleading. If he records his findings at each visit to a given process and plots them on a graph a tendency to drift can be detected.

If the graph shows that the drift is random and small compared with the design tolerance on the piece part, no action need be taken. If the indications are that there is a continuous drift in one direction, even though still within tolerance, he will be alerted to possible need for readjustment of the process. At what point does this become necessary?

Variations in a process are either due to specific causes or to chance. Chance variations have a natural spread across the normal curve as explained above, for practical purposes $\bar{x} \pm 3s$. Any variation greater than this indicates that something in a process has changed. To take advantage of the effect of sample size, that is that the means of random samples will have a nearly normal distribution if the sample is large, the decision to readjust is based on sample means rather than individual measurements, justifying the use of the $3s$ limits.

The grand mean of the samples of 4, which we call $\bar{\bar{x}}$, and the mean of the individual observations, $\bar{x}$, are nearly the same and approach each other as the number of samples increases. The standard deviation for the samples of 4, represented by $s_{\bar{x}}$, will be much smaller than that for the individual observations because of the averaging effect within each sample. The relationship between $s_{\bar{x}}$ and s is given by

$$s_{\bar{x}} = \left(\frac{s^2}{n}\right)^{\frac{1}{2}}$$

where n is the size of the sample.

A control chart can now be constructed based on the normal conditions of the process, the upper and lower limits being $\bar{\bar{x}} \pm 3s_{\bar{x}}$ as shown in Figure 7.8. As the process runs, further sample means are plotted on the control chart. If the plot falls outside either limit readjustment is called for.

Figure 7.8 illustrates the principles of statistical quality control leading to the most economic inspection technique for the degree of control required. Modifications and additions will be needed to suit practical

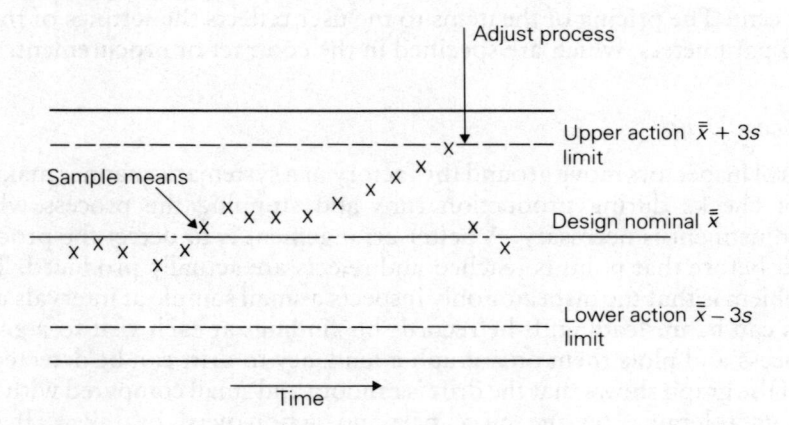

Figure 7.8 Process control chart

cases. Design tolerances and warning, as distinct from action, lines on the chart are typical of such features.

Maturity of Technology

A further influence on the design of a product and its related production processes is the degree of maturity of the technology involved. A useful division (Abernathy and Utterback, 1978) is into three stages which are described as 'fluid', 'transitional' and 'specific'. In each stage there is a change in the balance of innovation in product and process as set out in Table 7.1.

An innovative product embodying new technology meets new user needs and sells on performance. As more is learned about its capabilities and applications, partly from user experience, design changes are required to exploit the findings and cater for individual user needs. Processes must be flexible and will probably demand high levels of skill. Management will be entrepreneurial in a relatively small informal group.

After some experience at the fluid level the design tends to fall into a pattern of application areas and sales volume begins to increase. The demand for higher production levels leads to more formal manufacturing methods and some special process plant is justified. The organization grows, project and task groups appear creating a need for good liaison.

In the third stage, production consists mainly of standard models and there is a reluctance to undertake specials. The emphasis is now on cost reduction and most design changes are aimed at improving the price/performance ratio. The production system is more capital intensive

Table 7.1 Maturity of technology

	Fluid	Transitional	Specific
Competitive emphasis on	Functional performance	Product variation	Cost reduction
Innovation stimulated by	User needs, inputs	Expanding internal capability	Price/Performance improvement
Type of change predominant	Frequent product changes	Process changes – rising volume	Product & process increment
Product line	Diverse, custom design	At least one with significant volume	Mainly standard products
Processes	Inefficient flexible, changes accommodated	Changes in major steps only, rigid	Efficient, capital intensive, rigid, cost of changes high
Production equipment	General purpose skilled labour	Some automation	Special purpose, semi-skilled
Materials	Generally available	Some specialized materials	Specialized. Vertical integration if not available
Plant	Small scale located near technology	General purpose, some special	Large scale specific to products
Organization	Informal, entrepreneurial	Liaison relationships, project teams	Emphasis on structure, goals and rules

and rigid, making modifications expensive. The process plant is special purpose, automatic and specific to products. The organization introduces more structure, goals and rules into its operation.

The Make or Buy Decision

It is unlikely that any company would find it an economic proposition to make all the components it embodies in its products. In some cases the technology involved is not within the company's competence; in others it is so critical to the performance of the product that the company wishes to have it under direct control. Combined with the economics of manufacture and purchasing, these factors create a complex set of conditions to be considered in making the decision (Bergen, 1975). A company would normally wish to:

Make (1) those items that are profitable and within its competence;
(2) those items that, by reason of security or performance, demand a degree of control not otherwise assured;
Buy (3) those items not in class 2 where cheaper prices can be obtained by doing so.

In practice, this type of decision is taken quite often and in various parts of the company. It is helpful if the decision is approached in the same way, using the same criteria, in all departments, to ensure that all such decisions support company policy. For a typical company the above policy statement might be expanded into guidelines as follows:

Buying is indicated to:

(1) Extend the capacity of the factory.
(2) Obtain special technology in an open market.
(3) Obtain better prices.
(4) Improve commercial position.
(5) Avoid capital investment.

Buying is contra-indicated:

(1) Unless there is an open and competitive market.
(2) If in-house capacity exists.
(3) If subcontracted work cannot be brought in-house when factory load falls.
(4) If high added value is involved.
(5) If single sourcing would result and
   (a) supplier reliability is doubtful.
   (b) supplier's normal technology would be stretched.
(6) High supervision level would be required.
(7) If 'special' and low volume to supplier.
(8) If 'in depth' knowledge of the component is important to the company.

With so many parameters to consider, it is helpful to have a system ensuring that the criteria are consistent and applied in the same order. One way to achieve this is by means of a logic network as shown in Figure 7.9. Each lozenge in the network is a question box requiring a 'Yes' or 'No' answer. If the answer is 'Yes' the exit from the box is vertically downwards. If it is 'No' the exit is horizontally to the right or left. The questions relate to the current situation. Question 1 means 'have we the appropriate process in-house now?' not 'is there a process we could bring

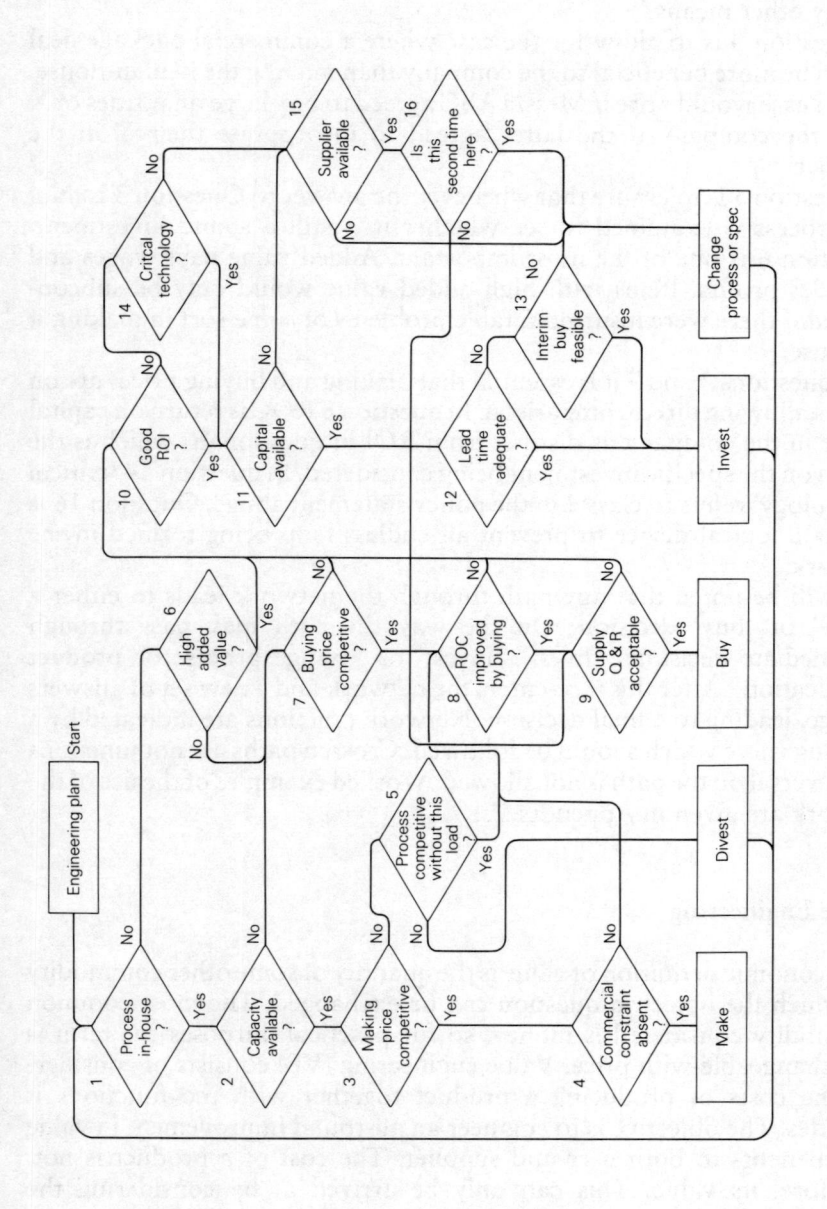

Figure 7.9 The make or buy decision

in?'. Competitive means 'the same quality could not be obtained cheaper by any other means.'

Question 4 is to allow for the case where a commercial package deal would be more beneficial to the company than making the item in-house. Such a case would arise if Messrs ABC agreed to buy large quantities of X from the company if the latter agreed to incorporate their Y in the product.

Question 5 is to ensure that whenever the answer to Question 3 is 'No' the process is examined to see whether it is still a sound investment. Question 6 is one of the most important. Added value pays wages and provides profits. Items with high added value would only be subcontracted if there were insurmountable problems of some sort in making it in-house.

In questions 3 and 7 it is essential that making and buying prices are on a basis allowing direct comparison. In question 8 ROC is return on capital in use in the company as distinct from ROI in question 10 which is the return on the specific investment being considered. In question 14 'critical technology' refers to class 2 in the policy statement above. Question 16 is simply a logical device to prevent an endless loop being formed in the network.

It will be noted that any path through the network leads to either a 'make' or 'buy' decision. On the way the path may pass through intermediate decisions 'divest', 'invest' or 'change process or product specification'. After this it re-enters the network and a new set of answers emerge, leading to a final decision. Network junctions are indicated by a merging curve which should be followed. Crossed paths are not junctions and reversal on the path is not allowed. Worked examples of the use of the network are given in Appendix 7.1.

Value Engineering

The economic definition of value is the quantity of some other commodity for which the object in question can be exchanged. The most common commodity considered is money, so for practical purposes the term is interchangeable with price. Value engineering (VE) consists of considering the costs of producing a product together with the functions it provides. The objective is to engineer an all-round improvement in value with benefits to both user and supplier. The cost of a product is not, therefore, its value. This can only be arrived at by considering the functions it performs.

VE does not initially consider manufacturing methods, as would a cost reduction exercise, but starts by questioning the necessity of the functions

The R&D/Production Interface

and the means by which they are performed. It asks, for example:

What is it?
What does it do?
What does it cost?
What else will do the job?
How much will it cost?

VE is a structured approach to answering these questions. The key steps are

Selection
Information
Speculation
Evaluation
Investigation and planning
Implementation
Summary

Because all aspects of the product must be considered, VE is essentially a team operation, bringing in those people with specific knowledge, from anywhere in the firm as required, as part-time members. There should be one full-time member, the VA co-ordinator, whose task it is to maintain continuity, collect and analyse information, schedule meetings and produce agenda and records. He will be able to perform these duties for more than one team.

Team Composition

A VE team engaged in an engineering design exercise would typically consist of:

R&D engineer
Designer
Production/methods engineer
Cost estimator
VE co-ordinator

Representatives of other functions such as marketing, finance, materials management, servicing and quality assurance are co-opted as required to deal with specific problems. An individual who has no product knowledge but has imagination can often stimulate ideas. The co-ordinator is the only full-time member of the team and it is his task to ensure that the others, who should be sufficiently senior to be able to take decisions on actions proposed, feel involved and committed to the value improvement concept. He does not do this by behaving as if it were his personal project, but by quietly ensuring that things get done as decided.

Selection

The products, or parts thereof, selected for VE should be those that will provide the best return on the considerable investment in time and money that VE demands. Pareto analysis is a conventional way of establishing this. This consists of measuring or estimating financial factors such as cost or profit associated with the products being considered and drawing a histogram of money against product or element type. The bars of the histogram are arranged in descending order of size and it will usually be found that 80 per cent of the money will be associated with 20 per cent of the products, to a first approximation – the origin of the well-known 80–20 rule. This identifies the group of items likely to give the best return on the exercise and puts them in an order of priority.

Information

The scope of the exercise is established and information on costs, specifications, requirements, etc., collected and analysed. The VE co-ordinator should prepare all this data, in conjunction with engineers, designers and cost accountants as appropriate. This phase aims at listing all the necessary functions and the costs of providing them, ending with a complete function/cost analysis identifying the areas of high cost and/or poor value.

Speculation

The complete team for this exercise is assembled and briefed on the problem by the co-ordinator. Each member is encouraged to speculate on alternative methods of performing the functions at lower cost. It is essential that a chairman capable of controlling the meeting be appointed; no negative or critical comment must be allowed at this stage. Judgement must be suspended and as many ideas as possible, no matter how fanciful, collected and recorded, from any source. The notion that ideas come only from the professional specialists in the field must not be allowed to obtrude, nor the traditional 'we tried that and it didn't work' story. While none of the first set of ideas may be feasible or even relevant, they can be built on, allowing the flow to continue freely no matter how perverse the line of argument. No good intention, however illogical, must be lost at this stage.

Evaluation

When all ideas have been exhausted, and recorded by the co-ordinator, each is reviewed briefly. Rough estimates of cost are used to create a priority list of the most promising cases for further study. A systematic assessment of the advantages and disadvantages of each low-cost idea is made to establish the lowest-cost means of performing the function under discussion. Taking into account both costs and functions, the better-value proposals are identified for further development. No impractical idea, however attractive, must get through this stage.

Investigation and Planning

The selected ideas will now be thoroughly investigated by the team members by model making, testing, cost estimating, obtaining quotations and any other actions necessary to prove their viability. Any approvals for making the changes are obtained and the changes themselves are planned.

Implementation

If an existing product is involved, the normal modification procedure will be used, the VE co-ordinator being responsible for observing the formalities. If a product is under development, the changes become the responsibility of the project leader to ensure incorporation. In either case the co-ordinator makes a summary report for the record.

Function/Cost Analysis

Cost analysis is the starting point not only for deciding the subject of the exercise but also of the exercise itself. A simple air pressure control valve as used in aircraft is shown in Figure 7.10 to illustrate the procedure. Table 7.2 is a breakdown of the costs of each of the component parts.

The analysis of function requires concise and unambiguous definition of the functions performed by the part investigated. To achieve this it is helpful to use two words, a verb and a noun, to describe each function. A part may have more than one function. Thus a case may 'provide protection' and 'provide mounting' and 'provide screening' for the components within.

The two analyses are combined in a matrix structure as shown in Table 7.3. The functions are listed horizontally and the parts vertically. The total cost of the part and the percentage of the total cost it represents is entered in the last two columns and the same is done for the function costs in the bottom three rows. The lowest row provides for identifying high-cost functions that should be given special attention. The costing of functions is done by estimating the proportion of the part cost that can notionally be attributed to each function to which it contributes. The sum of the allocated function costs must, of course, equal the part cost.

Table 7.2 Cost analysis

Parts or assemblies	Cost £
Banjo assembly	1.07
Valve body	6.62
Spring	0.39
Diaphragm assembly	2.14
Cover	2.24
Lug	0.10
Nuts, bolts and washers	2.34
Assembly cost	4.58
Total	£19.48

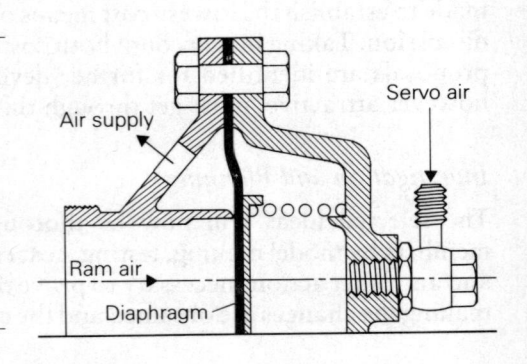

Figure 7.10 Air control valve

The VE team now has the data displayed in a manner allowing it to spot anomalously high costs of performing any function. In a given product range, experience with the procedure rapidly creates a set of norms for functions and any increase in cost above these is very obvious. This in itself is a great help to designers even before any analysis of their new product is undertaken.

It may appear surprising that three parts in the valve have been found to have no function at all and that they amount to over 5 per cent of the total cost. Not surprisingly they have been labelled 'High'. This is not an uncommon result of this type of analysis and stresses the difficulty of the craft of the designer, particularly under time pressure. Study of the operation of the valve shows that the servo air will completely seal the valve without the aid of the spring and that it and the diaphragm plate can therefore be eliminated together with the turned spigot inside the cover.

The other notable high cost function is 'connect parts' which accounts for over 60 per cent of the total. By building this function into other basic parts of the valve, such as the body assembly and cover, as in Figure 7.11, the associated cost is reduced from 12.08 to 2.14, halving the percentage of the total. This is achieved by eliminating not only functionless parts but also unnecessary machining operations and simplifying the shape of the sand castings. The overall cost reduction is from 19.4 to 6.29 without any loss of performance, as seen in the analysis of the new design in Table 7.4.

The cost, including the opportunity cost, of value analysing existing products and implementing the results is significant and involves people from a wide range of company functions. Before embarking on an exercise it is important to establish that the increase in profit and/or sales

Table 7.3 Function/cost analysis

Parts	Stop air	Sense ram air	Sense servo air	Sense cabin air	Connect parts	Provide mounting	Resist corrosion	Provide support	Provide interchangeability	No function	Total cost	%
Banjo assembly	0.4		0.2		0.4			0.47			1.07	5.5
Valve body		1.0			2.82	0.8	0.8		0.6	0.6	6.62	34.0
Spring									0.39		0.39	2.0
Diaphragm assembly	0.6	0.1	0.1		0.94	0.2	0.1				2.14	11.0
Cover			0.4		1.2	0.1	0.34	0.1			2.24	11.5
Lug										0.1	0.1	0.5
Nuts, bolts and washers					2.14	0.1		0.1			2.34	12.0
Assembly					4.58						4.58	23.5
Total	1.0	1.1	0.7	0.1	12.08	0.9	1.24	0.67	1.09		19.48	100.0
Total %	5.1	5.7	3.4	0.5	62.0	4.6	6.4	3.4	5.6			
High or low					H				H			

Table 7.4 Function/cost analysis (new design)

Parts	Stop air	Sense ram air	Sense servo air	Sense cabin air	Connect parts	Provide mounting	Resist corrosion	Provide seal	Provide interchangeability	Provide testing	Total cost £	%
Cover and connection	0.15	0.25	0.50	0.10	0.25	0.30		0.15		0.06	1.76	25.5
Body assembly	0.15	0.20	0.25	0.45	0.40		0.25	0.30	2.18		31.5	
Diaphragm assembly	0.15	0.10	0.25	0.20	0.25	0.10		0.20		0.03	1.28	18.5
Valve assembly	0.05		0.05	0.05	0.15					0.05	0.66	9.5
Fasteners, nuts, bolts, etc.					1.04		0.31				1.04	15.0
Total	0.50	0.55	1.05	0.80	2.14	0.80		0.91		0.17	6.92	100.0
Total %	7.2	7.9	15.1	11.6	30.9	11.6	13.2		2.5			
High or low					H							

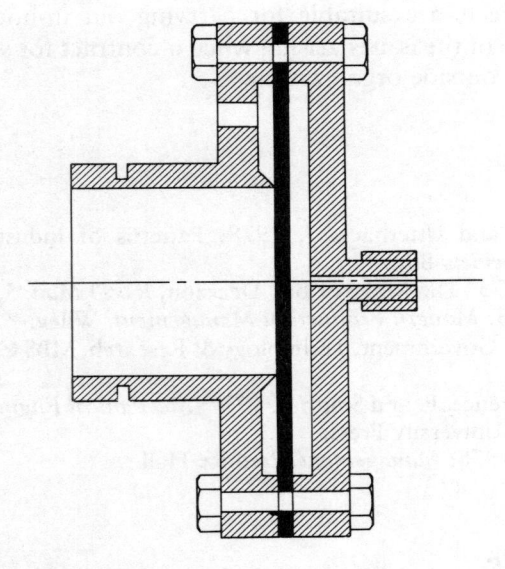

Figure 7.11 Redesigned air valve

and market life of the product will together produce a significant benefit after recovering the costs, particularly those of implementation. If the overall effect is to increase profit but not volume the resources may be better utilized in creating a new product. The increase in production volume that the new product will generate will distribute overheads more thinly and hence reduce costs on the whole range of products, causing a double increase in profits.

A preferred time for introducing the procedure is in the design phase of the development project. The time and cost is minimized and the need for modifications when the product is in production, wasting the effort spent on initial production engineering, is avoided.

Review

This chapter has:

(1) Described the product structure tree and Gozinto chart.
(2) Described the concept of quality control.
(3) Described a sampling plan.
(4) Described the maturity of technology concept.
(5) Presented a logical basis for the make or buy decision.
(6) Described a procedure for value engineering.

Not all projects are suitable for carrying out in-house. Chapter 9 considers some of the issues arising when a contract for such a project is placed with an outside organization.

References

Abernathy, W. and Utterback, J. 1978: Patterns of Industrial Innovation, *Technology Review* 80, 7.
Bergen, S. A. 1975: The Make or Buy Decision, *R&D Man.* 5, 2.
Buffa, E. S. 1983: *Modern Production Management*. Wiley.
Davies, D. 1980: Government, Technology & Research, MBS Conference, *R&D Man.* 10, 51.
Hutton, S., Lawrence, P. and Smith, J. 1977: *Mechanical Engineers in the FRG*. Southampton University Press.
Stoner, A. F. S. 1978: *Management*. Prentice-Hall.

Further Reading

Moroney, M. 1976: *Facts from Figures*. Pelican.
Robson, M. 1982: *Quality Circles*. Gower.
Tooley, D. F. 1981: *Production Control Systems*. Gower.

Appendix 7.1 The Make or Buy Decision – worked examples

Example No. 1 – 4BA nuts

There has been in past years a steady requirement for 4BA nuts. It is now diminishing as metric sizes were adopted some time ago. They are produced in-house on an auto.

Q1 The answer is Yes. Go to Q2.
Q2 The answer is Yes. Go to Q3.
Q3 The answer is certainly No since there is a free market of specialist suppliers operating on a much larger scale. Go to Q5.
Q5 If the prices of the present load are not competitive and the auto only produces nuts and screws, the process is not competitive. The answer is No leading to the decision divest and re-enter the logic network at Q1.
Q1 The answer is now No. Go to Q6.
Q6 The added value cannot be high on such items. Go to Q7.
Q7 The answer is Yes since they can be bought in an open and competitive market. Go to Q8.

The R&D/Production Interface 113

Q8   The answer is Yes since there is no longer a capital investment to finance and buying is at competitive prices. Go to Q9.
Q9   The answer is Yes for the same reasons as Q7. The final decision is therefore 'Buy'.

If the answers to Q5 and Q9 were both Yes, indicating that the process is competitive without the 4BA load and that the supply Q&R is acceptable, buying would again be indicated via Q8 since buying small quantities of mass-produced items rather than investing in equipment to make them in-house must improve the company ROC.

Example No. 2 – Opto-electronic widgets

OEWs are essential components of ABC's high technology products. Their manufacture demands a high investment in capital equipment and know-how. ABC does not consume a sufficient volume to justify the investment, and its corporate plan does not include component sales. The OEWs are proprietary devices available from several suppliers on the open market so they do not rank as critical technology. The route is therefore via Q1 to Q6 where the answer is Yes, leading to Q10.

Q10   The answer is No. Go to Q14.
Q14   The answer is No. Go to Q15.
Q15   The answer is Yes. Go to Q16.
Q16   The answer is No. Go to Q9.
Q9   The answer is Yes as there are established suppliers in an open market. This leads to the 'Buy' decision.

Example No. 3 – Replacement of capstan lathes

One or two autos in the machine shop have excessive maintenance costs and require frequent re-setting due to age. They have high reject rates and hence uncompetitive prices.

Consider a fictitious part that might be made on them in order to go through the network.

Q1   Yes.
Q2   Yes.
Q3   No – due to old age.
Q5   No – same reason. This leads to the Divest decision and re-entry into the network.
Q1   No.

Q6   Variable load – sometimes Yes.
Q7   No, if new capstans produce attractive prices.
Q10 Yes.
Q11 Yes leads to invest decision and re-entry into network.
Q1   Yes.
Q2   Yes.
Q3   Yes.
Q4   Yes. This leads to final 'Make' decision.

ABC is led into an equipment replacement exercise by a series of logical steps.

8 R&D/Production Relationships

Most of the studies of relationships between R&D and production in recent years have been of a qualitative and often anecdotal nature. This has led to several misjudgements as to cause and effect. In an effort to establish a qualitative foundation for this relationship the author, over a period of years, conducted a quantitative analysis by comparing results in four developed countries. This involved designing a questionnaire and applying it to quantitative observations of a sample of companies in the same type of industry in each country.

The first step was to construct a set of hypotheses expected to influence variables relating to (a) operations management and (b) R&D project management factors measuring company performance and project success. A set of five descriptors was then constructed for each variable, representing five levels of the variable and carrying scores from 1 to 5. The order of ascending scores was such that the greatest benefit to the company attracted the highest score (Tables 8.1 and 8.2).

In doing this it would have been helpful to include profitability or value added as the independent variable but in all countries there were many companies which did not know or would not release these figures in relation to individual products. A variable directly affected by operations management and project management, the productivity index, was therefore used as representing the impact of the R&D function on profitability. The productivity index, for this purpose, was taken as the company income divided by the personnel strength of the company. Though this would not satisfy purists, the only factor that would invalidate the productivity index for this purpose would be if some companies had widely different subcontract proportions in their outputs; these would have apparently higher figures than the others. In the UK, the FRG and the USA the proportions varied between 6 and 10 per cent, which was not enough to make a significant difference. Japan is known to have a high subcontract content in many companies but the figures were not available; the difference between Japanese and other productivity figures was, however, so great that conclusions drawn were not invalidated.

Methodology

In the UK, the FRG and Japan the data were collected by means of on-site visits. In the USA a questionnaire was sent by mail to a proportion of respondents. The target industry was scientific instrument manufacture and, with the exception of Japan, some 30 per cent of listed companies in each country were interviewed.

The data collected fell into two categories: those related to operations management and those related to R&D project management. The operations management data are largely those given by companies in their annual report and accounts, with the difference that they were collected directly from company executives and not as published for the benefit of shareholders.

In the first category there were 13 variables of the type normally expressed numerically. They are listed in Table 8.1. The productivity index, described above, was the dependent variable used as a measure of the productivity of the company.

Some of the project management variables are of the same type as the operations data, that is, numerical. In the remaining cases scoring was by means of descriptors, describing the manifestation of the variable in five increasing stages. A score of 5 was awarded for 100 per cent presence of the variable and a score of 1 for a minimal presence.

The analysis of the data thus obtained was in two parts. In the first part the variables were tested for correlations. Significant population

Table 8.1 Operations management variables

	Name	Scale
1	Total no. of employees	100s
2	No. of employees in R&D	100s
3	% of employees in R&D	0–100
4	Company income	£m
5	Income per employee	£k
6	R&D expenditure per annum	£m
7	R&D expenditure as % of income	0–100
8	Expenditure per head in R&D	£k
9	No. of technologies in products	Number
10	Typical selling price	£k
11	Typical annual production	100s
12	Typical market life	Years
13	Typical project duration	Years

differences were tested for in the second part to establish the probability of variations being due to systematic effects or to chance. These analyses were carried out using the SPSS package at Manchester Business School.

The data analysed represented 65 developments from 54 companies in the four countries. Where companies provided data on more than one project they came from separate divisions within the firm, thus representing 65 separate R&D organizations with their own management. The samples represented 13 UK, ten FRG, 23 US and nine Japanese companies. The low number of Japanese companies was not due to the companies themselves but rather to the poor organization of the Japan External Trade Organization (JETRO) in London.

Each respondent was asked to select a project of which he had detailed knowledge and that had been completed within the previous two years. They had all reached the market with varying degrees of success. It was noted that a significant number of respondents, having grasped the intention of the study, asked whether data on successful or failed projects were preferred. No preference was stated; recent personal knowledge was given as the criterion.

This procedure permitted comparison between operations in the four countries and projects in the four countries. In addition project outcome correlations with project-independent variables were calculated on the pooled data.

Operations by Country

Table 8.2 defines the variables used in Table 8.3, which displays the comparative data on company operations in the four countries.

The average company sales and number of employees in Japan are greater than in the other countries. Sales were four times those of the next highest country (USA) and the number of employees was 1.7 times the next highest (FRG). Compared with the UK, sales were 20 times greater and the productivity index over four times higher in Japan. Since it is known (Clarke, 1984) that Japanese manufacturing companies in general often subcontract a significant amount of their production, the last ratio should not be taken seriously. A further problem with this aspect of the analysis is the changes in exchange rates over the period of the study. Discounting ratios by large amounts to allow for these factors does not change the nature of the findings, however.

The comparisons of scores for R&D manpower are not subject to these uncertainties and should be disturbing to the West. In the UK and FRG an average of 9 per cent of company employees worked in R&D and this had been the traditional level in the industry for several years.

118 R&D/Production Relationships

Table 8.2 Project management variables

Score	Descriptor

1 Degree of technical success
- 5   High success technically. All objective and performance specs met or exceeded. Very few modifications after drawing release
- 4   Technical success. All performance specs met without undue modifications because of technical problems
- 3   Moderate success. Project completed; all technical problems overcome by normal resources. Performance acceptable. Some technical loose ends
- 2   Low success. Did not meet target spec. Some technical problems not solved. Not as good as competition
- 1   Technical failure. Project scrapped through failure to solve technical, production, quality or cost problems

2 Degree of adherence to R&D programme
- 5   Complete production data released before planned date
- 4   Released 0–1 month after planned date
- 3   Released 1–3 months after planned date
- 2   Released 3–6 months after planned date
- 1   Released 6–12 months after planned date

3 Speed through production departments
- 5   Product available to marketing 2–3 months after drawing release
- 4   3–5 months
- 3   5–8 months
- 2   8–12 months
- 1   12–18 months

4 Education of project leader
- 5   7–9 years at university level
- 4   5–6 years
- 3   4 years
- 2   3 years
- 1   1–2 years

5 Experience of project leader
- 5   5 years' experience in same position, following 5 years' experience in same industry after qualifying
- 4   Less than 5 years in post after 5 years in industry
- 3   No experience in post; 5 years plus in same industry
- 2   Less than 5 years' experience in the industry in any capacity
- 1   No relevant experience

6 Degree of CEO involvement in project
- 5   Active in new product decisions. Knows project leaders/managers and talks to them. Is well informed on technology, project progress and market potential

R&D/Production Relationships 119

    4   Reviews project proposals constructively. Spends less than 5 per cent of his time on new product policy and progress
    3   Does not react to project progress until planned completion date is near. Reviews product policy decisions taken by others
    2   Makes contact with project only on request of other managers
    1   Delegates product policy decisions. Is unaware of project progress

7 Degree of R&D project subcontracted
    5   75–100 per cent including production drawings
    4   50–75 per cent
    3   25–50 per cent
    2   Up to 25 per cent
    1   Zero

8 Degree of flexibility of operation
    5   No compartmentalization. Individuals to do what they see as appropriate and desirable, free from departmental constraints
    4   Individuals from different departments co-operate to solve problems on their own initiative without respective managers' instructions
    3   Individuals will co-operate across department boundaries when instructed by respective managers
    2   Individuals complain that 'they' have not done something, but require instructions to give them the relevant information
    1   Strict conformity with departmental structure of tasks. Information does not cross departmental boundaries horizontally

9 Absence of Status Consciousness
    5   No status problem. Ideas, directions and proposals considered on merit irrespective of source. Acted on if perceived sound. Recipient will investigate
    4   Critical but positive attitude to external ideas. Acted on if self evidently sound
    3   Critical neutral attitude to external ideas. Requires to be given proof before considering action. Recipient will not investigate on own initiative
    2   Automatic objections to ideas from other departments, trades, disciplines, lower seniority, etc.
    1   Refusal to accept ideas, proposals from other departments, etc.

10 Level of decision making on new products
    5   Detailed decision making on product policy, R&D budget, product specifications, made by CEO
    4   Decisions on product policy and R&D budget made by CEO. Specification decisions by technical and/or marketing directors
    3   Product policy and R&D budget decisions by technical and/or marketing directors. Specifications by departmental heads
    2   Product policy by departmental heads, specs by R&D and/or marketing specialists

120 R&D/Production Relationships

Table 8.2 (*cont.*):

Score	Descriptor
1	All new product decisions left to R&D and/or marketing specialists

11 Ratio of research to total R&D budget
5	Zero on research
4	Less than 5 per cent on research
3	Less than 10 per cent
2	Less than 20 per cent
1	Less than 30 per cent

12 Degree of ability to do job
5	Completes all tasks; achieves or exceeds objectives without help or supervision from seniors
4	Completes tasks, achieves objectives with some help and supervision in minority of cases
3	Completes great majority of tasks, but with considerable help and supervision in a minority of cases
2	Tends to achieve objectives in some cases. Not a good finisher. Looks for help and supervision
1	Frequently fails to achieve objectives. Does not appear able to benefit from supervision and help

13 Degree of motivation
5	A 'self-starter'. Needs controlling rather than motivating. Produces many suggestions for improvement of group results
4	Once started, maintains impetus and interest in task without external stimulus
3	Once started on task which interests him maintains impetus as long as interest of superior is evident
2	Needs occasional pep talk and positive signs of encouragement from superior
1	Works as long as supervision maintains drive

14 Degree of integration
5	Project leader has authority over all aspects of project, supported by top management, in all departments
4	Project leader responsible for R&D and design and liaison with production departments. Authority delegated by R&D manager/director
3	Project coordinator has no direct authority; liaises with and advises all relevant departments
2	Project liaison engineer reports to department manager on progress of project. Access to all information, no authority
1	No form of integrator; all authority with department head

15 Degree of participation in design

- 5   Production engineers formally involved with R&D in all phases of design as full-time members of project team
- 4   Production engineers part-time members of project team. Formal engineering committee discusses design progress. Production engineers approve drawings
- 3   Any non-standard design solutions fully discussed with production engineers before being embodied. No routine meetings
- 2   No routine or formal participation in design phase by production engineers. Designer consults production engineers when he considers it useful to do so
- 1   Design by design office based on data from R&D and released to production without discussion

16 Degree of joint reward system

- 5   R&D and production personnel take part in formal joint reward system based on success of project
- 4   Individuals rewarded by department on success in solving department-related problems in project
- 3   Some departments give merit and achievement awards; others do not
- 2   Occasional merit awards for individual achievement at the discretion of management
- 1   No performance award system in use

17 Clarity of problem definition

- 5   Statements such as 'No problems have ever been due to lack of clarity in design data, drawings or problem definition'
- 4   'Very occasionally we have to ask for clarification of problem or information so that we can complete our task. We always receive it quickly'
- 3   'In quite a few cases we can't get on because of unclear statements of problem or design data. This does not hold the job up very much'
- 2   'Much of the time we are going backwards and forwards asking for clarification so that we can get on'
- 1   'Problem definition and design data are never initially clear enough for us to work on. We lose a lot of time sorting it out'

18 Clarity of understanding of problem

- 5   Statements such as 'If the information is complete we/they never have difficulty in understanding the problem'
- 4   'Even when the information appears to be complete we occasionally have to go over it with them to ensure that we all understand it'
- 3   'There is always a lot of informal discussion to clarify problem and design data'

122 R&D/Production Relationships

Table 8.2 (cont.):

Score	Descriptor
2	'We/they always have difficulty in understanding their/our problems and the information they/we provide'
1	'We always provide complete information on the project, but a lot of time is still spent trying to get over what it means in their terms'

19 Completeness of information

5	'Information we receive is always complete. We very seldom have to ask for additional data'
4	'Occasionally information is incomplete and we have to ask for the missing data. It seldom holds up the project'
3	'On some occasions we can't get on for lack of information and spend some time trying to get it'
2	'We lose a lot of time on the project because they don't provide us with all the information we need'
1	'They are very secretive about their projects. We have to solve our own problems'

The average in Japanese companies was rather more than twice this percentage. In the USA the average is lower at 7 per cent but this is offset by a much higher expenditure per head on R&D workers.

In terms of percentage of income invested in R&D the USA scored lowest and the FRG highest, Japan being only slightly above the USA. However, these figures must be related to average company incomes to have much meaning. The UK, in these terms, invests least at a third to a half of the investment in the USA and FRG, and a twelfth of that in Japan.

Japan has 400 universities producing 100 000 engineers annually (Rawle, 1983) compared with the UK's 15 000 (Central Statistical Office, 1984) and this has resulted in Japan having the world's highest proportion (53 per cent) of qualified scientists and engineers (QSEs) in industry. Lower labour mobility than elsewhere combines with this effect to keep salaries down and, crucially, to encourage a relatively high investment in training. The low expenditure on in-service training in the UK is stigmatized in Coopers & Lybrand (1986). The high level of training and re-training is a major factor in Japanese industrial success (Rawle, 1983).

Expenditure per head in R&D has a significant correlation with productivity, as seen in the next section.

Differences in selling price are largely due to the FRG's selling a

Table 8.3 Operations Variables – means by country

	UK	FRG	USA	Japan
Total no. of employees	584	1404	909	2389***
Percentage of employees in R&D	9	9	7***	19***
Company income, £m	9.2	34.4	45.7	215.4***
Company income per employee, £k	18.5	25.9	67.5	89.4***
R&D expenditure as percentage of company income	7.5	7.6	5.6	6.1*
Expenditure per head in R&D, £k	14.7	28.6	49.2	34.2***
Typical selling price, £k	6.9	3.0	10.8	135.3
Typical market life, years	7.7	7.0	7.5	7.0
Typical project duration, years	3.3	3.2	2.1	2.2
Number of companies	12	10	23	9

*, $p<0.05$; ***, $p<0.001$.

smaller proportion of large systems than the others, and the Japanese figure is distorted because one company is a high outlier in this sense. The analysis is not significantly affected by omitting this company. As would be expected in an international market, product life does not vary greatly between countries. Though not statistically significant there is a logical tendency towards low R&D resources linking with longer project duration and market life. The USA and Japan both got their new products to market faster than the UK and FRG but the differences are not statistically significant.

Projects by Country

Table 8.4 presents scores of project variables by country. There are no significant differences by country between the three variables indicating project success. Of the independent variables the degree of CEO involvement in the project is higher in the FRG than elsewhere and absence of status consciousness is highest in Japan. To a lower statistical significance team ability and motivation are highest in Japan, as is clarity of problem definition. Clarity of problem understanding is highest in the UK.

Use of 'joint reward system' deserves special mention as it indicates management problems in implementation. No high scores were found in any country and during the interviews respondents often asked about methods of administering such systems. Yet, as will be seen in the next

Table 8.4 Project variables – means by country

	UK	FRG	USA	Japan
Technical success	3.8	3.8	3.6	4.3
Adherence to programme	2.5	2.1	2.3	2.6
Speed through production	3.1	2.6	2.8	3.1
Education level of project leader	2.9	3.4	3.3	3.1
Experience of project leader	4.2	4.2	4.2	4.3
CEO involvement	3.8	4.9	3.9	3.9***
% R&D project subcontracted	1.4	1.7	1.5	1.6
Flexibility of operation	3.5	3.8	3.8	3.9
Absence of status consciousness	3.2	3.4	3.7	4.7***
Level of new product decision making	4.0	3.9	3.7	4.0
% R&D budget on research	4.0	3.9	3.7	3.9
Team ability to do job	3.5	3.7	3.4	4.3*
Motivation of team	3.4	3.9	4.0	4.5*
Degree of integration	4.0	3.8	4.0	4.4
Use of joint reward system	1.3	1.8	2.0	2.8?
Clarity of problem definition	3.7	3.6	3.2	4.1*
Clarity of problem understanding	4.3	3.8	3.2	3.6**
Completeness of information	3.4	3.5	3.4	3.8
Number of projects	16	17	23	9

?, $p<0.1$, *, $p<0.05$; **, $p<0.01$; ***, $p<0.001$.

section, there were quite strong correlations between the scores for this variable and project success.

Absence of status consciousness is worth commenting on further as an effect of national culture on scores. The nature of the variable is best explained by reference to the relevant descriptors in Table 8.2. In Japan, Miyajima reported, questions on status and information transfer puzzled the respondents. It appeared that they did not represent national cultural concepts in Japan. This is interesting since there is evidence (for example, Tung, 1984) that Japan is a strongly hierarchical culture and that status and face are emphasized.

Status consciousness was included by the designer of the interview structure expressly because of experience of its manifestation in UK companies. The UK scored lowest for this variable.

There is a widespread perception in the UK that top management is ever ready to give responsibility to project leaders/managers but seldom to delegate corresponding authority. A variable, degree of project integration, was therefore defined in terms of the project leader's breadth of authority in the company to permit inter-company comparison. From Table 8.4 FRG has the lowest score for integration, but this is misleading. In fact project integration is high in the FRG for two reasons. The high degree of CEO involvement already noted is an integrating factor and another is the strong orientation of FRG industry to a standards and systems approach. As a result of this FRG project leaders are able to predict and influence reactions in other departments because all are working to the same well-developed system. One of the attributes of such a system is that it makes available to all concerned the information they need to discharge their responsibilities. Because of this, supra-departmental authority is not needed by the project leader to ensure that his ideas are implemented – hence the low FRG score for degree of project integration.

The UK national culture seems to be anti-systems and engineers often regard standards as restrictions on their creativity rather than as an efficient means of communication. In the absence of authority to impose their ideas successful project managers are obliged to resort to persuasiveness, personal influence and the 'old boy' network. UK national culture is reflected in the low score for absence of status consciousness and the high score for clarity of problem understanding. The latter is consistent with the UK emphasis on science and individual creativity.

The significantly higher score for team ability in Japan is consistent with the higher investment in training and the high score for motivation with the high scores for project integration – a strong project leader increases team motivation – and the higher score for joint reward systems.

The US sample scores lowest for clarity of problem understanding and production involvement in design, probably representing the standing of the production function in the USA in this industry and the communication gap separating it from R&D, another cultural factor.

Variable Correlations within Countries

The scores for the variables were tested for correlations using the Kendall τ and the Pearson r statistics. The results of the two tests were very similar. Multiple stepwise regression analysis was also applied. There are reservations as to its validity because of the small samples and the non-parametric nature of some of the variables. The close correspondence between the τ and r results suggests that the deviation from interval scale is slight and hence that the effect on results may not be radical (Siegal, 1956). The results will be discussed here because they lead to an interesting speculation upon the optimum level of investment in R&D and identification of variables explaining major proportions of variances in indicators of success.

Productivity

In both the UK and the FRG, and in the pooled data for these two countries, there was a strong positive correlation (0.75, $p<0.001$) between productivity and expenditure per head in R&D, explaining 40 per cent of the variance. In both the USA and Japan the strongest correlation with productivity was a negative one, selling price (0.25 in the USA, 0.4 in Japan), explaining 25 per cent of the variance in the USA and 40 per cent in Japan. Thus productivity is influenced in the UK and FRG mainly by a management factor, the level of expenditure on the R&D worker, and in the USA and Japan by a product factor, selling price.

The regression equations for the UK show a positive correlation with percentage of employees in R&D. Japan scores twice as high as the UK for this variable with a significance of $p<0.001$, but with a *negative* correlation. One can speculate that a positive slope for this regression line confirms investment below the optimum level in the UK and the negative slope in Japan indicates investment above the optimum level. A further speculation is that the optimum must lie between these two values. If the mid-point were taken arbitrarily the implication is that the UK manpower in R&D could be increased to 13–14 per cent of total manpower with continuing improvement in productivity. Further research with larger samples is needed on this subject.

Project Variables Correlations

Correlations between the variables measuring project success and the independent variable were tested for and the results are presented in Tables 8.5 and 8.6. These give the sign and significance of the Pearson r. The Kendall τ was also used to examine the non-parametric variables: no differences of consequence were found. The stepwise multiple regression equations, with the reservations already mentioned, are as follows:

UK Prod=6.3+1.2(exp. per head in R&D)+2.2(% employees in R&D)
$R^2 = 40\%$ $R^2 = 20\%$

FRG Prod = 1.9+0.7(% employees in R&D)−0.14 (market life)
$R^2 = 34\%$ $R^2 = 10\%$

USA Prod = 49.5 − 0.5 (selling price)
$R^2 = 25\%$

Japan Prod = 98.0 − 0.8 (selling price) +6.4 (market life)
$R^2 = 83\%$ $R^2 = 5\%$
−0.9 (% employees in R&D)
$R^2 = 3\%$

The dependent variable, Prod, is the productivity index and R^2 is the percentage of the variance explained by the independent variable.

Table 8.5 Correlations between project technical success and the independent variables

	Overall	UK	FRG	USA	Japan
Adherence to programme	?pos	?pos	?pos		
Speed through production departments					
Education level of project leader					
Experience of project leader		?pos			
CEO involvement					
% R&D subcontracted	?neg				
Flexibility of operation				POS	
Absence of status consciousness	?pos	?pos			
Level of new product decision making					
% of R&D budget on research				POS	
Team ability to do job				?pos	
Integration of project			?neg	?neg	
Production involvement in design				POS	
Use of joint reward system		?pos			
Clarity of problem definition	POS				
Clarity of problem understanding	POS				
Completeness of information	POS	POS	POS	POS	
Number of projects	66	17	16	24	9

POS, $p<0.05$ positive; NEG, $p<0.05$ negative; ?pos, ?neg, $0.15<p<0.1$.

Project Technical Success

Table 8.5 presents the correlations between project technical success and the independent variables. Overall the strongest correlations are with clarity of problem definition, clarity of problem understanding and completeness of information. This group can be considered as three elements of communication. It may be significant that it is the only instance where pooling the data has a strengthening effect on the correlations, supporting the view that communication problems are at the root of a large number of industrial problems in all cultures.

Table 8.6 Correlations between adherence to programme and the independent variables

	Overall	UK	FRG	USA	Japan
Technical success	?pos	?pos	?pos		
Speed through production departments	POS	?pos	POS		
Education level of project leader					
Experience of project leader		?pos			
Degree of CEO involvement					?neg
% of R&D subcontracted	?neg				?neg
Flexibility of operation	POS	?pos	POS		
Absence of status consciousness	POS			POS	
Level of new product decision making		POS			
% of R&D budget on research			?neg		NEG
Team ability to do job	POS	?pos			?pos
Motivation of team					
Degree of integration of project					
Completeness of information	?pos				
Production involved in design					NEG
Use of joint reward system	?pos		POS		
Clarity of problem definition				?pos	
Clarity of problem understanding					

POS, $p<0.05$ positive; NEG, $p<0.05$ negative; ?pos, ?neg, $0.15<p<0.1$.

The overall low significance correlation with adherence to programme is probably the unsurprising finding that projects which are technically successful at most stages tend to slip less than those which are not.

There is no across-the-board agreement on the importance of the independent variables; the pooled data, except in the case mentioned above, weaken rather than strengthen the analysis. There appear to be underlying differences present, possibly of a cultural nature.

In the UK, completeness of information is the most significant positive correlation and explains 40 per cent of the variance. Experience of the project leader and absence of status consciousness also seem to be advantageous, but the effect of CEO involvement is disadvantageous. This may link with the lower average level of technical qualification among the UK chief executive officers.

In the FRG the most significant variables are flexibility of operation and clarity of problem definition. The negative influence of 'project leader formal authority' probably reflects potential conflict with the national systems orientation.

In the USA the important positive correlations are with per cent R&D expenditure on research, production involvement in design, and completeness of information. There are low significance correlations with team ability (positive) and with project leader authority (negative). These are consonant with the perceived communication gap between the R&D and production functions in many US companies. The regression analysis indicates that 50 per cent of the variance is explained by these variables.

In Japan the only – but interesting – clues to technical success come from the regression equation. High mean scores are found for absence of status consciousness, experience of project leader and team ability, together explaining 71 per cent of the variance. All three are *negative* correlations. These attributes would be expected to lead to new and better solutions to problems in the UK and it seems that the apparent anomaly may be of cultural origin. Much has been published about the Japanese group culture, company loyalty and risk-averse management. There is much discussion of creativity in Japan but the practical approach is that of 'keihakutansoka', the art of 'making things lighter, slimmer, shorter and smaller', leading to creative individuals being constrained and having to work 'under the bench' to make progress (Clarke, 1984). Bottom-up decisions are not common in this context. One can speculate that, since the data largely represent the views of senior company people, project success is judged against this policy and the negative correlations appear.

It seems that the average level of technical success in Japan is high, which would correspond to general perception, with individualism, where present, seen as an undesirable influence detracting from realization of company policy.

Adherence to Programme

Overall the important factors in launching new products on schedule are speed through production departments, flexibility of operation, absence of status consciousness, and team ability (Table 8.6). Subcontracting part of the project is likely to lose time rather than gain it. Technical success, use of joint reward system, and completeness of information all have positive correlations with low significance.

In the UK, level of management decision on projects correlates positively. Experience of the project leader, flexibility of operation and team ability correlate at low significance.

In the FRG, as overall, speed through production departments and flexibility of operation have significant positive correlations and use of joint reward systems correlates with a high significance. The presence of research in the project is likely to delay completion.

In the USA there is a high significance correlation with flexibility of operation, suggesting that the ability to overcome the communication gap between R&D and production noted previously has its major benefit in adherence to programme. This correlation is confirmed in the regression model which also shows a negative correlation with education level of project leader. These two variables together explain some 45 per cent of the variance, suggesting that practical commonsense is more important than academic achievement in avoiding slippage.

In Japan there are negative correlations with per cent of research and with production involvement in design, which may relate to the tentative hypothesis offered about the negative correlations with technical success. The culture seems to prefer low-risk projects – no research – and informal interaction between functions – high scores for production involvement in design mean increased formality. CEO involvement and subcontracted R&D, if anything, delay completion of the project.

Speed Through Production Departments

There are smaller differences between countries for this variable than for the other dependents, and the overall significant correlations are reflected to some extent in all countries except Japan.

Adherence to R&D programme, flexibility of operation, degree of integration of project, together with clarity of problem definition and clarity of problem understanding, which are measures of quality of communication, correlate positively with efficient progress through production in the overall case.

In the UK much the same pattern is found with a very high significance ($p<0.0001$) attaching to flexibility of operation.

The same is true of the FRG with the addition of a possible positive influence from motivation and production involvement in design. The already noted systems orientation in the FRG lends credibility to the last correlation in spite of the low significance from the sample tested.

In the USA there is a departure from this pattern. The degree of CEO involvement and completeness of information have positive correlations as does flexibility of operation at a lower significance. CEO involvement may mean that the project gets preferential treatment on resources and manpower and/or a personal contribution to the project. The former seems more likely in larger companies and the latter in small, particularly new, companies. The regression analysis indicates that completeness of information and team ability correlated positively, per cent of research correlated negatively and the three variables explained 45 per cent of the variance between them.

Japan again showed low variance of the dependent variable and no significant Pearson r coefficients. The regression equation explained 45 per cent of the variance in terms of the degree of integration, measured as the breadth of authority of the project leader.

Discussion

There are clear differences in the productivity of the scientific instrument manufacturing industries in the four countries studied. The relative productivity indices are as follows:

UK 100
FRG 140
USA 360
Japan 480

The respective managerial cultures are apparently influential. In the UK and FRG there is a strong correlation between expenditure per head in R&D and productivity. This is not found directly in the USA and Japan but, if the product of per cent of employees in R&D and expenditure per head in R&D is taken as an index of R&D resources, the figures are:

UK 100
FRG 190
USA 250
Japan 480

The two league tables have the same range and the countries are roughly in the same positions in both.

The FRG is low in the productivity league table and slow in getting new products to market. Research content and subcontracted R&D are adverse effects on both and adherence to R&D programmes appears to be the main factor for reaching the market in reasonable time.

USA productivity was 75 per cent of that of Japan; its overall position would benefit from greater involvement of senior management, more manpower in R&D, greater participation of production in design and greater completeness of information. It is pointed out that more manpower in R&D will be needed to cope with the additional design changes and modifications they will produce.

Japan had the highest productivity and consistently high average scores for indicators of project success and cultural factors confusing to Western minds. The sample is too small for reliable analysis and the speculations within the text are probably all that this study justifies.

Review

This chapter has:

(1) Constructed a set of hypotheses to measure company performance and project success.
(2) Collected data representing 65 R&D departments from 13 UK, 10 FRG, 23 US and 9 Japanese companies.
(3) Described operations by country, projects by country and productivity by country.
(4) Described multiple regression equations by country.
(5) Discussed the relative productivity of scientific instrument manufacturing industries in the UK, FRG, USA and Japan.

References

Central Statistical Office 1984: *Facts in Focus*. HMSO.
Clarke, R. 1984: *Aspects of Japanese Commercial Innovation*. Technical Change Centre.
Coopers and Lybrand 1986: A challenge to complacency. In Challis H., *Engineering News*, April 1986.
Rawle, P. R. 1983: *GEC Commissioned Report*. London Business School.
Siegal, S. 1956: *Non-Parametric Statistics*. McGraw-Hill.
Tung, L. R. 1984: *Business Negotiations with the Japanese*. Lexington Books.

Further Reading

Bergen, S. A., Miyajima, R. and McLaughlin, C. P. 1988: The R&D/Production Interface in Four Developed Countries. *R&D Man*. July No. 3, 201.

9 Contracts

The make or buy decision enters into project as well as product tactics. A project set up to generate a new product or process may be an in-house activity utilizing the company's own staff and resources, or it may be contracted out to another organization. This is done, for example, in order to provide an economical method of introducing a new technology into the company by using an established expert, or when in-house resources are temporarily so stretched that it is the only feasible expedient.

Conditions for Successful Contracts

When companies enlist the services of consultants and contractors, two factors are observable. The companies most likely to go to outside parties for this type of service are those who are best equipped internally. Those who have little in-house capability make least use of consultancy services in all fields. Secondly, and a possible explanation for the first phenomenon, only those companies having on their own staff a group or individual of at least the same calibre and ability as the outside group are likely to achieve success in this type of collaboration. Without this provision there is likely to be a disastrous failure of communication.

While the general principles of project management are much the same in the two cases, a number of important aspects that are implicit in the first case, in that they are built in as part of the company procedures, must be made explicit in the second. Much common knowledge of how the company operates and the lessons of past successes and failures in both technical and personnel terms are shared between company departments. They tend to communicate in a form of shorthand based on this common database and can to some extent predict each other's reactions to normal situations. Any gaps in information can often be filled by informed guesswork. Admittedly the predictions and guesses will sometimes be wrong, but the situation can, with goodwill, usually be recovered. The absence of any such shared background with an outside organization makes it imperative to formalize procedures to a much greater extent and to provide more information specific to the work to be carried out. This leads to the concept of the outside organization accepting a contract as a means of defining the nature of the work to be done and the responsibilities of the two parties towards it.

Legal Definition of Contract

A contract may be defined as an agreement enforceable at law. Not every agreement is such, even though it may constitute a moral obligation. There must be an intention on both sides for there to be legal consequences in the event of a breach, in order to constitute a binding contract. There are other legal points to note (Light, 1960):

> A contract may be written or verbal, but the intention of the verbal form may be more difficult to determine at a future date.
>
> There must be an offer and an acceptance of the offer. The offer must be specific. A priced article in a shop window is not an offer, simply an invitation to negotiate.
>
> There must be a consideration. This is the legal term for value promised in exchange for performance of the contract. In the absence of consideration the agreement is not a contract unless it is written and sealed, as with a deed. Gratuitous promises cannot be enforced at law.
>
> There must be capacity. The parties to the contract must be legally competent and authorized to enter into it.
>
> The purpose of the contract must not be illegal.

Form of Contract

The task of the customer's representative is to get a satisfactory job done as economically as possible. That of the contractor is to ensure a profit in doing so. This is more difficult to analyse in those cases where the uncertainty is high, for example research projects, than in those where it is lower, as in production contracts.

In the past it has been the practice for research and development contracts to be on a 'cost plus' basis. The contractor reports the costs to the customer who pays an amount equal to the costs plus an agreed percentage of them as profit. This has led to waste and inefficiency since the definition of a good hour of work is one that can be charged to the contract rather than one in which some progress has been made. This has been particularly remarked on in government contracts and has led to pressure to move towards fixed-price contracts.

Fixed-price contracts have been normal for production contracts but on occasion this has led to claims that excess profits have been made and in a few cases repayment of the excess has been enforced. Some form of fixed price plus incentive payment offers a partial solution, the aim being to share the risks between the contracting parties. In all types of contracts, particularly the last, definition of the risks it is intended to cover and the manner in which they will be allocated is of great importance.

The Learning Curve

In the case of production contracts, which will be repeated over a period of time, pricing is sometimes based on historical rates with the learning curve applied to reduce them year by year. The learning curve (Hirschman, 1964) concept originated in pre-war manufacturing operations in the US aircraft industry. Historical records showed that every time the quantity manufactured doubled, the cost per unit reduced by the same amount. If the fifth batch of ten cost 80 per cent of the fourth batch then the fortieth batch would cost 80 per cent of the thirty-ninth. Plotted on double logarithmic graph paper this emerges as a straight line making forecasting of costs for projected future batches of the same product a simple exercise as long as conditions are not seriously altered. The slope of the line is specific to the product and the production organization and is arrived at from historical figures. It is common in this type of contract to use this curve in fixing the prices for further batches. It must be stressed, however, that this is what can be achieved by effort, innovation and good management in production, rather than what happens in a *laissez-faire* atmosphere.

Specification

In all cases it is of the essence to specify the work to be done in an unambiguous form and to make it quite clear which party is responsible for which elements. The customer will almost certainly have to supply the contractor with something. It may be information or it may be components for incorporation in the contractors activities. In either case the content and timing must be specified so that there can be no confusion at a later date when the agreement on who does what is no longer fresh in the mind.

In many cases of R&D contracts the outcome will be subject to considerable uncertainty. It will be necessary to specify procedures, tests, reports and completion dates since the contractor will not accept a contract based on an outcome with a low probability of achievement. In such a case it may well be advisable to draw up the contract to cover stages that can be defined in this way and make contracts for succeeding stages conditional upon achieving agreed criteria of success for prior stages.

The completion date for the stage or project must be defined both in terms of time and criteria of success. The incentive aspect may be brought in at this stage to define a reward for the contractor for finishing on or before the contract completion date and compensation to the customer for finishing late.

Documentation

The starting point for a contract is frequently a published 'Invitation to Tender'. The contractor responds to this and obtains the 'Conditions of Tender', a written specification of the form in which the tender must be submitted and any special undertakings required from the contractor before he is regarded as qualified to tender. He will then be supplied with:

(1) The conditions of contract.
(2) The specification.

In tendering he will supply:

(3) Information explaining his proposal, possibly including drawings, models, photographs, etc.
(4) The resources it is proposed to apply to the contract, and some indication of how they are costed.
(5) A formal quotation.
(6) Any correspondence on which important aspects of the negotiations have been based.

If the quotation is accepted by the customer he will send the contractor:

(7) Formal acceptance of quotation.
(8) Order or letter of intent.

The final stage is the contractor's

(9) Acceptance of order.

Before taking this step there should be a final review of the conditions of contract, specification and proposal to ensure that no false impressions as to feasibility and probable profitability exist. All the documents should be filed together and stored securely and accessibly. Final acceptance by the customer of the work done, and payment for it, will depend upon their provisions being demonstrably met.

Drafting a Contract

In the vast majority of cases contracts of the type discussed do not result in litigation. The costs of going to court are likely to be higher than the value of the contract and the only beneficiaries are typically the lawyers. This does not excuse imprecision in writing the contract. A good contract is one which brings benefits to both sides and this is the result that should be aimed at in negotiations; it should be written, however, as if every point were to be used as evidence at a later date.

Literary English is a beautiful rather than a definitive language. In the hands of a good writer it can convey atmosphere and emotion, but it works to a large extent by analogy rather than definition. This can, and does, lead to ambiguity. If there are any legal points of substance in the contract terms they should be dealt with by professionals.

The engineer will be expected to contribute to the technical aspects of the specification and to those points associated with the running and timing of the project. This should be written in short grammatical sentences with the minimum of dependent clauses. It is not advisable to indulge in elegant variation; repetition of the same word a dozen times to convey the same meaning in the same paragraph is better than risking ambiguity. This is not a competition for the Nobel prize for literature but a protection against potential accusations of lack of clarity. Professional jargon should be avoided as far as possible. Where essential to the sense of the passage any such terms must be defined in the same document.

Qualifying adjectives and adverbs should be avoided and the use of unadorned nouns and verbs relied on. The meaning of a sentence should not be allowed to depend on punctuation. Filler phrases such as 'in respect of', 'in the context of', should be avoided. It is good practice to go through any document before parting with it and eliminate any word that is not essential to conveying the precise meaning intended. There will be some of these no matter how much care goes into the first draft. The whole of the first paragraph of a first draft can usually be removed without loss.

Quite apart from the drafting of contracts the task of the engineer involves a great deal of communication, much of it by the written word. The use of words to formulate ideas is a good discipline for ensuring that the ideas themselves are relevant, coherent and logically presented. As Arthur Koestler put it in *The Act of Creation*:

> Words are essential tools for formulating and communicating thoughts, and also for putting them into the storage of memory, but words can also become snares, decoys or straight jackets.

These are the basic considerations for getting ideas accepted and one should consciously work towards improving skill in this direction. A useful text to have when writing anything is *The Complete Plain Words*, originally by Sir Ernest Gowers, published by HMSO (Fraser, 1983), from which the above examples of filler words are taken. Reference to this well-structured book will go far to deal with any points on which there is doubt. Happily it is readable as well as informative. Another essential item for reference is a dictionary.

Drawings

Contract drawings, together with the specification, must define completely the work to be done and the standards with which it must comply. Conventions used on the drawings must be explicitly stated. The type of projection and the symbols used for components, finishes, limits and the conventions for dimensions, scale and component values must be presented where they can be seen in using the drawings. The drawings must follow a consistent pattern so that comparison between them is not misleading.

Incentives

In some research and development contracts the degree of technical uncertainty may be such that the requirement cannot reasonably be specified in terms of an end result. An alternative is to break the overall requirement down into elements that can be defined by activity rather than result. An example of the tactic would be a project aimed at establishing the suitability of a material for a given task. A defined series of tests would be the work content and the delivery of the report on the test results in a specified format would be the defined completion of a first contract. After consideration of the first set of results, it would be decided whether to abandon the material or to investigate further. In the latter case the operation would be repeated with a second set of tests. The risk and the cost to the customer is thus under control and there is a relationship between cost and reduction of risk.

Where such a step-by-step approach is not appropriate, and it does restrict the contractor's freedom to use his own judgement in areas where he may be better informed than his customer, an approach that divides risk and reward on a reasonably equitable basis between customer and contractor may be a useful option. The figures are regarded as targets rather than as criteria. They are adjusted so that if the project were completed on time to specification the contractor would realize a reasonable profit. The principle to be applied is that any departure from the target represents a loss or gain to be shared on an agreed basis between the two parties.

Targets may be set for any parameter that can be measured as the project proceeds, such as cost, time and performance. The requirement to be able to measure must be taken into account when drafting the specification. If the cost exceeds the target cost the contractor will be paid his costs, plus his target profit, less a proportion of the overrun. If the cost is less than the target figure the contractor is paid his costs, plus his target profit, plus a proportion of the cost saving. Upper and lower limits may be applied to prevent a runaway condition in the event of really bad estimating. The method is illustrated in Figure 9.1.

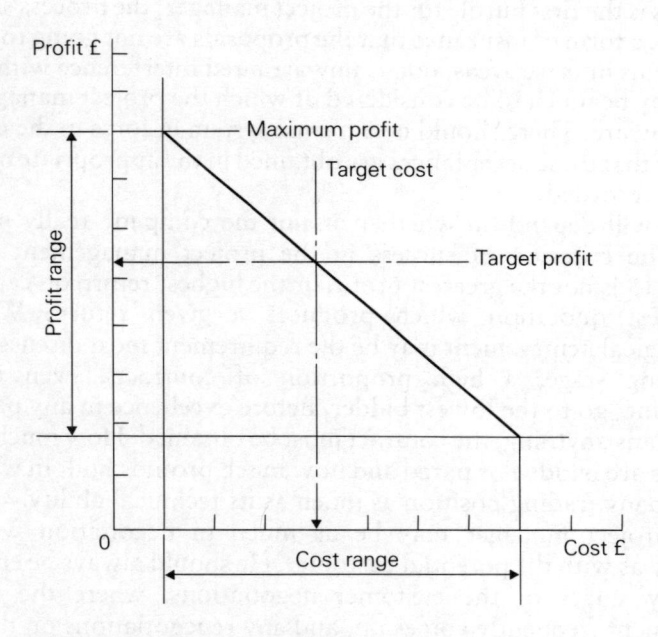

Figure 9.1 Incentive scheme

There is a possibility that applying an incentive scheme to one parameter only may attach undue importance to it. The customer would probably be unhappy if the project were completed well ahead of time at the expense of some key quality aspect. The inclusion of incentives judiciously applied to several parameters will reduce the danger. In setting up the scheme, care must be taken to judge the range and slopes of the lines so as to maintain the desired balance in the minds of the contractor's engineers.

The Quotation

Only when a project manager has reached a fairly high level in a company hierarchy will it be necessary to deal with the whole of the tendering process. The terms of contract, costing, pricing and the delivery promise will be among the aspects of the task that overlap with other company functions as illustrated in Figure 1.1. There may be legal, estimating, pricing, marketing, sales, financial control and other departments, depending on the size of the company, all with an interest and a responsibility for ensuring that the tender, if accepted, will benefit the company. Getting acceptance of the technical specification by these functions is the first hurdle for the project manager; the process should be viewed as a form of insurance that the proposals are not going to give rise to problems in these areas, not as unwarranted interference with the job. There may be much to be considered of which the project manager is not initially aware. There should be a formal system in force in the company to ensure that these acceptances are obtained in the appropriate order and properly recorded.

Much will depend on whether or not the company really needs the order. The criterion of success in the project management game in Chapter 18 is not the greatest profit, or the highest return on capital, but the lowest quotation which produces a given return. While the technological achievement may be the requirement most discussed in the negotiating stage, a high proportion of contracts, even in space engineering, go to the lowest bidder. Before excellence in any part of the work means anything, the contract must be obtained. How much the cost estimates are padded or pared and how much profit is built in will reflect the company trading position as much as its technical ability.

The project manager may be as much in negotiation within his company as with the potential customer. He should always be engaged in the early stages of the customer negotiations, where the technical commitment frequently comes up, and any renegotiations on that basis. In either case adequate preparation should be made, so that the relevant facts and estimates are in a presentable state. The reinforcing effect of repetition and simple visual exhibits should not be overlooked. He should think himself into the position of the other person, whether in-house or customer, and try to anticipate his approach and reactions. This is one of the main reasons for the statement that an engineer can only do his own job well if he understands those of the other functions in his company. People tend to remember those facts that (a) they want to know, (b) they hear often, (c) they hear last and (d) are presented simply and logically.

Review

This chapter has:

(1) Defined the legal requirements of a contract.
(2) Explained a basic condition for success.
(3) Explained the need for a greater information content in contracts than in in-house projects.
(4) Explained cost plus, fixed price and incentive contracts.
(5) Described the learning curve.

The next chapter discusses the project life cycle, forms of organization for controlling it, and styles of leadership.

References

Fraser, Sir B. 1983: *Plain Words*. HMSO
Hirschmann, W. B. 1964: Profit from the Learning Curve. *HBR*, Jan.–Feb.
Light, H. R. 1960: *Legal Aspects of Business*. Pitman.

Further Reading

Ruskin, A. M. and Estes, W. E. 1982: *Project Management*. Dekker.

10 Organization and Control

The most important resource in any company is the people. Nowhere is this more true than in R&D and engineering generally. A manager's prime task is to optimize the collaborative efforts of a number of people, being responsible for both the task and the people. The project manager or leader has this dual responsibility for his project.

Project Life Cycle

In principle the task of the project manager is to plan, organize and lead a group of people to complete a project life cycle of the type illustrated in Figure 10.1. The longest cycle starts with the market analysis aimed at defining customer needs, and ends with the manufacture of a product to meet those needs in a manner calculated to make a profit for the company over the life of the product. In doing so the project will move from a generalized concept through progressive degrees of refinement and detail, removing uncertainty and increasing knowledge at each stage over the duration of the project. Chapter 5 discussed ways of subjectively quantifying decreasing uncertainty as the project progresses.

Some projects may have a much shorter cycle. If a relatively simple redesign of an existing product is to be carried out it will start in the appropriate box, for example that labelled design and development, and that labelled prototype/testing may or may not be invoked, depending on the confidence level that the task can be successfully carried out. A project to develop a new production process requires a similar selective use of the concept.

In all but the very smallest of projects a number of people will be involved, some with specialist knowledge not necessarily in the possession of the project manager. It will be the latter's task to optimize the results of the joint efforts of these people in the presence of personal differences of education, training, temperament and maturity. The extremes of management approach to the problem are management by discipline and management by project.

Organization and Control 143

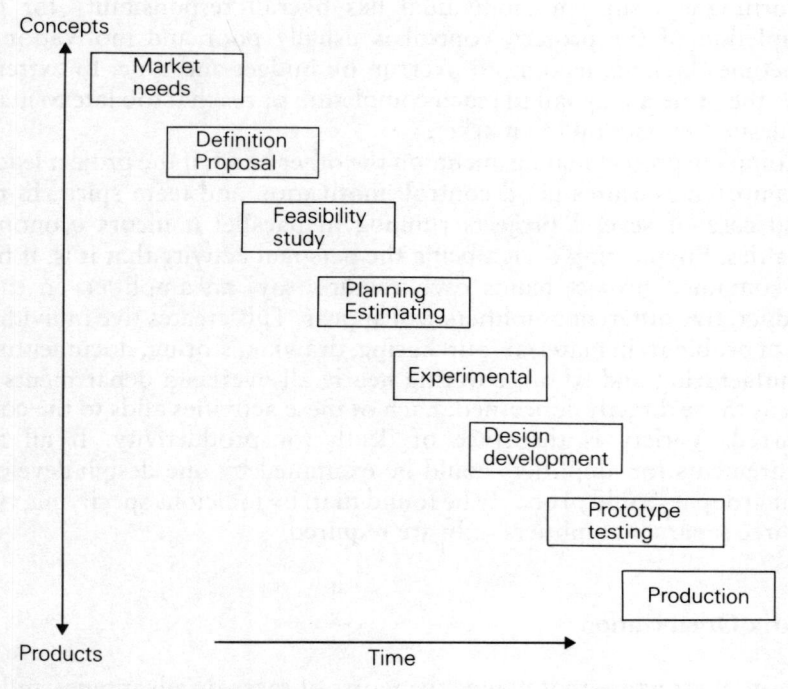

Figure 10.1 Project life cycle

[Figure shows staggered boxes along a time axis from Concepts/Products to Time, labeled: Market needs, Definition Proposal, Feasibility study, Planning Estimating, Experimental, Design development, Prototype testing, Production]

Management by Discipline or Project

In the first case a series of functional departments, each with its own manager and dedicated to one or more specific disciplines, provide the knowledge and resources to carry out the range of activities needed to develop the new product. The responsibility for doing this rests with the department managers. Particularly in multi-discipline products the number of such departments may be large. In the second case a manager is appointed with authority, delegated by top management, to control what happens to the project in all functional departments, and to whom functional department managers are required to provide an adequate service. For this purpose they second members of their departments to the project manager. These last, while reporting on standards in their own technology to their departmental manager, report to the project manager on all matters directly concerning the progress of the project.

Management by discipline, in which each technology is the responsibility of a specific department manager, results in some very good technology and the creation of centres of competence in each discipline. Unfortunately, since no individual has overall responsibility for the completion of the project, control is usually poor and motivation is sometimes lacking, leading to overrun on budget and time. In extreme cases the project may fail to reach completion or reach it too late to make the desired impact on the market.

Complete project management, on the other hand, if the project leader is competent, ensures good control, motivation and team spirit. In the usual case of several projects running in parallel it incurs economic penalties. Engineering design being the personal activity that it is, if five self-contained project teams each require, say, an amplifier, in their product, five different amplifiers will appear. This creates five individual sets of problems in materials purchasing, drawing, storing, documenting, manufacturing and so on, covering nearly all overhead departments as well as those directly concerned. Each of these activities adds to the costs incurred. Variety is the spice of death for productivity. If all the requirements for amplifiers could be examined by one design/development group it would probably be found that, by judicious specifying, two or three separate amplifiers only are required.

Matrix Organization

A form of structure that avoids the worst of these disadvantages and in appropriate cases presents some benefits, is matrix organization (Davies and Lawrence, 1977).

In this case the departments are in two classes. Service departments are responsible for standards of technologies used in the company products and product departments are responsible for the products embodying the technologies. A project leader is appointed from the most appropriate department; if a new product is the objective this leader will probably come from the associated department. If the project concerns a standard electronic package to go into several products, the project leader may well come from the service department concerned. He is allocated specialists from the service departments to form the project team, but not on a permanent basis. Project progress is reviewed at appropriate intervals and resources, both people and equipment, are allocated as needed by the project for the next period. The senior specialist from each department is probably seconded to the project leader for the duration of the project but the more junior people can be more flexible. It will probably be found that, for example, detail draughtsmen are required in two or three intensive sessions on each project, between which they would be underemployed. They can be moved to other projects in these intervals, improving departmental productivity. Figure 10.2 illustrates the form of organization. A 'product line' structure is created which can, with advantage, be extended throughout the company to include production engineering and commercial. Good communications are encouraged by doing so, and each product line can be encouraged to see itself as a profit centre, a company within the company, making for commitment to that element of the company objectives.

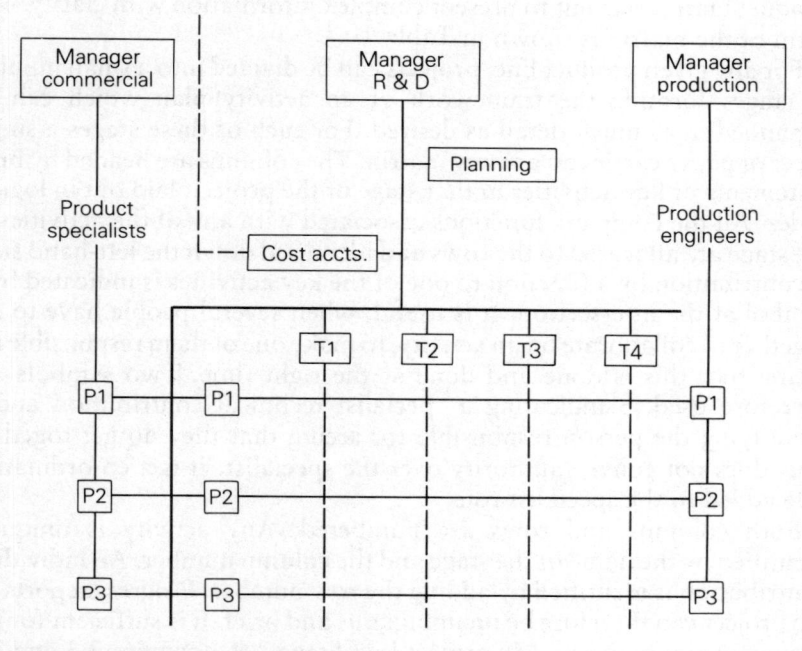

Figure 10.2 Matrix structure

The Activity Matrix

A reason why a number of companies that have adopted some form of matrix management have declared it a failure is to be found in inadequate preparation and briefing of those involved. To someone pitched into a matrix and left to find his or her own way the prospect is unsettling. It often appears unclear as to who is responsible for what, where the orders come from and how many bosses there are. What is needed is an adequate route map to enable everyone to find their way around the system (Bergen, 1975).

Peter Drucker (1967) makes a useful distinction between clarity and

146 Organization and Control

simplicity. A Gothic cathedral is a complex design, but when standing inside it the individual knows where he or she is and how to reach any other point in it. It has clarity. A modern multi-storey office block is a very simple design. Without help in the form of floor and room numbers, however, the individual within it is completely lost and disorientated. It does not have clarity.

Because of the large amount of information to be displayed in an adequate route map, there is no hope of one that is not complex. The new product matrix sets out to present complex information with clarity. The form of the matrix is shown in Table 10.1.

For any given product line, projects can be divided into a small number of stages forming the framework of an activity plan which can be expanded in as much detail as desired. For each of these stages a single sheet of paper carries an activity matrix. The columns are headed by brief statements of key activities in that stage of the project, laid out in logical order. All the company functions associated with any of the activities in the stage are allocated to the rows and identified down the left-hand side. A contribution by a function to one of the key activities is indicated by a symbol at the intersection. It is useful, when several people have to get together to collaborate on an activity, to make one of them responsible for seeing that this is done and done at the right time. Two symbols are therefore used, S indicating a specialist technical contribution and E identifying the person responsible for seeing that they do get together. This does not convey authority over the specialist; it is a co-ordinating role added to the specialist role.

Both columns and rows are numbered. Any activity is uniquely identified by the name of the stage and the column number. An individual contribution is identified by adding the row number. Progress reports on the project can therefore be unambiguous and brief. It is sufficient for the project manager to say 'My project is at Stage 2.9, activities 2.3 and 2.5 have been omitted (or delayed)'.

The bottom row of the matrix indicates typical lead times for starting activities in order to complete the stage by the date scheduled for the go/no-go meeting which is the last activity. This is not part of the project plan but an aid to the project leader in creating one with an adequate safety margin. The lead times are useful in planning other activities dependent on this stage being completed. There is thus the initial data for work load planning for all functions involved comprising activity description, its approximate timing, a list of the other functions involved and the identity of the co-ordinator. Aggregating this data for all projects indicates the total work load by functions; staggering the projects in time allows most efficient use of resources.

There is space at the top of the column for only a brief description of the activity. This may be insufficient for newcomers to the company. The foot of the column carries a numerical reference or references. These references lead to specific paragraphs in a procedures manual where full information is given when necessary. The information in the matrix may, in fact, be expanded indefinitely. Instead of leading to a write-up, the reference can lead to another matrix, expanding the single column in the first, and so on to any degree of detail required. The amount of information per stage can be expanded at any desired rate while preserving the hierarchical presentation in levels of detail, combining accessibility and clarity. For the duration of a project stage the individual has only to look at one sheet of paper to see the position reached, moving directly to further specific information if and when necessary.

Because it takes the form of an overlay on the traditional organization tree and provides a mass of accessible information it does much to dispel the individual's worries as to who is responsible for what. Each person's contribution is clearly laid out for the project and it can be seen how it will proceed from activity to activity. For the same reason department managers do not feel that their authority is being attacked. In practice the system, once accepted, generates an element of co-ordinating authority of its own, based on its information content. If presented as a guide, not a rule book, and project leaders are free to reject any of its provisions, they do not do so irresponsibly. The fact that everyone has a copy means that a delay in a project, due to neglecting a provision, is known to all and the project leader responsible is very exposed. The best way, though time consuming, of setting up such a system is by a participative approach. Involving all relevant functions in discussion and decision lays many misconceptions to rest at all levels and generates a helpful commitment to the system.

Resource Allocation

A feature of matrix organization is that it permits a useful degree of resource switching between projects. This must not be taken too far and it must be done with thought for the project leader's attitudes. The senior members of the team in each discipline should be switched to other jobs as little as possible as they must have an on-going responsibility for their area. There are, however, often specific periods of, usually, intense activity, followed by periods of inactivity. An example of this is the detail draughtsmen whose services are required to convert feasibility sketches into experimental drawings from which the model shop produces models for test. After this they have little to do that is essential until the models are proved and the experimental drawings must be modified and converted into production drawings. They can be allocated to other projects in the inactive periods provided that this is done in a proper manner.

Table 10.1 New product matrix

New product guide	Stage 2																													
Function E = executive S = specialist	Activity	Check target specification								Experimental (X)													Evaluate XI						Go/no go heading	
		1	2	3	4	5	6	7	8	9	10	11	12	13	14	15	16	17	18	19	20	21	22	23	24	25	26	27	28	29
Project leader		E	E	E	E					E	E	E	S	E	E	E	E	E	E	E		E	E	E	S		E		S		1
Drawing office			S								S	E	S			S	S	S	S	S		E		E							2
Electronics			S	S						S	S			S		S	S	S	S	S		S									3
Model shop										S												S									4
Production engineering																	S	S		S						S					5
Article engineering																										S					6
Estimating					S												S	S			E		S	S							7
Quality assurance											S				S									S	E				S		8

	1	2	3	4	5	6	7	8	9	10	11	12	13	14	15	16	17	
Service tech. pubs												S						9
Product specialist	S	S				S	S	S					S	S				10
Value eng. co-ordinator		S					S											11
Dev. resources controller			S															12
																		13
																		14
Development dept. manager		S				E	S								S	E		15
Heads of dev. mktg																S		16
Typical lead time — months (minus D)	10	10	10	10	9	9	9	9	9	8	7	7	6	2	1	1	D	17
New product manual References	40.3.2	40.3.2;43	40.3.3		40.3.4	40.3.5	40.3.6	40.3.7	50	40.3.8	40.3.9;41;45	40.3.10;31;35	40.3.12	40.3.13	40.3.14 40.3.15	40.3.16	40.3.17 40.3.18;56	
Related activities	E.1			E.2								E.4 40.3.11		S1.2.2.10 E.15	S1			

New product manual documents referred to:

PU/31 Functions of the estimating Dept.   PU/45 V.A./V.E. Programme
PU/35 Estimator's check lists   PU/50 Standard of safety requirements for laboratory apparatus.
PU/40 Project check list   PU/51 Environmental testing
PU/41 Value engineering procedure   PU/56 X1 Go/no go meeting
PU/43 Project teams

150 *Organization and Control*

The most important consideration is that the allocation must be done in a completely open and transparent way. If this is not achieved every project leader rapidly convinces himself that his project is being deprived of resources in order to benefit others favoured by the department manager. This demotivates the project leader and the team. As the effect is due to lack of information rather than any hard evidence of the situation, it can be removed by ensuring that everyone knows where the resources have been allocated and why. In a small department it may be possible to have all the project leaders present at a meeting to make the decisions. In a larger organization, where this is not possible, the heads of both project and technology groups should be present, with equal standing so that the immediate superior of every project leader has first-hand knowledge of the reasons for the allocation, took part in the decision, and can explain it.

The resources are allocated periodically at a review meeting which is preceded by individual project leaders assessing their own progress and estimating their needs for the next period. These are entered in the appropriate place in the form shown in Table 10.2 which acts as both the agenda and the minutes of the meeting. In a larger organization the

Table 10.2 Resource allocation

Project	Department man-hours						Comments	Project man-hours	Cum. cost	Cost to complete	Budget
	1	2	3	4	5	6					
Other activity											
Totals											

resources controller can be of great use in ensuring that the original requests for resources do not add up to much more than is available, in preparing and circulating the form in its agenda stage, then collecting the decisions at the meeting, entering them on the form alongside the requests and recirculating it. It forms a record of not only the resources allocated, but also those requested, and after a few months of operating the system the project leaders' requests become realistic and they even strike agreements with each other on timing and amount of resources in advance of the meeting.

The vertical columns of Table 10.2 represent the department providing the resources and the horizontal rows the projects and activities using them. In addition to the projects, rows are provided for detachments, holidays, sickness, etc., so that the total at the base of each column gives the full strength of the department, disposing of any arguments about resources not accounted for. Opposite each project the number of man-hours/days requested from each department is entered before the meeting. At the meeting the amount agreed is entered alongside the first figure, in the same column. The columns on the right of the form show the total allocation to each project for the period and to date. The latter figure is entered in money terms in the next column. The penultimate column shows the estimated cost to completion and the last one the budget for the project.

The Project Leader/Manager

Any of the above forms of project management pose considerable strain on the project leader, perhaps the matrix form most of all because of the sophistication of the concept. Some management writers take the view that a matrix should not be resorted to if it can be done without. Davis and Lawrence (1977), however, state 'a significant outcome of matrix organization is its apparent capacity to foster innovation. In those industries where continuous product innovation is a criterion for survival and success, organizations that have adopted the matrix seem to fare well ... benefits of standardisation are coupled with the capacity to respond to change – a way to have your cake and eat it too'.

The role of the project leader takes a number of forms depending on his level of authority. It is noticeable that managements are more willing to give responsibility to the project leader than they are to delegate commensurate authority. Some appear to think that they can delegate responsibility; in practice the roles listed in Table 10.3 are frequently found.

The project leader in many of these roles has to face a number of

Table 10.3 Project leader roles

Title	Role	Authority
Liaison engineer	Reports progress to dept manager	None. Has access to information
Project co-ordinator	As above plus indicates action to correct error	Indirect – team exposed if action not taken
Project leader (R&D)	Leads R&D team	Over R&D team delegated by R&D manager
Project leader	As above plus liaison with production depts	Over R&D team. Persuasion and personality in other departments
Project manager	Functional authority over all aspects of project up to defined end	Delegated by company management

ambiguities (Wilemon and Cicero, 1970). This situation is considerably eased by the structure and information content of the new product matrix approach. Typical of these problems are those listed in Table 10.4.

This being so it is not surprising that being a project leader is not a universal ambition nor a job for which all are suited. It is possible to obtain some guidance in selecting project leaders from the work of J. Gooch of Brunel University. This postulates that there are two types of management jobs. Type A jobs are where the responsibility is for completing a finite task in a finite time, the typical project leader situation. Type B jobs are where the responsibility is for maintaining a level of competence and efficiency in an on-going activity, a departmental management role. The next section contains a questionnaire, the answers to which indicate the individual's preferential adaptability to the A or B job. Appendix 10.1 provides the analysis of the scores and it should be noticed that it is the ratio of A and B scores that is significant, not the absolute values. Only when the imbalance is large should the result be regarded as meaningful. It is likely to produce more reliable results if the questionnaire is completed by a third party with a good knowledge of the applicant. It can, of course, be used for self-testing, but is likely to be less than objective in its finding.

Table 10.4 Project leader ambiguities

Personal	Individual versus company goals
	Problem solving versus organization
Technical versus managerial	Over-involvement in technology demotivates specialists
	Inability to delegate increases involvement
	Interest in technical detail confuses management and technical roles
Project risk versus professional risk	Acceptance of final responsibility
	Technical obsolescence anxiety
	Tendency to remain in admin roles
Organization	Autonomy of project manager versus centralized project control
	Bureaucratic complexity leads to use of informal means to achieve goals

Self-test Questionnaire

Circle the number on each line which you feel most closely represents your own behaviour.

Factor no.			
1	Never late	5 4 3 2 1 0 1 2 3 4 5	Casual about appointments
2	Not competitive	5 4 3 2 1 0 1 2 3 4 5	Very competitive
3	Anticipates what others are going to say	5 4 3 2 1 0 1 2 3 4 5	Good listener
4	Always rushed	5 4 3 2 1 0 1 2 3 4 5	Never feels rushed even under pressure
5	Can wait patiently	5 4 3 2 1 0 1 2 3 4 5	Impatient whilst waiting
6	Goes all out	5 4 3 2 1 0 1 2 3 4 5	Casual
7	Takes things one at a time	5 4 3 2 1 0 1 2 3 4 5	Tries to do too many things at once

8	Emphatic in speech	5 4 3 2 1 0 1 2 3 4 5	Slow deliberate talker
9	Wants recognition of performance	5 4 3 2 1 0 1 2 3 4 5	More concerned with satisfying himself
10	Fast eater, talker, etc.	5 4 3 2 1 0 1 2 3 4 5	Slow doing things
11	Easy going	5 4 3 2 1 0 1 2 3 4 5	Hard driving
12	Hides feelings	5 4 3 2 1 0 1 2 3 4 5	Expresses feelings
13	Many outside interests	5 4 3 2 1 0 1 2 3 4 5	Few interests outside work
14	Satisfied with job	5 4 3 2 1 0 1 2 3 4 5	Ambitious

To compile your scores see Appendix 10.1.

Management Relationships

There are two separate issues in considering relationships between the project manager and his team. The first is the number of relationships and the second is their quality.

Nearly everyone will agree that the problems of managing a project grow with the number of people for whom the project manager is responsible. It is not generally realized how rapidly the number of project manager–team relationships increase with the size of the team. There are not only one-to-one relationships between the project manager and the individuals in the team, but also potential relationships between the manager and the team in groups of two or more. The potential numbers of relationships was stated many years ago (Graicunas, 1933) as

$$R = n(2^{n-1} + n - 1)$$

where R = the number of relationships and n = the number of subordinates. Examples of the numbers involved are shown in Table 10.5.

In the normal course of events by no means all of these potential relationships will exist, but in an emergency, when the project manager may feel constrained to supervise all individual and joint activities, very large numbers are clearly possible if organizational steps have not been taken to provide effective control. It is for just such situations that the army plans and trains, and many years of trial and error have resulted in a hierarchy in which the number of subordinates at most levels is between 3 and 6. The quality of the relationships is greatly affected by the approach to them and to the task adopted by the project manager.

Table 10.5 Project relationships

Number of subordinates	Number of relationships
1	1
3	18
5	100
7	490
10	5210

Leadership Styles

A program of research into leadership styles has been in operation at Ohio State University since 1945. Hersey and Blanchard (1977) have presented the main ideas developed. Leader behaviour can be described in two dimensions:

(1) Task behaviour — This describes the leader's behaviour in forming relationships between himself and his coworkers, in forming patterns of communication and working methods for the group.

(2) Relationship behaviour — This describes the leader's behaviour indicative of friendship, mutual trust and respect in his relationship with the group.

This enables leader behaviour to be assessed by followers on two axes as shown in Figure 10.3, forming a 2 × 2 matrix that depicts four basic styles of leadership, none of which is inherently superior to any of the others. The appropriate style in any case depends on the relationship between the leader and the follower, expressed in terms of the maturity of the follower. If a scale of maturity of the follower is placed beneath the task behaviour scale the appropriate style is indicated by the intercept of the score on the maturity scale with the bell-shaped curve on the matrix.

When maturity is low the style is Hi T/Lo R. This is described as 'telling' the follower what to do. As his maturity increases the style moves up to the Hi R/Hi T quarter; the leader 'sells' to the follower decisions already made. In the Hi R/Lo T quarter the leader discusses and agrees with the follower what his task shall be; the style is 'participative'. In the last quarter, with a mature follower, the leader defines the problem but leaves the analysis and solution to the follower. He 'delegates' the task.

156 Organization and Control

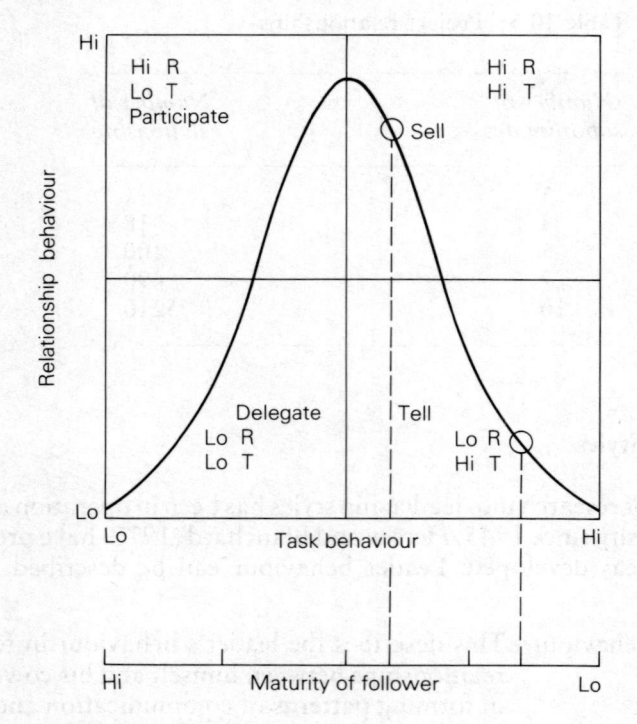

Figure 10.3 Leadership styles

There are some psychological difficulties in the approach, particularly with the more mature follower. The latter may, for instance, feel that if he is regarded as competent to take on the task by himself he ought to be in charge of his own department and that the manager is intentionally blocking his promotion. So he withdraws and avoids all contact with the manager. The manager may think he has delegated when he has effectively abdicated. Some guidance in analysing these potential situations is available via transactional analysis, described in Chapter 11. This type of problem stems from the fact that no one is equally mature in all facets of his personality. Many mature technologists are politically immature and vice versa. A practical method of dealing with the situation is by objective setting.

Objective Setting

Communication between leader and follower must take place in as many dimensions as there are levels of maturity to be considered. Drucker

(1967) makes the statement:

> The focus on contribution, by itself supplies the four basic requirements of human relations:
>
> > communications;
> > teamwork;
> > self-development; and
> > development of others.

Objective setting does just this in relation to the project in which leader and follower share responsibility.

A distinction should be made between an objective and a job description. The latter attempts to answer the question 'What am I expected to do?' Objective setting is a dialogue discussing the question 'What shall I think about?' A job description may be necessary for administrative reasons but its relevance to R&D work is questionable. If a knowledge worker is hired to think, it is valid to tell him what to think about; it is doubtful whether he can usefully be told what to think.

The management approach to setting up the system is important. It is worth going to some trouble to ensure that those involved understand that they are not facing an inquisition or a witch hunt but directly influencing management in their area. It is useful for the leader to start initial discussions by asking general questions such as 'How are we doing in your area?', conveying joint responsibility and leading the follower into expressing views on how to improve performance. He then helps the follower into formulating these views into agreed objectives, which are recorded as shown in Table 10.6.

Table 10.6 Objective setting

Objective	Criterion of success	Source of data	Suggestions for improvement	Review

Objectives

An objective is a quantitative statement of improvement over time of some aspect of the follower's activities. The breadth or narrowness of the statement is the leader's means of tailoring the task to match the maturity of the follower.

In the same technological area the leader might, for an immature follower, emerge with the objective 'evaluate the performance of the XYZ transducer for use in our ABC analyser', stating the agreed date for completion of the report. For a more mature worker it might read 'report on the feasibility of a detector for ABC analysers with 20% improvement in linearity and sensitivity and a 200% longer life'. For a highly mature follower the objective might be 'proposals for replacing our ABC analyser in 5 years time, taking advantage of likely technological advances, with the aim of doubling our market share'.

The same approach would deal with management and personnel objectives within the follower's sphere of responsibility. The lower the maturity, the more specific the objective and the lower the uncertainty involved. The objective must be accepted by the follower and the time estimates should be his own. Some of the objectives should be his own proposals.

Criteria

Unless there is a quantitative criterion there is no objective, only a pious hope of better times. The criterion must be agreed as part of the dialogue. It must define the target and the date by which it is to be achieved.

Source of Data

An important, but often neglected, requirement is to specify the source of the data that will be used in judging success or failure. There are multiple records of the same activities in nearly all companies and frequently no two of them agree. It is essential to specify clearly, at the time the objectives are agreed, which record will be used.

Suggestions for Improvement

The objective having been agreed, suggestions for actions to achieve it and the resources needed are discussed. Where agreed, they are entered into this column. The follower is encouraged to put forward suggestions, including any for action by the leader to help to achieve the agreed objective.

Review of Objectives

The objectives are reviewed at the agreed intervals which will differ with the maturity of the follower. The objectives of immature followers will be reviewed at shorter intervals than those of mature workers. The results will be noted and success or failure explained where possible. The suggestions for improvement will also be reviewed and note taken of those completed and those unfinished. This analysis is often more important than the basic result. The inability to carry out an agreed suggestion may indicate that neither the follower nor the leader had really understood the problem when the objective was set. This may be the most important outcome of all.

The historical record over a few cycles of objective setting and reviewing is a means of evaluating the progress of the follower on the sound basis of how he thinks about his job and how he carries it out. It avoids the psychological pitfalls of some appraisal systems that do not stick to this safe ground for discussion. It records the developing relationship between the leader and the follower and teaches each about the other.

As an illustration of the procedure, such a dialogue with the chief designer of a company produced an objective of reducing the number of drawing errors. A measure of the errors was agreed as the number of errors expressed as a percentage of the number of drawings issued. The criterion of success was agreed as 5 per cent in twelve months time and a number of suggestions for improvement were recorded.

At the review a year later it had sadly to be admitted that far from achieving the objective the rate was nearer 20 per cent. All the suggestions for improvement had been adequately implemented so the conclusion could only be that neither party had grasped the size and nature of the problem. This was the beginning of realistic assessment of the situation. Further analysis of the data now available led to a more practical objective of 10 per cent for the following year and a new list of suggestions for improvement, this time with more relevance to the problem. This initiated a sustained attack on the problem which produced the desired result eighteen months later.

Review

This chapter has:

(1) Described the project life cycle.
(2) Outlined project management by function and by project.

(3) Described the matrix compromise and some of its merits.
(4) Described project leader/manager roles and ambiguities.
(5) Described the Ohio State University approach to management style analysis.
(6) Described the procedure and benefits of the objective setting technique.
(7) Presented a self-test questionnaire for potential project leaders/managers.

The recommendations of this chapter depend upon communication for their success. In the next chapter exercises are used to demonstrate some of the problems of communicating. Some of the problems are analysed and some methods of minimizing them are suggested.

References

Bergen, S. A. 1975: The New Product Matrix, *R&D Man.* 5, 2.
Davis, S. M. and Lawrence, P. 1977: *Matrix*. Addison-Wesley.
Drucker, P. 1967: *The Effective Executive*. Pan Piper.
Graicunas, V. A. 1933: Relationship in Organisation, *Bull. Int. Man. Inst.* 7.
Hersey, P. and Blanchard, K. H. 1977: *Management of Organisational Behaviour*. Prentice-Hall.
Wilemon, D. and Cicero, J. P. 1970: *The Project Manager – Anomalies and Ambiguities*. *Ac. Man. J.*, Fall.

Further Reading

Baker, B. N. and Wilemon, D. L. 1977: Managing Complex Programs, *R&D Man.* 8, 1.
Newman, A. D. and Rowbottom, P. W. 1968: *Organisation Analysis*. Heinemann.

Appendix 10.1   Compiling Self-test Scores

(1) To compile your A score add up the numbers which you have circled to the right of the central zero for factors 2, 5, 7, 11, 12, 13 and 14, and the numbers you have circled to the left of zero for factors 1, 3, 4, 6, 8, 9 and 10.
(2) To compile your B score add the numbers to the left of zero for factors 2, 5, 7, 11, 12, 13 and 14 and numbers to the right of the zero for factors 1, 3, 4, 6, 8, 9 and 10.

The A score reflects your leaning towards the project management type of finite task, bounded by specification, time and money constraints.

Your B score reflects your leaning towards the management of a departmental type of on-going unbounded organization on a minimum variety basis.

The actual scores in the two cases have little significance. A large difference between scores suggests a preference for the type with the higher score. A small difference between scores should be ignored. (Source: J. H. Gooch based on work by Bortner and Rosenman.)

11 Communication and Structure

Inadequate communication is at the root of a wide range of industrial problems. The flexibility and power of the English language can lead to ambiguity in communication. A well-designed communication structure can do much to mimimize this by recognizing the fact that words do not have specific meanings until they are defined for a particular purpose. The thesis is illustrated by a set of exercises.

Communication Exercises

The problems of communication and an indication of the benefits of structure can be demonstrated using the following exercises. A 'sender' is selected from the class, the remainder being 'receivers'. The sender is seated facing away from the others in a position where he is not overlooked. The exercise is in three parts. For the first the sender is given a sheet of paper with a diagram drawn on it similar to that shown in Figure 11.1 and the following instructions:

(1) Face away from the class.
(2) Describe the diagram in your hand so that the receivers can draw it.
(3) Do not answer any questions from the receivers.
(4) Verbal communication only, no signs or gestures.

The receivers are informed that they are not allowed to ask questions nor to demand repeats of words or phrases. This constitutes an open-loop communication system. An analogy from control engineering would be a kettle on a gas ring. The only means of controlling the temperature of the water in the kettle is the gas tap. Nothing in the system tells the operator when he has reached the desired temperature; he can influence the temperature but he has no direct means of knowing the result.

After being given a few minutes to study the diagram the sender is told to go ahead and the time is noted. This exercise will take about five minutes. On completion the time is noted and the duration recorded. The receivers are asked to display their results. Although the diagram is simple and highly repetitive, few will get it completely correct.

The second exercise is a repeat of the first with some significant changes

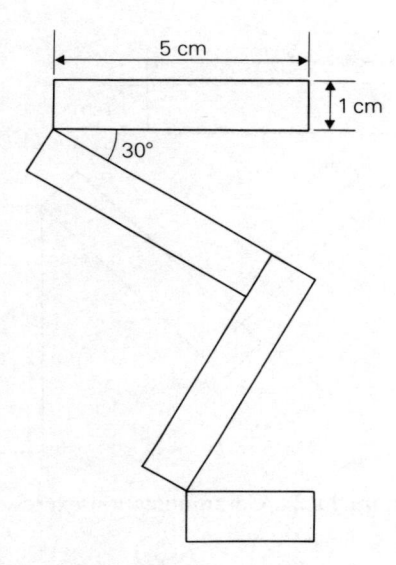

Figure 11.1 Communication exercise 1

in the rules and the use of Figure 11.2. The sender now faces the receivers so that he can see their reactions and they are allowed to ask questions to which he will reply. Verbal communication is still the only medium permitted. The exercise is timed as before. This is now a closed-loop system. The analogy is now the addition of a thermometer in the water in the kettle with its dial visible to the operator. He can see the effect of his manipulation of the gas tap and adjust the latter to stabilize the system at the desired temperature. The system now employs feedback to tell the operator whether or not he is achieving the desired result and, if not, the size of the error.

This time the proportion of receivers getting the diagram right will be greatly increased largely because of the introduction of feedback in the communication system. However, the time taken will be greater. It will be determined by the receivers rather than, as in the first exercise, by the sender. The noise level in the multi-channel communication system will be higher, both literally and in terms of communication theory. Since the amount of information to be conveyed remains much the same this means that the signal-to-noise ratio will be worse. In an automatic attempt to improve this the sender will find himself repeating the same statements several times, with variations, in response to repeated questions from the receivers. In communication terms he is introducing redundant information to make good the loss in the system. For all these reasons the

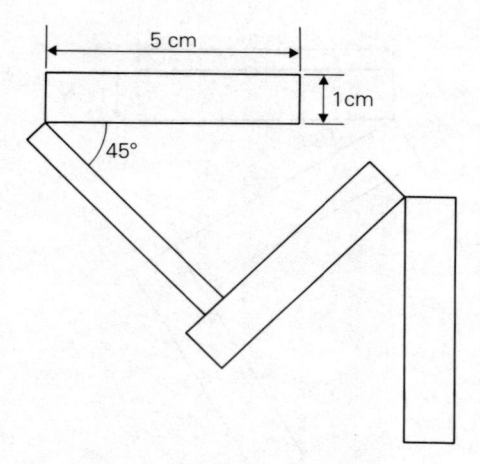

Figure 11.2 Communication exercise 2

additional time and effort involved in achieving the improved results, compared with the first exercise, will be significant.

It would thus appear that the choice lies between a fast, simple, single channel, open-loop system with a high incidence of error and a relatively slow, complex, multi-channel, closed-loop, more costly system that produces a much higher proportion of correct answers.

Communication Structure

A third approach to the problem can, in suitable cases, achieve the accuracy of the feedback system with the speed of the open-loop system by employing feedforward. Its suitability will depend on two factors: the ability to define the information content and the will to invest in developing the system.

The ultimate in feedforward communication is probably to be found in the forces. At the Trooping of the Colour it is manifestly impossible for the troops at the back of the massed formations to understand any of the words uttered by the OC parade on the opposite side of Horse Guards. Yet they all move together in the right way at the right time to carry out part of a complicated manoeuvre. The communication is of very high quality.

The reason is, of course, that there is no need for words to be understood as such in this situation. Everyone present knows what is to be done, indeed has rehearsed it, and all that is needed to trigger the next move is a loud noise from the expected direction. Even in the more difficult case of an unrehearsed drill movement, the order given will be one of a small set of possible orders which fit into a structure made familiar to all concerned by training. Each order triggers a practised response. Since it is one of a small set of possible orders there is little chance of ambiguity if the structure has been absorbed.

Happily, this appears to be the way that the human memory works. A given set of words appears to trigger retrieval of an image, which may be quite complicated compared with the information content of the words. It has been built up by observation and/or training, and stored. Various devices such as mnemonics can be used to improve retrievability and accelerate training. If these devices can be designed into the communication structure its effectiveness is improved. The design strategy is to define the possible information content of a message in terms of the necessary minimum of variations, then to design the structure so that it has a maximum content of standardized information and requires the minimum number of specific triggers to identify the variation to be conveyed.

The process may be regarded as feeding forward to the receiver a set of standard options, which are (a) understood and (b) embodied in a structure, together with a trigger identifying, in conjunction with the structure, the option to be conveyed.

Feedforward Structure

Relating these principles to Figures 11.1 and 11.2, it will be seen that they comprise, despite the problems already encountered in describing them on an *ad hoc* basis, only a small number of variants. The elements are all rectangles, and some dimensions are given. They form the links, at various angles to their neighbours, of a continuous chain. The chain can be described adequately by specifying the first rectangle and then relating the next one to it by the four statements in Table 11.1.

Taking the top rectangle of Figure 11.2, it can be specified as a rectangle with the dimensions 5 × 1 cm, the longer side horizontal, at the top of the page.

The second rectangle is first imagined as superimposed on the first then moved vertically downwards 1 cm and rotated 45 degrees clockwise about its own top left corner. For the moment its dimensions are not revised. This to make the next rectangle simpler to specify.

The third rectangle is initially visualized as superimposed on the second. It is then rotated 90 degrees clockwise about its lowest corner. This is its final position.

166 Communication and Structure

Table 11.1 Communication structure

(1)	Superimpose	Place an identical rectangle on top of that specified.
(2)	Translate	Move the superimposed rectangle along an axis and in a direction such as to achieve the desired position or an intermediate one.
(3)	Angle	If necessary, rotate the rectangle about a specified point.
(4)	Revise	If necessary, revise the dimensions of the rectangle.

The second rectangle, having simplified the specifying of the third, now has its smaller dimension revised to 0.5 cm from the highest corner.

The fourth rectangle, starting from the third, is moved 1 cm on an axis normal to the longer dimension of the third rectangle and then rotated 45 degrees anti-clockwise about its highest corner.

The four statements of Table 11.1 have sufficed to generate Figure 11.2 unambiguously and with no more effort than in the open-loop case. Feedback and repetition are no longer necessary. Furthermore, there is a mnemonic content in the initial letters of the names for the four statements in that, taken in the order in which they were used they spell STAR.

Structure Development

While Table 11.1 conveys the notion of using structure to simplify communication, it still leaves the possibility of some ambiguity in conveying the provisions of the four key statements. This can be reduced to negligible proportions by further development of standardized definitions and statements. The elements of the rectangle chain may be defined as in Table 11.2.

Retaining the mnemonic STAR to identify the set of statements appropriate to the chain, the statements themselves can be standardized in mnemonic form. Figure 11.3 shows how this set of definitions and statements can be presented on one sheet of paper with the mnemonics relating to them. The mnemonics ensure that after a minimum of experience with the structure it is no longer necessary to refer to Figure 11.3 when transmitting or receiving.

Table 11.2 Element specification

Specify rectangle	X dim, Y dim, position
Specify angle	Degrees clockwise
Identify rectangle	Number in order drawn
Identify corner	Number clockwise from vertical through C of G
Identify line	Two corner numbers
Identify axis	Angular degrees clockwise from vertical

Specify, superimpose $x = 5$ cm, $y = 1$ cm

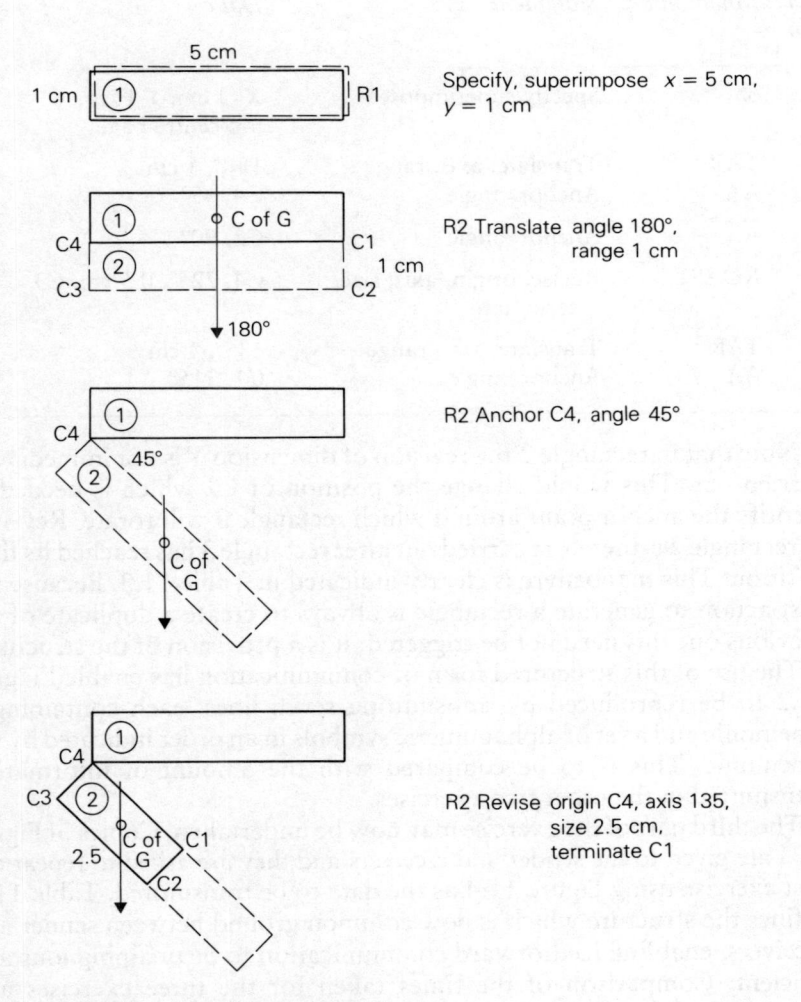

R2 Translate angle 180°, range 1 cm

R2 Anchor C4, angle 45°

R2 Revise origin C4, axis 135, size 2.5 cm, terminate C1

Figure 11.3 Structure presentation

168 Communication and Structure

The use of the structure may now be illustrated using Figure 11.2 as the design to be transmitted. Table 11.2 gives the complete list of rectangles, mnemonics, statements and data involved in doing this. After a little practice the full statements may be omitted as the mnemonics will ensure that the data is transmitted in the correct sequence. Table 11.3 is the complete description of Figure 11.2.

Table 11.3 Structured transmission

Rect. no.	Mnemonic	Statement	Data
1	SS	Specify/superimpose	X 5 cm, Y 1 cm, top centre page
2	TAR	Translate, axis, range	180°, 1 cm
	AA	Anchor, angle	C4, 45°
3	AA	Anchor, angle	C2, 90°
2	ROAST	Revise, origin, axis, size, terminate	C4, 225°, 0.5 cm, C3
4	TAR	Translate, axis, range	135°, 1 cm
	AA	Anchor, angle	C1, 315°

Note that in rectangle 2 the revision of dimension Y is not immediately carried out. This would change the position of C2 which is needed to identify the anchor point around which rectangle 3 will rotate. Revision of rectangle 2 is therefore carried out after rectangle 3 has reached its final position. This manoeuvre is clearly indicated in Table 11.3. Because the first action to generate a rectangle is always to create a duplicate of the previous one this need not be triggered; it is a provision of the structure.

The use of this structured form of communication has enabled Figure 11.2 to be reproduced by transmitting seven lines, each containing a mnemonic and a set of alphanumeric symbols in an order indicated by the mnemonic. This is to be compared with the amount of information transmitted in the other two exercises.

The third part of the exercise may now be undertaken. Copies of Figure 11.3 are given to the sender and receivers and they are asked to repeat the first exercise using Figure 11.4 as the data to be transmitted. Table 11.3 defines the structure which is now common ground between sender and receivers, enabling feedforward communication to be unambiguous and efficient. Comparison of the times taken for the three exercises and discussion of the accuracies found will generate further insights into the subject of communication.

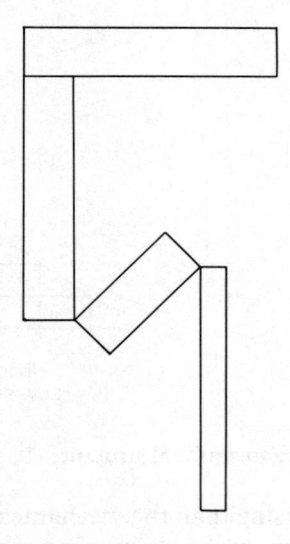

Figure 11.4 Communication exercise 3

Organizational Structure

The question 'who must communicate with whom?' is in principle dealt with in Figure 1.1. The detail of the answer, however, is influenced by a number of factors specific to the company, its products, its market and the people in it. Lawrence and Lorsch (1969) provide some insight into the potential difficulties.

They describe two types of organizational structure which they classify as high structure and low structure as illustrated in Figure 11.5. High structure is appropriate to, for example, a manufacturing organization producing a simple mechanical device, the design of which is mature and stable, embodying a single technology. The organization is represented by a tall narrow-based triangle. The manager may be visualized at the apex of the triangle issuing orders largely concerned with batch quantities and frequency. Since the people making the devices know all they need to know about them, no other information is needed. They report back to the manager on the progress of the batches. This is a single-channel communication system. It is adequate because there are no unknowns in the situation. A high degree of certainty permits a high structure.

Particularly in a multi-discipline product company the R&D situation is quite different. There are always conflicts between the demands imposed by the several disciplines. The electronics package will demand

Certainty
High structure

Uncertainty
Low structure

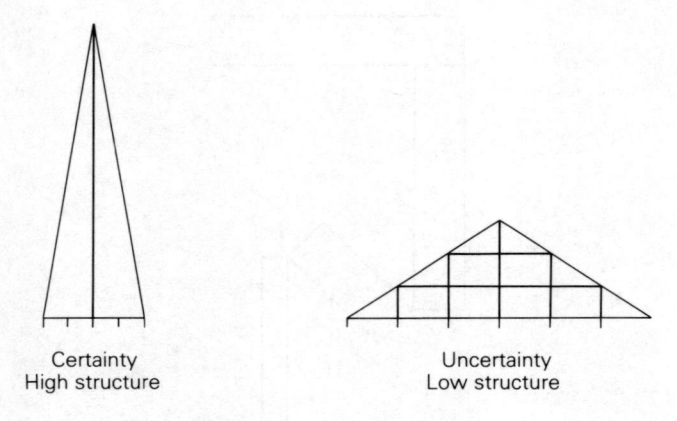

Figure 11.5 Organizational structure

more space within the casing than the mechanical engineers can provide. The latter in turn might want the electronic package split in two parts to ease the problem, to the detriment of the circuit design. There must therefore be discussion and compromise in order to achieve an overall optimum result. The decisions must be made where the knowledge is and this is by no means always in the manager's office. The specialists must be able to communicate with each other directly and efficiently. This means a multi-channel system and a low structure arising from the uncertainties to be dealt with. A low degree of certainty calls for a low structure.

Differentiations

One cause of communication difficulties, particularly in the absence of a well-designed structure, is what Lawrence and Lorsch have called differentiations. These are factors such as education, training, language and responsibility which colour the thinking of people so that different impressions result from the same data. Some examples are given in Table 11.4.

In the case of time constant, a production worker tends to be focused on the production schedule for today or this week. An R&D worker is aware that what he does today will not affect company output in this order of time span. It may be months or years before his work today makes an impact: in the case of a project failure it may never do so. Words such as 'hurriedly' and 'quickly' are likely to be associated with different orders of time spans in the minds of the two people. Salesmen are probably in between these two. They have in some cases a weekly or monthly schedule

Table 11.4 Differentiations

Time constant	Short term		Long term
	Production	Sales	R&D
Attitude	Task centred		Relation centred
	Production	R&D	Sales
Structure	High		Low
	Production	Sales	R&D

of orders to win but the long-term relationship with their customer is also of great importance and the weight to be put on the two factors at any one time calls for the exercise of judgement.

In terms of the leadership style factors described in Chapter 10, different attitudes arise from different responsibilities. Production workers are likely to be more concerned with the task and to work in a high structure organization. Salesmen are relationship centred since both today's sales and their longer-term future is influenced by their relationship with the customer. R&D workers are between these extremes. They have tasks to complete but their ability to do so may depend on their relationships with centres of competence, both internal and external to the company, providing them with information.

Organizational structure has already been referred to. Production organizations are likely to be high structures and R&D departments low structures. Sales are somewhere in between since although there is a structured sales department, individual salesmen operate much of the time on their own. They often make their own decisions on how to deal with their customer's problems and requests.

The hypothesis is that, when there is no formal communication structure to ensure that the symbols used trigger the same reaction everywhere, differentiations such as those above have the effect of making it probable that they will trigger quite different responses in different people. When attempting to communicate in the absence of adequate structure, care should be taken to learn enough about any differentiation to be able to predict the effect it will have and make allowance for it.

First Language Effect

Most people readily accept that speaking in a foreign language presents a major differentiation and there are hilarious anecdotes in all multinational companies to support this view. What is not so widely appreciated is that even after problems of vocabulary and fluency are overcome a more fundamental differentiation remains.

Words are in many ways the tools of thought; they are what the individual uses to formulate as well as express his ideas. It is the view of current educational theory, the Jesuits and transactional analysis psychology (see Chapter 13) that attitudes and patterns of thought are formed and, to a large extent fixed, in the first five years of life. It follows that an individual's patterns of thought are conditioned by the nature of his or her first language.

Some languages are more sophisticated than others and have a greater vocabulary. English is of this type, as can be seen in any multiple language notice, say on an international flight. The English notice is always the shortest. There is such a large vocabulary that one can differentiate between slightly different meanings without resorting to qualifying words which add to the length of the statement. The tendency is for English language based thinking to see things on a grey scale because of the relative ease with which nuances of meaning can be expressed. Languages that do not share this ability lead to thinking in a more black and white mode. Those with this type of first language may see the result as a tendency for native English speakers to talk around the subject instead of making black and white statements and decisions. The English speaker may initially have the perception that some other nationalities come to more black and white decisions than themselves, on the same evidence, and are therefore more competent or more rash, according to the context.

Feedback versus Feedforward in Project Management

Two extremes of communication structure already mentioned are feedback and feedforward. They can be represented as in Figure 11.6.

The component parts of communication can be seen as clarity of problem definition, completeness of information and clarity of problem understanding. If any one of them is defective, communication is degraded. Feedback and feedforward are two methods of ensuring that all three come together. Both start with inputs in the form of market needs and company objectives which must be converted into clear definitions of the problems to be solved to create a product supplying the market need in a manner profitable to the company. When this has been satisfactorily completed a specification for the new product can be drafted. At this point the paths diverge.

Communication and Structure 173

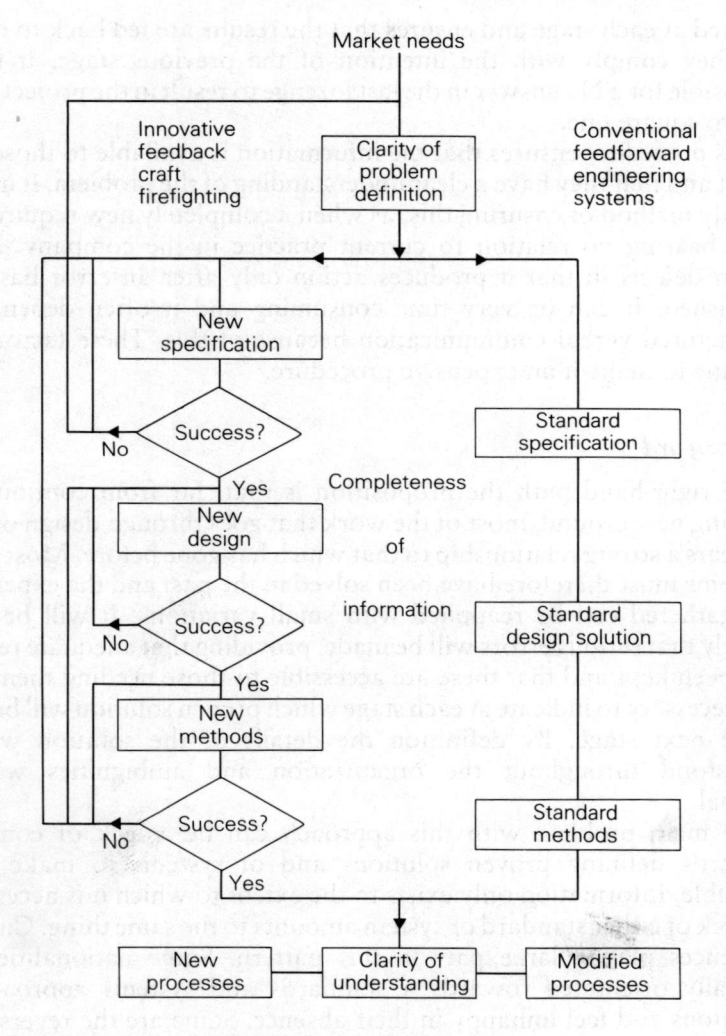

Figure 11.6 Feedback and feedforward

Feedback

Every activity in the left-hand path is treated as if it were being undertaken for the first time. When the new specification is raised the network asks the question 'is it successful in meeting the market need profitably?' If the answer is Yes a new design is undertaken based on the specification. If the answer is No the network returns to the first activity and reconsiders it in the light of the objections raised in the question lozenge. This procedure is repeated at each stage and ensures that the results are fed back to ensure that they comply with the intention of the previous stage. It is not impossible for a No answer in the last lozenge to result in the project going back to square one.

This procedure ensures that the information is available to those who need it and that they have a clear understanding of the problem. It may be the only method of ensuring this, as when a completely new requirement arises bearing no relation to current practice in the company. It has certain defects in that it produces action only after an error has been established. It can be very time consuming and it often depends on unstructured verbal communication because of this. These factors can combine to make it an expensive procedure.

Feedforward

In the right-hand path the proposition is that, far from continuously breaking new ground, most of the work that goes through design offices, etc. bears a strong relationship to that which has gone before. Most of the problems must therefore have been solved in the past and the experience thus gathered can be reapplied with small variations. It will be most unlikely that serious errors will be made, providing that adequate records have been kept and that these are accessible to those needing them. It is only necessary to indicate at each stage which proven solution will be used in the next stage. By definition the details of the solution will be understood throughout the organization and ambiguities will be minimal.

The main problem with this approach can be a lack of company standards defining proven solutions and of systems to make them accessible. Information only exists to the extent to which it is accessible. The lack of either standard or system amounts to the same thing. Cultural differences play a large part in this pattern. Some nationalities are culturally orientated towards a standards and systems approach to operations and feel unhappy in their absence. Some are the reverse and feel that individuality is under threat when they appear. These latter tend to accord creativity and inventiveness a higher status than incremental progress.

Communication Structure

The form of communication structure in a company must relate to the problems and activities of that company. It is unlikely that even the simplest company can use the armed forces technique but the principle is widely valid. As much as possible of the message should be contained in the medium: as Marshall McLuhan pointed out, the ability of advertising to convey a message and influence people is due to success in achieving this.

There are examples of communication structures in all companies. The drawing system, if it is any good, is highly structured. The drawing number alone can tell one what size it is, where to find it, what product or process it describes, in how much detail, whether it is on micro-fiche, how many times it has been modified. A simple coding system can be used since it is required only to indicate which of several options has been adopted. On the drawing is found, in standardized positions, such data as the nature of the modifications, when they were introduced, what product serial numbers they affect, which other drawings are relevant. A mass of technical and manufacturing detail is present in a codified standard form. Where there is often a weakness is in the drawing retrieval system. This should permit a draughtsmen to see instantly whether the part that he has been asked to design exists already somewhere in the company. Such a system is needed in order to be able to use the right-hand path in Figure 11.6. In too many cases the draughtsman finds it quicker to design a new part than to search through hundreds of drawings for one that fits his task.

The make or buy decision approach described in Chapter 7 is an example of a structure designed for a specific purpose to ensure that a series of related questions are asked and answered in the same ordered sequence by everyone.

Value engineering, as described in Chapter 7, is a structured method of considering the functions and costs of a product together in order to provide overall improvement in value, providing benefits for both user and manufacturer.

Engineering and other standards are valuable in the first place as structured communication. The UK conversion to metric standards removed ambiguities from an area of international affairs because it was widely understood and accepted rather than because of any intrinsic merit. The establishment of preferred standards takes this further. There is a tendency for some engineers to regard all standards as a constraint on their talent. This may be so in the individual case but the effect is outweighed by the cumulative effect on company results when the whole is considered. Standards of this type, made accessible to all by a well-developed system, are needed to achieve the benefits of the feedforward approach of Figure 11.6.

Much of the value of the market/product analysis technique of Chapter 2 is in the structured presentation of the information. The structure is simple to explain and clarity of understanding is rapidly achieved by all. The structure overcomes the differentiations between the people who

176 Communication and Structure

must discuss the findings. It does the same in the case of the new product matrix, another communication structure described in Chapter 10, by relying less on words and more on defined symbols.

A major merit of network planning systems such as PERT is that the structure ensures that the work content and logical sequence of jobs is not stated in potentially ambiguous groups of words but by a combination of the layout of the network and the defined symbols forming it. The information to be conveyed can be wrong, but not ambiguous.

Review

This chapter has:

(1) Illustrated some communication problems by means of class exercises.
(2) Illustrated the communication structure concept.
(3) Described problems caused by differentials and organizational structure.
(4) Described the 'first language' effect.
(5) Described the feedforward and feedback concepts.

When communication has been established the project manager can begin to motivate and manage his team. In chapter 13 some work by social scientists and psychologists offers some insight into the factors influencing motivation.

References

Lawrence, P. and Lorsch, J. 1969: *Developing Organisations*. Addison-Wesley.

Further Reading

Epton, S. R. 1981: The Role of Communication in R&D, *R&D Man.* **11**, 4.
Holroyd, P., Richer, M. and Woods, M. F. 1983: Microcomputers and Decision Making, *R&D Man.* **13**, 1.
Pruthi, S. and Nagpaul, P. S. 1978: Communication Patterns in Small R&D Projects, *R&D Man.* **8**, 2.

12 Computers in R&D

The impact of computers on almost every aspect of industrial life has been most marked and it would be strange if R&D and project management had escaped. Contrasted with the large-scale effects in some other areas, such as office work, warehousing and process control, the impact on R&D type activities has been slower to develop and is still a fairly new phenomenon other than in its basic role as an aid to designers.

Because of the discontinuous nature of project management there is as yet little standardization of hardware, systems or software. Despite the fact that there are quite a number of commercial packages available, much of the software is written in-house, often as a part of the research or development project in which it will be used. The man-hours involved in writing programs of any complexity, and particularly in debugging them, are such that, as in other areas of use, this phase will probably pass in favour of the economics of buying a proven package from a reputable source, as suitable suites of programs become available.

Any published note on the subject at the moment can only be a snapshot of a rapidly moving situation; the applications can be classified but the individuality and absence of repetition of R&D projects would make detailed descriptions of specific applications of very narrow interest. The current status of computers and microcomputers in R&D, and the probable course of development in their use, is a more useful area of study and has been taken up by a group at Manchester Business School, UK (Morse, 1984).

The research was based on a postal questionnaire to 490 of the main research centres and elicited a positive response from 36 per cent. A high proportion, 77 per cent, of respondents were from government or quasi-government establishments. Sizes in the sample ranged from less than 50 employees (20 per cent) to over 1000 (3 per cent). Some 15 industries were represented in the sample; no significant variation in facilities was found between them. Some organizations (6 per cent) had no computing facilities at all. These organizations all had less than ten QSEs working in R&D and tended to be those expected to do relatively little quantitative analysis. In the main, R&D establishments tended to have stand-alone computers with a high proportion of microcomputers, nearly nine out of ten having one or more.

The general categories of applications reported were as follows; in most cases more than one category was present in the same organization.

(1) Management
(2) Experimentation
(3) Calculation
(4) Modelling
(5) Information handling
(6) Other

Some respondents reported that a number of applications were only possible on a microcomputer. Experimentation and data logging were quoted by half those making this point.

Within the broad categories of usage above, the applications broke down into a wide range of tasks.

(1) Management
    Network analysis
    Resource planning
    Research planning
    Spreadsheet program
    Financial modelling
    Decision tree analysis
    Cost–benefit analysis
    Ranking models
    Expert systems
    Forecasting
    Management information

(2) Experimentation
    Process control
    Process monitoring
    Data logging
    Equipment control

(3) Calculation/analysis
    Statistical analysis
    Data analysis
    Technical calculation

(4) Modelling/design/simulation
    Mathematical modelling
    Scientific modelling
    CAD/CAM
    Simulation

(5) Information handling
　　Word processing/report writing
　　Data presentation
　　Data storage
　　Information access
　　Database systems

(6) Other
　　Software development

Well over three-quarters of the respondents said they would be purchasing a microcomputer or additional software within the next year. The applications were expected to be the same as those already noted. Half of those making this statement thought they would use it for experimentation and over 40 per cent for information handling. When asked for their views on longer-term future applications the emphasis was again on the increase of information handling, with management applications falling as a percentage of the whole.

The general view was that microcomputers would continue to be used extensively for automating laboratory operations and even more for recording, analysing and interpreting results. Applications of artificial intelligence based systems were envisaged by very few.

If present staffing levels are maintained, the ratio of microcomputers to QSEs will fall from the present 1 to 8 to about 1 to 3. There was no correlation between this figure for individual industries and their 'nearness' to computing as an activity.

The overwhelming consensus amongst respondents was that microcomputers had made a significant impact on their organizations. The conclusions reached by the Manchester Business School team were:

(1) Diffusion of microcomputers into R&D has been rapid and the pace will increase, except perhaps in small establishments.
(2) Applications have tended to be *ad hoc*, with software generally written in-house.
(3) The individual researcher has been the prime mover, seeking to satisfy his own needs.
(4) R&D is at an infant stage in integrating microcomputers and information technology into its activities. Management does not appear to have encouraged it actively.
(5) Microcomputers will be the chief medium through which knowledge engineering and artificial intelligence will enter the R&D laboratory. Management approaches will have to change if this transition is to be made smoothly.

PC Planning Systems

There are a number of modestly priced programs with a reduced range of facilities designed to run on PCs. One of them, written by the InstaPlan Corporation of California, has the additional merit that it is sold in several packages starting from the basic planning system. This allows the small company with little planning expertise to gain experience for an outlay at the £100 level.

They can then add a Tracker unit, which will monitor the progress of the work, effort and expenditure as the project proceeds. This can be followed by the Note Pad unit on which to record decisions and the reasons for them as they are made. This can be a critically important action as the human memory is notoriously selective, and looseleaf and logbook notes are prone to be separated from the project plan.

Finally, a unit can be added to print out a complete network diagram. Following the PERT conventions this displays the logical dependences of the project activities very clearly, as indicated in Chapter 6.

The minimum hardware requirements for InstaPlan are 640k of random-access memory (RAM), MS–DOS 2.0 or higher and a floppy disk. In theory the program will run with 512k but this may leave the planner with inadequate memory for data associated with the plan. In this form it will handle 600 activities; a memory expansion unit to raise this figure to 3000 activities is expected to be available in 1990.

The program defaults to interpreting all activities as Finish to Start sequential operations. It can on demand change this to either Start to Start or Finish to Finish.

The first stage of planning is to list the main activities on the processor outline. These can now be studied in turn in greater detail and the original list can be edited, moved and deleted as the plan develops. Immediately the activities and their durations are entered the Gantt bar chart and the end date are displayed. The relationships can now be changed, delays between activities inserted and the whole built up into a complex network that can be displayed as a PERT chart by using the optional unit.

The planning, however, is done on the Gantt chart with the critical path clearly shown by colour or shading. This is the oldest system and probably the best understood by most people whatever their backgrounds. Its main disadvantage, the sorry state the diagram reaches when manually drawn out versions are used for monitoring and are continually amended, is no longer a disadvantage when a computer is used.

The basic program can outline several projects so that the total effect on resources can be displayed and individual calendars can be constructed for each person. If there are mandatory finish dates InstaPlan will tell you when the activity must be started. When repetitive steps are present in either activities or resources a copy command performs these with minimum effort.

Tracking

The actual progress of the project together with the effort and cost to date are recorded in the project history database. They are all displayed on an analytical spreadsheet. The resource loading can be shown for a single assignment or the entire plan, with actuals, plans and overloads by time period. If you enter time, money and percentage progress of each activity, the program will report on performance against schedule, budget and manpower plan. It should be noted that, in particular, the percentage completion is a difficult subjective judgement, probably made by the project leader, and is not part of the program. Based on reported progress and remaining work for each assignment the program will forecast cost and work to complete project.

Notes

Unlimited notes can be kept on disk and displayed at a keystroke for activities, assignments and resources. These can be printed out or included in reports. A cross-indexing system locates related comments with a single keystroke. A calculator 'pops up' for quick calculations.

Reports

Planned, actual or progressive value for any time period in value or hours can be exported to Lotus, Borland or Microsoft spreadsheets. The Gantt chart bars are partially filled to show percentage progress. A spreadsheet report printing activities versus resources or activities versus time can be provided. A resource report shows assignments for a specific time period with planned, actual and notes in a convenient format. Resource charts show money, manhours, mandays, manweeks, percentage reference as the vertical scale and can focus on a single assignment, project or the entire plan to form a cost–schedule graph.

PERT Option

The PERT option prints a complete network diagram of any project developed as described above. PERT nodes are shown as boxes connected by lines illustrating the logical connections, with planned delays marked on them. Critical path and group indications are shown on the box frames. Activity data such as dates, slack and status can be selected and displayed. A strip on the left-hand side of the screen provides a key to the symbols in use and a square for issue date and approval.

Shareware

There is an even cheaper method of starting to use computers for a wide variety of tasks. The Association of Shareware Professionals is an international body providing floppy disks of programs in the public domain at about £5 a disk and encouraging the buyer to copy them. The small snag is that it costs considerably more than the purchase price to buy a licence to use them and a licence is required for each computer.

The local agents provide an extensive catalogue of programs available at a nominal charge. One such is Easy Project, written for the IBM PC and 100 per cent compatible instruments. It can be used on a hard disk computer or a floppy disk type with two disk drives. It is supplied on a single disk and the Install program deletes the Easy Project data from it after translating it to a blank data disk in the second drive, leaving the A disk as systems disk. The program can receive a maximum of 20 project phases and 1000 tasks per project. There is no limit to the number of resources per project.

Easy Project is an efficient method of planning, tracking and controlling all types of projects. Movement of the cursor is controlled by several nominated keystrokes and the program itself is menu-driven. The components of the Main Menu are as follows:

(1) Project: Create project numbers, descriptions, phase descriptions and define holidays
(2) Task: Maintain task data
(3) Quick-input: Mass input for new tasks
(4) Schedule: Schedule work plans automatically
(5) Gantt: Produce Gantt charts for a project detailing planned versus actual progress
(6) Reports: Generate reports, including work plans, status reports and summary reports
(7) Utilities: Configure system and sundry utility file handling
(8) Licence: Print licence and registration form
(9) Exit: Return to DOS

When creating a new project the procedure to be followed is the following.

(1) Choose 'Project' from the Main Menu and enter a project number, descriptions, phase descriptions and project holidays.
(2) Choose 'Resource' from the Main Menu and add resource data for the project. Resources will be identified by assigning them a unique user-defined code.
(3) Choose 'Task' from the Main Menu to enter and maintain tasks in the project.
(4) If you want Easy Project to calculate estimated schedule dates, choose 'Schedule' from the Main Menu.
(5) Gantt charts and/or reports may be produced at this point.

A sample project is included on the system disk and this may be viewed. The system disk has a file named README.DOC which gives more details on setting up projects, resource maintenance, task maintenance and notes on entering tasks. There is also a quick-input method which, with some limitations, allows up to 19 tasks to be entered from one screen.

There are options for calculating the critical path only and for each phase or network to be scheduled from the project start date, permitting multiple phases to be scheduled at the same time.

The Report Menu comprises nine different reports which can be further processed by your Word Processor; they are all dBASE compatible.

Review

This chapter has:

(1) Reviewed the progress of computers in communication and control of R&D projects.
(2) Reported some speculations on the future use of computers in R&D.
(3) Described two programs designed to aid planning, tracking and control of a wide range of projects.

Reference

Morse, G., Ong, C. H. and Pearson, A. W. 1984: Computers in R&D; a UK Survey, *R&D Man.* **14**, 4.

Further Reading

Chandor, A. 1981: *Dictionary of Microprocessors*. Penguin.
Holroyd, P., Richer, M. and Woods, M. F. 1983: Microcomputers and Decision Making, *R&D Man.* **13**, 1.
Lewis, C. 1982: *Managing with Micros*. Blackwell.

13 Motivating Project Teams

People problems are at least as difficult and often more important than the technological problems. People are the most important resource in a company and the one we understand least well. Some of the relevant work of management theorists is reviewed in this chapter.

Management Theory

There can be said to be at least three main schools of management theory addressing the people problem: the classical school embodying the work of F. W. Taylor and Henri Fayol, the behaviourist school founded by Elton Mayo and the quantitative school which appears to have had its origins in the operations research techniques developed during World War II. Some practical experiments carried out by Mayo in the early 1930s produced results of interest to the project manager.

The Hawthorne Experiments

Mayo and his colleagues at Harvard were invited by Western Electric to join in a study of productivity at their Hawthorne plant in 1927. A department, in which women were employed wiring the back plane of telephone exchanges, had been divided into a test group and a control group. As a first experiment they improved the lighting for the test group and were pleased to find that productivity improved, but puzzled to find that productivity also improved in the control group. They improved the lighting further and obtained a further improvement in productivity in both groups. They then reduced the lighting level and were even more puzzled by the fact that productivity improved once more.

Mayo repeated this type of experiment in more sophisticated conditions with salaries, coffee breaks, working hours and other variables. Always both groups reacted positively to any change in the test group conditions in whatever direction.

Many possible direct effects were ruled out by the test program and Mayo eventually concluded that a complex emotional chain had been behind the productivity changes. Because both test and control groups had been singled out for special attention a group pride had developed and this became the motivation for improved performance. A sympathetic attitude by supervision had reinforced this effect.

Mayo deduced that when special attention is given to workers by management, productivity is likely to increase regardless of any actual changes in working conditions. This has become known as the Hawthorne effect.

A massive interview program convinced Mayo that informal working groups created a social environment that greatly influenced the productivity of the employees. The pressure exerted by such groups had a stronger influence than management demands. His conclusion was that these groups could be turned into productive forces by giving the employees a sense of being appreciated. This stresses the social needs of man, such as job relationships and response to work-group pressures rather than management control, replacing the older concept of motivation by rational personal economic needs only.

Transactional Analysis

Surprising experimental findings, though of a quite different nature, were also the foundation of transactional analysis (TA). A Canadian brain surgeon, W. G. Penfield, found that direct stimulation of specific parts of the human brain by a very low voltage electrode, under a local anaesthetic, consistently produced recollections, which the patient could describe, of the same past event and the associated feelings. He concluded:

(1) The human brain contains a record of every event experienced.
(2) The event and the feeling associated with it are inseparably locked together in the brain.

The consequences for behavioural psychology were developed by Berne (1964). Everyone has a brain recording of every experience of internal and external lived events and associated feelings. The most important of these, from a behavioural point of view, are held to happen in the first five years of life. In addition, there are within everyone his or her own parents in the form of received data and, with maturity, a third contribution from his or her own adult experience.

Berne concluded from his behavioural observations that the unit of social intercourse is a 'stimulus' followed by a 'response', and he developed definitions and a language permitting description and analysis. The 'stimulus followed by response' unit was given the name 'transaction'

Motivating Project Teams 187

and the psychological states corresponding to the three inputs were named 'Parent', 'Adult' and 'Child'. These terms do not imply relationships nor are they roles to be played. P, A and C are actual psychological states due to the three functions of the brain in recording, recalling and reliving. Every individual contains all three.

Parent

P is a record of imposed, unquestioned events internalized between birth and age five. It is a taught concept, represented by Figure 13.1, containing largely 'how to' data.

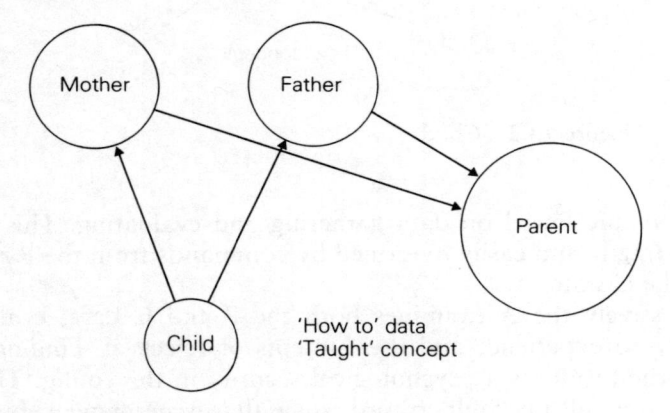

Figure 13.1 Parent

Child

The C state is a recording of internal events in response to external events mainly associated with the P state as shown in Figure 13.2. It also contains genetic urges to move, express feelings and make a noise, often in conflict with social demands. At the time these recordings are made the infant cannot yet relate cause and effect, so approval and reward for good behaviour tend to produce confusion. This leads to negative feelings of the type 'it must be all my fault'. A premise is that the infant has been exposed to virtually all possible feelings by the time he or she goes to school.

Adult

The A state begins to be formed as early as 10 months, as awareness leads to initiatives and discovery. As data accumulates there begins a thought

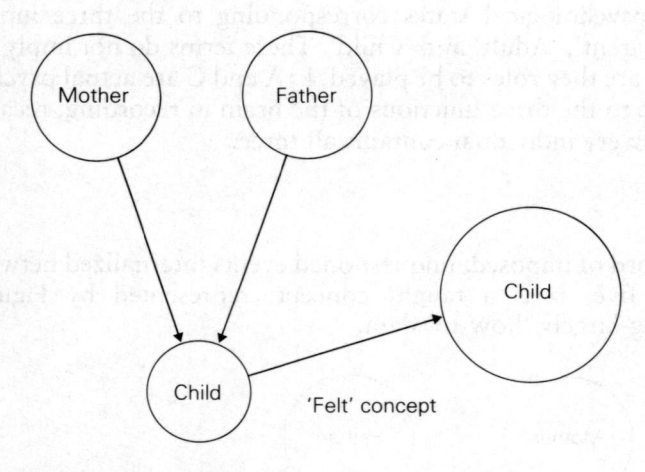

Figure 13.2 Child

(Mother and Father arrows point to Child; Child arrow points to another Child labelled 'Felt' concept)

concept of life based on data gathering and evaluating. This stage is initially fragile and easily overruled by commands from the P state and fear in the C state.

Progressively the A examines both the P and C data, evaluates it according to experience and then accepts or rejects it. Finding that P data is true produces a psychological security in the young. This does not erase the 'all my fault' record, since that is permanent, but it can switch it off. This stage, shown in Figure 13.3, is built up gradually. Even when quite mature, however, severe stress conditions may cause reversion to the stored P or C state where response is instantaneous. The process by which the A state evaluates data is slower than this, hence the advice 'count to 10' when provoked. The idea of probability develops in this period of life. The child has no such concept. His world is one of unpleasant alternatives, such as 'no greens, no pudding'.

Conflict is produced when what the parent says does not seem true to the adult. This occupies the evaluation faculty of which there is a finite amount. This suggests that the undisciplined child, contrary to some ideas on 'progressive' education, is not more creative but less so. The disciplined child does not have to use his evaluation faculty on conflict and can devote it all to education.

The physical child response to stroking is extended to the psychological equivalent in terms of praise and reward. When the parent or child dominates, the outcome is predictable. When the adult is in charge, the outcome is not always predictable and the possibility of failure, success and change is introduced.

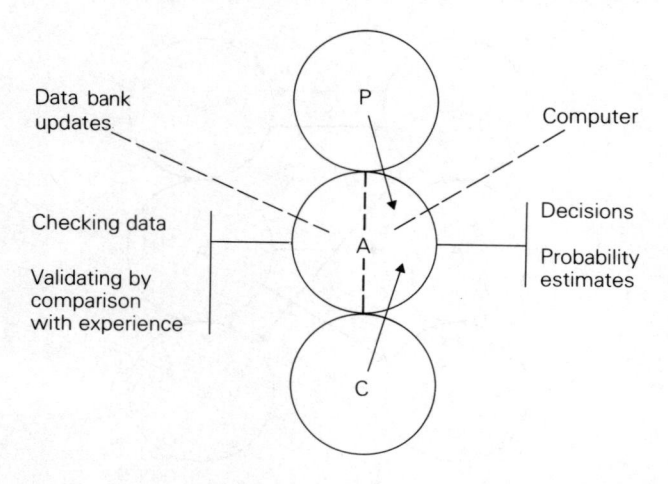

Figure 13.3 Adult

Transactions

The TA concept is that of every individual consisting of all three P, A and C states and a transaction consisting of two such individuals, one providing a stimulus and the other a response, as in Figure 13.4. TA theory states that if both stimulus and response emanate from the P state (X) the transaction will carry on, since both are airing their prejudices and neither is analysing the data. In the same way, a C–C transaction continues as an interplay of genetic urges and expressed feelings.

If a stimulus is from P to C and the response from C to P, that is, the second individual accepts that he is in a child/parent relationship with the first, the transaction will continue. If, on the other hand, he refuses to accept this relationship and responds from his own adult (Y) on a 'don't talk to me like that' basis to the adult or child of the first individual, this is a new stimulus and the transaction has broken down.

The general rule is that when stimulus and response are parallel lines the transaction will continue, but when the stimulus and response lines cross, communication stops. The key questions in TA are 'who is stimulating?' and 'who is reacting?' Crossed stimulus and response lines create stress but if one party to the transaction can say honestly 'that was my parent speaking' the stress is relieved.

The lessons to be learned from TA are (Harris, 1973) as follows:

(1) Learn to recognize your child, its fears, vulnerabilities and methods of expression.

190 *Motivating Project Teams*

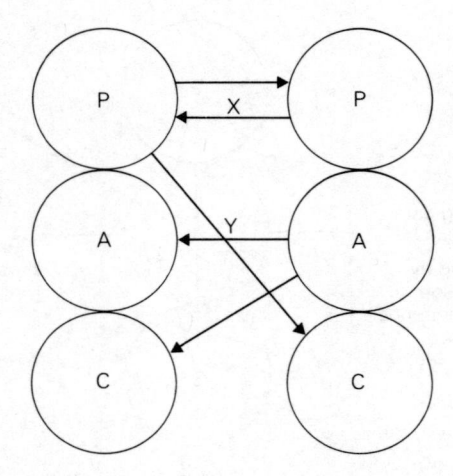

Figure 13.4 Transactions

(2) Learn to recognize your parent, its prejudices and dogmas.
(3) Be sensitive to the child in others, stroke it.
(4) Count to ten when necessary, give your adult time to process the data.
(5) When in doubt, leave it out.
(6) Work out a system of values. Decisions need an ethical framework.

Leadership Styles Revisited

The leadership style analysis of Chapter 10 can profitably be re-examined in the light of TA. Referring to Figure 10.3, the first quarter 'telling' can be seen to be a P–C transaction. The immature newcomer to the department will almost certainly accept this relationship initially, so no breakdown of the transaction is to be expected as long as there is adequate stroking by the adult. The second quarter represents a stimulus from an adult with a response from a transitional child/adult. Because of this the 'selling' of the idea to someone not yet fully mature is likely to be a workable relationship. Consciousness of being invited rather than ordered will usually provide adequate stroking.

In the third quarter 'participative' style is an adult–adult transaction with both stimulus and response attempting to improve the outcome of the transaction. Achievement provides most of the stroking and fosters the relationship.

The fourth quarter can be less straightforward. It can be indicative of full maturity of the follower, now left to run his own activities without supervision. He may, however, begin to think that, being judged capable of running his own show, he should be given a department of his own. If he expects immediate reaction to this suggestion his child is contaminating his adult. The leader must treat this possibility with care. If he thinks he is in an adult–adult transaction while the follower has moved to a child–parent response, because he thinks the leader is refusing to accept the point he is making, communication has ceased. The stimulus/response lines have crossed.

The follower may, of course, be right. Perhaps the leader's parent has taken over under the stress of pressure, on the one hand from top management to complete the project and on the other from the follower for promotion, thus breaking up the team. The parent attitude would be 'do it thus because I tell you to', again crossing the stimulus/response lines.

Another possibility is that the leader perceives the high achieving follower as a threat to his own position, and withdraws. His adult is progressively contaminated by his child. If the stress is high enough and he is basically insecure – his adult has not turned off his child's 'all my fault' – his child takes over with a 'nothing to do with you' response.

At any stage of development of leadership style the description arising from the Hersey and Blanchard analysis may contain a number of possibilities. Transactional analysis offers help in identifying the specific case and objective setting is a means of moving the leader/follower relationship towards the adult–adult transaction while focussing discussion on contribution to the task for which they share responsibility. This is the most basic common ground in the relationship, the safest, and that which supplies, in Drucker's words, the four basic requirements of human relations.

Motivation

Frederick Herzberg (1968) put forward the two-factor approach to motivation after an extensive study of job attitudes among engineers and accountants. He concluded that satisfaction and dissatisfaction with the job do not come from the presence or absence of one set of factors. In his view there are satisfiers, which he calls motivating factors, and dissatisfiers, which he calls hygiene factors.

Those in the first category include achievement, recognition, responsibility and advancement. Their absence appeared to have little to do with employees' dissatisfaction. The dissatisfiers were such factors as salary, working conditions and company policy. The absence of problems in these areas did not satisfy but created conditions in which the satisfiers, when present, could motivate people, hence the term hygiene factors. Briefly, the satisfiers were related to the job content and the dissatisfiers

192 Motivating Project Teams

were related to job context, mainly company policy and environment.

The reactions of people to any given stimulus are so individual, however, that generalizations are dangerous. There will always be exceptions to this classification of factors influencing motivation. Much of the interest in the recent past in job enrichment programmes has sprung from this and other work by Herzberg. Some of these programmes have been successful and some have not. Some have been initially successful and then suffered a relapse, suggesting that at least some of the cases owed their success more to the Hawthorne effect than to a deeper understanding of people. At a much simpler level, engineers being what they are, recognition of achievement is an effective motivator that is always to hand and, as long as it is 'felt fair' by peers, runs no great risks in being applied. A quantitative study (Bergen, 1983) supports this view for both the UK and West Germany.

Contingency Model

The Fiedler (1977) model is based on the notion that group performance is contingent upon the circumstances. The four variables are (1) the leader's relations with the members of the team, (2) whether the task is highly or poorly structured, (3) whether the leader has a high or low level of authority and (4) the leader's style in terms of the Hersey and Blanchard two-dimensional analysis already described.

Table 13.1 Contingency leadership model

Situation characteristics								
1 Relations	Good				Poor			
2 Task structure	High		Low		High		Low	
3 Leader authority	Strong	Weak	Strong	Weak	Strong	Weak	Strong	Weak
Category	1	2	3	4	5	6	7	8
Favourable to leader?	Favourable		Moderately favourable				Unfavourable	
Probable leader performance								
1 Relation motivated	Poor		Good		Good?		?	Poor
2 Task motivated	Good		Poor		Poor		?	Good

Leader–member relations are good if they all look forward to working together and there is mutual trust and respect. They are bad when these conditions are not present. A task has high structure when the goal and the methods of achieving it are well understood and agreed upon – see Chapter 10, Objective Setting. It is poorly structured when any of these features is absent.

The leader's level of authority can arise from his position in the company or from his personal expertise. His style has been discussed in Chapter 10.

Assuming that the success of the leader and of the team are inseparable, combinations of the four variables give rise to eight categories. These give some guidance on how successful a given leader is likely to be and how favourable a given situation is likely to be from his point of view. These factors are displayed in Table 13.1.

Review

This chapter has:

(1) Described the Hawthorne effect.
(2) Described the transactional analysis concept and its bearing on management style analysis.
(3) Indicated the TA basis of objective setting.
(4) Described the two-factor motivation model.
(5) Described the contingency leadership model.

References

Bergen, S. A. 1983: *Productivity and the R&D Production Interface*. Gower.
Berne, E. 1964: *Games People Play*. Grove Press.
Harris, T. 1973: *I'm OK, You're OK*. Pan Books.
Herzberg, F. 1968: How do You Motivate Employees? *HBR*. **46**.
Pugh, D. S., Hickson, D. and Hinings, C. R. 1984: *Writers on Organisations*. Penguin.

Further Reading

Fayol, H. 1930: Industrial and General Management, *Int. Man. Inst.*
Fiedler, F., Chemers, M. and Mahar, L. 1977: *Improving Leadership Effectiveness*. Wiley.
Taylor, F. W. 1947: *Scientific Management*. Harper & Bros.

14 Failures and Successes

Over the years much research effort has gone into trying to understand the reasons for success and failure of R&D projects in commercial terms. The best known of the earlier endeavours is probably Project Sappho, which was carried out by the Science Policy Review Unit (SPRU) based at the University of Sussex. It adopted the then new methodology of selecting inventive products which had reached the market and making pairs of companies of which one had been successful and the other unsuccessful.

An extensive questionnaire was designed, proved and applied on site to 28 pairs of companies and the answers were analysed on a computer. The largest computer available in the UK at that time was ATLAS and the data collected saturated the machine.

As in other cases the results were not completely conclusive. Statistically the strongest correlation was between understanding of the market and commercial success. The fact that this was the only major correlation emphasizes that creative development is by no means easy and is always expensive. It usually takes a great deal longer than is originally planned and hence, to a lesser degree in most cases, a larger amount of resources. A selection of case studies was reported, illustrating the mixed results that emerge from apparently similar projects.

The EMI Scanner

A non-invasive diagnostic method of internal examination of patients had been a long felt want in the medical profession. The discovery of X-rays by Roentgen in 1895 led to the development of imaging systems that displayed internal pictures of bone structure and harder tissues in the human body. Although these were of great use to the profession the benefit was reduced by the fact that (a) interfering tissues confused the image and (b) for health reasons the X-ray dose was kept as low as possible, reducing the contrast.

In 1967 Godfrey Hounsfield of EMI Central Laboratories reported that X-ray tomography had now become a practical proposition because of the advance of computers. An improvement of 100 times in the information content of existing techniques would allow the absorption coefficient of a transverse slice of an object to be calculated to an accuracy of 0.5 per cent.

X-ray techniques were well understood and the mathematical basis for Hounsfield's approach had been established in 1917 by the Austrian Radon. The clinical need for a non-traumatic method of exploration was stated by Oldendorf in the 1960s.

The company did not have a medical or X-ray background and was conditioned by three previous failures to exploit the medical systems market. There had been little internal enthusiasm for this project and it was largely due to the personal sponsorship of a new technical director, Dr John Powell, that the company, which had 48 000 employees and a £500m turnover, decided to exploit Hounsfield's work.

The Market

In 1975 there were 160 000 conventional machines in 97 000 hospitals world-wide. A replacement rate of 10 per cent per annum means a market of 10 000 machines. If 20 per cent of the replacement machines were scanners, and EMI had 25 per cent of this market a figure of 500 systems per annum is arrived at.

The initial instrument sold for £16 000, rising to £200 000 for the head scanner. The head and body scanner version was then introduced selling at about £250 000. The revised forecast of sales was £80m per annum rising to £250m. The price was high in relation to orthodox equipment but was held to be justified by patient throughput. The head-scan time in 1972 was five minutes, falling to 20 seconds in 1977. The group forecast is given in Table 14.1. The economic benefits were held to be significant. An initial investment of £250 000 was held to save £12 000 per annum in cancelled laparotomies alone. Sweden forecast 70 per cent reduction in encephalography and 60 per cent reduction in cerebral angiogram times.

The Rise and Fall

The X-ray Tomoscan has been authoritatively described as the greatest advance in radiology since its inception. Its development and rise at EMI is described above. A financial analysis for 1972–7 is given in Table 14.1. What are the reasons for its fall?

The dependance on the US market was a factor. Acceptance there involved long trials and modifications. Health costs in the previous four years had risen at 15 per cent per annum and the President instituted a

Failures and Successes

Table 14.1 Financial analysis

	1972	1976	1977 (second half)
Sales (£m)	58	207	80
Profits (£m)	1.4	26	(3) Loss
Medical personnel	20	3500 (including 3200 in acquisitions)	
R&D expenditure (£m)	0.6	12	12
Production of scanner	Nil	500 (65% to USA)	800
Share price (p)	161	254	141

requirement for certificates of need for any hospital expenditure over $150 000. The new body scanner was priced at $750 000; the market was cut by half.

The original contracts included a commitment to update body scanners free of charge. As performance of later models improved this proved rash and costly.

The growth of the division and the world-wide acquisitions increased expenditure. Nine companies were involved with EMI and there were 15 competitive companies in 1977.

GE of the USA had ten times the back-up staff and resources of EMI and were on first name terms with the key people in the medical world.

Two companies were claimed to infringe EMI patents. Several suits were filed and litigation costs in the USA are high. The legal process is long winded; it can outlast the life of the patent.

The specifications of competitive equipment demanded further increases in R&D expenditure by EMI. The scan times were reduced to three and five seconds and one competitor embodied 288 detectors compared with the 20 seconds and 30 detectors of EMI.

The electronics division of EMI was expected to continue to generate cash, initially at a higher level than the scanner operation and ending up at about the same amount. Unfortunately the music electronics contribution hit a slump at the critical time and was unable to meet expectations.

This was a well researched and market estimated project: for the reasons given above it ended with the sale of EMI to another company.

Discussion

The time needed to bring an innovation to the market is nearly always longer than the layman imagines and the accuracy of forecasts by those in the business leaves much to be desired.

Rutherford, after working from 1890 to 1930 on radioactivity, being universally recognized for his discoveries and awarded many prizes and honorary degrees, gave as his view, 'There is no appreciable energy available to man through atomic disintegration.' Winston Churchill said of atomic energy in 1939, 'It might be as good as present day explosives, but it is unlikely to produce anything very much more dangerous.'

Authors seem to have been more effective. Kipling described scheduled Atlantic air services in detail in 1904. Marie Corelli predicted the atom bomb in 'The life everlasting' in 1911.

It is difficult to make a case that the time lag in getting innovations to the market-place has decreased in recent years. The comments above and Table 14.2 are culled from a paper I presented to the IEE in 1963.

The list is not long enough to permit any meaningful conclusions to be reached, but one or two tendencies can be seen. Timing is important. The gyro-compass was delayed because precision ball bearings were not available and the self-winding watch because no British watch industry existed in the inventor's time. He attempted to subcontract in Switzerland but the manufacturers were not interested and he had to start a company in the UK for the purpose.

The initial research is generally a one-man job; the production is often best carried out by an established firm. The inventor may not be the best

Table 14.2 Time lags

Device	Inventor	Aided by firm	Time (yrs)	Special firm	Established firm	Time (yrs)	Total time (yrs)
Zip-fastener	Engineer	Yes	12	Failed	Success	18	30
Fluorescent lamp	Scientist	No	40	–	Success	40	80
Tape recorder	Scientist	No	5	Failed	Success	35	40
Self-winding watch	Engineer	No	1	Failed	Success	16	17
Gyro-compass	Scientist	No	13	Success	Success	43	56
X-ray micro-analyser	Scientist	–	8	–	Success	5	13

198 Failures and Successes

man to develop and manufacture the product. Edwin Land successfully marketed Polaroid and Bakeland began a new industry with Bakelite but they appear to have been exceptions. They are outnumbered by the failures.

Even in cases where industry has not neglected an invention, the major part of the time is consumed in development rather than research.

Many new ideas have originated outside the industry concerned. Kodachrome was developed by two musicians and the original automatic telephone exchange by an undertaker.

Chapter 1 of this book presents a case that good communications between all members of a firm and its customers are essential to its success. This has been recognized for a long time. A French scientist said 'Most of the work to be done in science and the useful arts is precisely that which needs the knowledge and co-operation of many scientists – that is why it is necessary for scientists and technologists to meet – even in those branches of knowledge which seem to have least relation and connection with one another.' These words were said by Antoine Lavoisier in 1793. He was guillotined in 1794.

Review

This chapter has:

(1) Described the Project Sappho.
(2) Described the development of the EMI scanner.
(3) Discussed the time lags in R&D.

References

Freeman, A. 1972: *Project Sappho*. SPRU, University of Sussex, Brighton.
Bergen, S. A. 1977: *EMI scanner Case*. Manchester Business School.

Further Reading

Bergen, S. A. 1963: Research, Development and Innovation. *J.IEE* November.
Rawle, P. R. 1983: *GEC Commissioned Report*. London Business School.

15 Creativity in R&D

One of the constraints in planning R&D has been the lack of a convincing model of the process. One of the important factors in R&D is that of creativity. Why, then, do so many of the clearly creative new products fail to achieve their planned market share and, as a result, turn out to be unprofitable? There must be some other factors that have not been taken into consideration properly at some stage in the passage from idea generation to marketing.

One of these factors may well be adequate knowledge of the technology. There are others, many of which do not call for creativity. What are they, and how do they interact?

Galbraith (1976) put forward the idea that in the technological world the technology is so demanding that a given new technology is handled in the same way anywhere in the world no matter what the local culture. He named this the 'technological imperative'. An opposing view from Child and Kaiser (1975) is the 'culture-free thesis'. This states that whatever the forms, organization and functions that a company believes it has, unless these correspond to the norms and expectations of the local culture they will remain purely superficial window dressing. The company will operate practically in conformity with cultural expectations.

If the first view is sound it removes the need for a model with cultural factors in it. Even casual observation makes this hypothesis improbable. It will be seen that the second view and the proposed model are mutually supportive, since the model can predict effects of cultural factors corresponding to observed results.

Discontinuity

In the literature of creativity one factor appears consistently, plays no part in conventional design and thus may be used to distinguish between the two. This is the concept of creative discontinuity. Many of the prescriptions for creativity embody means of enabling the worker to break away from established continuous patterns of thought, since such patterns of thought are held to hinder access to new ideas not contained in a logical sequence from the starting point of the problem. A 'flip-flop' action is postulated, analogous to the visual perception of the Necker cube. This is an optical illusion in which the diagram of a skeleton cube appears to the observer in either of two orientations. The transition from one to the other takes place after a few seconds of observation, is discontinous and cannot be stopped at in an intermediate position. The initial orientation cannot be predicted, but reversal after a few seconds' observation always takes place in the same way. The change itself is stable in form.

This form of discontinuity will be familiar to engineers. Electrical engineers will be reminded of the torque versus speed curve of an induction motor which exhibits an unstable and unmeasurable set of values as the curve turns back on itself at the pull-out torque. A mechanical analogy is the Euler strut, where a beam is stable on either side of a centre line but unstable on it, passing from one side to the other discontinuously.

A relative newcomer among theories sets out to generalize the description of discontinuities of this type to which its originator, Professor Rene Thom of the Sorbonne, has given the name 'catastrophe theory' (Zeeman, 1976). It provides a visual model of the effects of a small number of control factors acting in a field or potential. Thom identifies seven elementary catastrophes as the only possible results when not more than four control factors are present.

Cusp Catastrophe

A catastrophe model of the interaction of creative and conventional engineering is shown in Figure 15.1. The model is graphical in form and can be regarded as a curved surface with a pleat forming a cusp where the two fold lines meet − hence its name. The vertical axis is the potential, in this case the best possible solution to the design problem. The two horizontal axes are the control factors. Control factor 1 is creativity or invention and control factor 2 is logical rigour or conventional reasoning. All points on the top surface are stable and all points on the underside of the sheet are unstable or inaccessible. Points on the two fold lines are semi-stable.

Path a–b represents the approach to a problem via a conventional, logical, pattern of thought without attempting to introduce new and untested ideas. Conversely, path a–g indicates unconstrained, even random, thoughts about the problem, unhindered by considerations of feasibility. The first approach may produce an acceptable answer to the problem. If it does it will be a conventional engineering solution based on established practice. If it fails to do so the graph indicates a return down the slope to the lower or 'failure' surface.

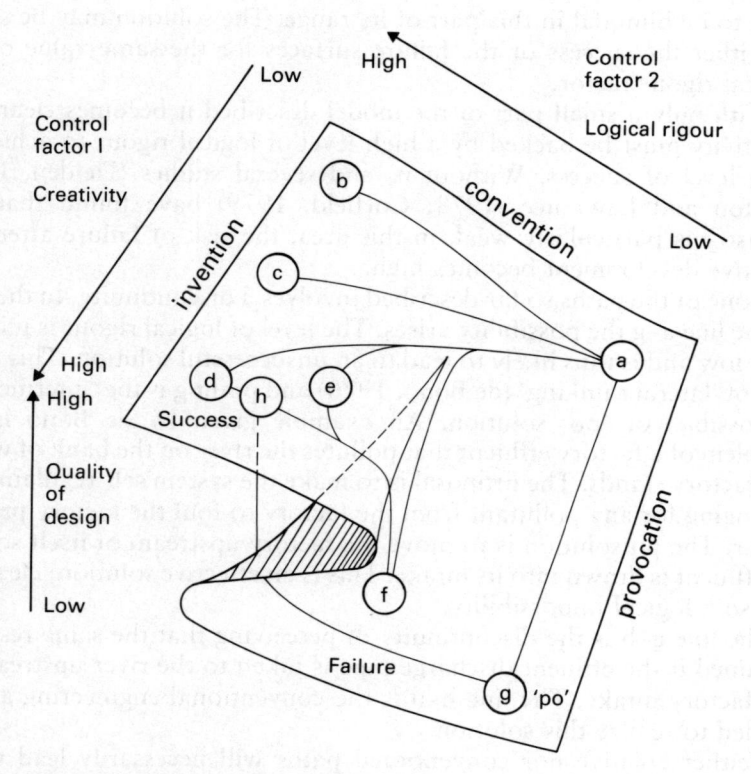

Figure 15.1 The cusp catastrophe

Path a–c is the path of a conventional engineering approach with a small creative content, probably giving a better solution than the strictly logical one from a theoretical point of view, but creating the possibility of a new set of problems, possibly in manufacturing. The personnel responsible for manufacturing will have no previous experience of the new problems: the problems of the previous product would be well known.

Path a–d is the case of a higher creative content, together with a high level of logical rigour, approaching an optimal solution.

Line a–f is the case of the failure of an approach with a high level of creativity but too low a level of logical rigour. It is seen that a very small change in logical rigour at this point in its range, perhaps a slight deficiency of knowledge in a subject, can have a disproportionate effect on the outcome. The alternative path a–d, by just reaching the higher side of the cusp, leads to a high level of success. The logic factor can be seen to be bimodal in this part of its range. The solution may be stable on either the success or the failure surfaces for the same value of the logical rigour factor.

With only a small part of the model described it becomes clear that creativity must be backed by a high level of logical rigour to achieve a high level of success. Without it, and several studies (Fielden, 1967; Hutton and Lawrence, 1978; Corfield, 1979) have found that UK industry is particularly weak in this area, the risk of failure attending creative development becomes high.

None of the paths so far described involves a discontinuity. In the case of the line a–g the possibility arises. The level of logical rigour is initially very low and is thus likely to lead to an unsuccessful solution. This is the line of 'lateral thinking' (de Bono, 1970) and point g is the 'intermediate impossible' or 'po' solution. An example given by de Bono is the problem of a factory effluent that pollutes the river on the bank of which the factory stands. The proposal is to make the system self-regulating by arranging for any pollutant from the factory to foul the factory process water. The po solution is to move the factory upstream of itself so that its effluent is drawn into its intake. This is an effective solution; clearly it is also a logical impossibility.

The line g–h is the discontinuity of perceiving that the same result is obtained if the effluent discharge pipe is taken to the river upstream of the factory intake. The line h–d is the conventional engineering action needed to realize this solution.

Neither creative nor conventional paths will necessarily lead to an acceptable solution in every case. If there were no possibility of obtaining the pipework needed for the above solution, the line h–f indicates the catastrophic failure in the general meaning of the word as well as that of Thom. It becomes an example of a phenomenon familiar to R&D workers: T. H. Huxley's 'Great tragedy of science – the slaying of a beautiful hypothesis by an ugly fact.' The logical path intended to be a–d may also fail to generate a solution and become distorted into the path a–e–f, returning to the failure level of the catastrophe surface.

The model represents most of de Bono's ideas on lateral thinking. Creativity can be seen to be complementary, rather than opposed, to conventional engineering, which must be present at an adequate level to permit a high quality solution. Success can be approached by either path or a mixture of both. After the event it may be difficult to say which path led to success; it will always be possible, with hindsight, to rationalize to a purely logical path to the solution. The provocative function of po is manifest in that the initial association of the path a–g is with failure, but it increases the possibility of the catastrophic leap to the success level along the line g–h.

Butterfly Catastrophe

The cusp catastrophe, in which the stable states are success and failure, has two control factors and three dimensions. It can be represented by a two-dimensional drawing as in Figure 15.1. In practice, of course, many cases fall between complete success and complete failure. These are compromise solutions from a technological viewpoint. They are acceptable rather than optimal.

Two further factors result in a five-dimensional model which cannot be represented by a two-dimensional drawing. Over part of its range, however, the butterfly graph develops a pocket providing a stable intermediate surface in the shape of a butterfly. If control factors 1 and 2 are held constant the three-dimensional shape then developed in that part of their range can be drawn as in Figure 15.2. The additional control factors are ability and constraint.

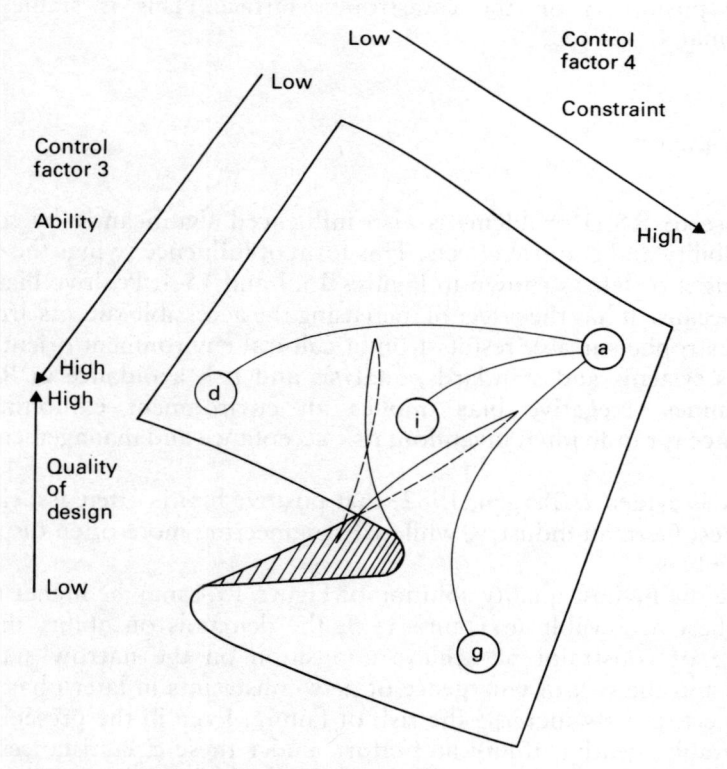

Figure 15.2 The butterfly catastrophe

The butterfly catastrophe contains the cusp catastrophe and for some values of constraint is qualitatively identical. At high levels of constraint the compromise pocket forms and as the level increases the pocket spreads. At the highest levels of constraint the pocket can eventually swallow up the point d, precluding the possibility of a higher quality solution. Again the model is descriptive of an intuitively expected result. The factors that determine the size of the compromise pocket are the relative strengths of ability and constraint, or feasibility.

High ability and low constraint will lead to a high quality solution. If the constraint is high and ability modest the path will tend toward the compromise pocket at i. A typical constraint in industry is that of time. An engineer may be well versed in the technique of value engineering; it includes methods of generating the creative discontinuity. He may be eager to make use of them. Often, however, he is under such pressure to complete the project by a given date that he accepts the first feasible solution he arrives at instead of working systematically towards the optimum. Even when possessed of high ability he is often forced to settle for the position i on the catastrophe surface. This is stable but suboptimal.

Bias Factors

Response to R&D problems is also influenced significantly by social acceptability and cultural effects. This form of influence swings the cusp to the right or left as shown in Figures 15.3 and 15.4. Positive bias, so called because it has the effect of increasing the accessible success area of the catastrophe surface, results from a cultural environment orientated towards systems and standards, analysis and risk avoidance in R&D programmes. Negative bias implies an environment exhibiting a preference for individual invention, risk acceptance and management by crisis.

There is evidence (Bergen, 1982) that positive bias is often associated with West German industry, while UK engineering more often displays negative bias.

While the highest quality solution of Figure 15.4 may be higher than the highest achievable in Figure 15.3, the demands on ability in the presence of constraint to achieve a position on the narrow success surface and the risk of emergence of new constraints in later phases of the project, greatly increase the risk of failure. Even in the presence of considerable creative ability and effort, under these circumstances the compromise solution may be the most economic answer.

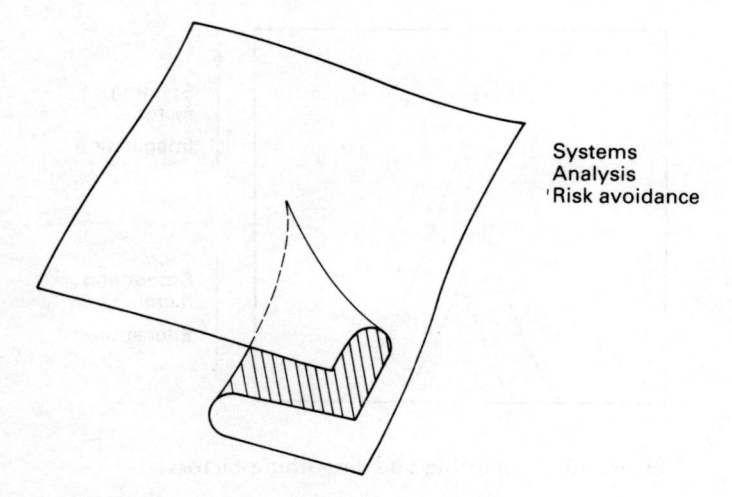

Figure 15.3 Positive cultural bias

Systems
Analysis
Risk avoidance

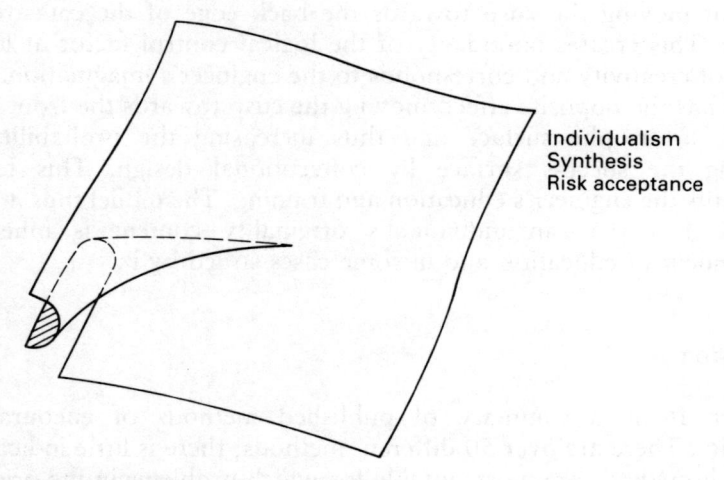

Figure 15.4 Negative cultural bias

Individualism
Synthesis
Risk acceptance

Smoothing and Splitting Factors

The fourth control factor in the five-dimensional butterfly catastrophe is shown in Figure 15.5. To simplify the figure, its effect is shown on a projection of the cusp onto a horizontal plane. It is the resultant of two effects, the splitting factor and the smoothing factor. The first has the

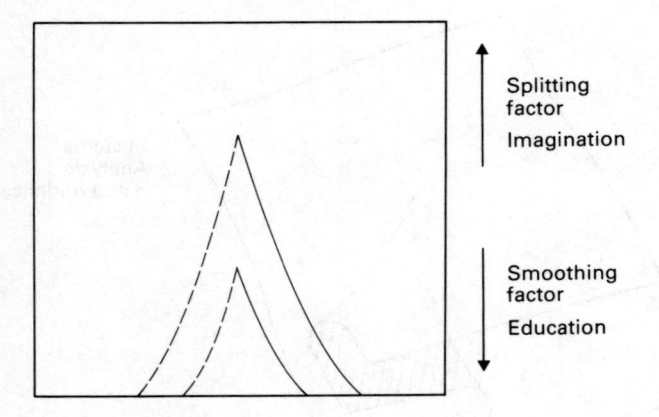

Figure 15.5 Splitting and smoothing factors

effect of moving the cusp towards the back edge of the catastrophe surface. This creates bimodality of the logical control factor at lower values of creativity and corresponds to the engineer's imagination. The second has the opposite effect, moving the cusp towards the front edge of the catastrophe surface and thus increasing the probability of reaching the success surface by conventional design. This factor represents the engineer's education and training. The model thus allows for the fact that an individual's originality content is inherent, independent of education and in some cases stifled by it.

Discussion

Chapter 16 is a summary of published methods of encouraging creativity. There are over 50 different methods; there is little indication of which methods are most suitable for which problems in the original papers.

Thom's main claim for his basic theory is that it provides a language enabling qualitative description of a system of moderate complexity embracing discontinuities. R&D is such a system and is capable of being described to a useful extent in catastrophe terms. The model permits comparison and discussion of techniques of approach to new product development in terms of five variables. Those chosen here reflect the environment and working conditions of the R&D engineer. The variables are:

(1) Creativity
(2) Logical rigour
(3) Feasibility (ability vs constraint)
(4) Cultural bias
(5) Personal attributes (imagination vs education)

Because the presentation is diagrammatic, needing no specialist knowledge to construct or discuss, it encourages discussion between workers of different disciplines and backgrounds who are collaborating on a project.

Review

This chapter has:
(1) Discussed the importance of discontinuity in the history of creativity.
(2) Introduced a form of catastrophe theory.
(3) Described the place of the butterfly catastrophe in R&D.
(4) Shown how the butterfly model permits discussion of
    (a) Creativity
    (b) Logical rigour
    (c) Feasibility
    (d) Cultural bias
    (e) Personal attributes

References

Bergen, S. 1982: Catastrophe Theory Model of the Engineering Design Process, *IEE Proc. Pt A* **131**, March.
de Bono, E. 1970: *Lateral Thinking*. Ward Lock Educational.
Child, D. and Kaiser, F. 1975: Culture Free Thesis. University of Aston Working Paper 39.
Corfield, K. 1979: *Product Design*. NEDO, London.
Fielden, K. 1967: *Engineering Design*. Department of Scientific and Industrial Design.
Galbraith, J. 1976: *New Industrial Estate*. Hamish Hamilton.
Hutton, S. P. and Lawrence, P. A. 1978: Production Managers in UK and Germany. University of Southampton report.
Zeeman, E. 1976: Catastrophe Theory. *Scientific American*, April.

Further Reading

Bergen, S. A. 1984: Catastrophe model of design process, *IEE Proc.*, May.
Zeeman, E. C. 1976: Catastrophe Theory, *Scientific American*, April.
Zeeman, E. C. 1977: *Catastrophe Theory Selected Papers 1972–1977.* Addison-Wesley.

16 Idea Generation

It was pointed out by Crawford and Hendrix of the University of Michigan in 1977 that, although the demand for new products had increased steadily as marketing became more important, little of use was known about successful idea generation that led to successful new products. The situation has not changed much in the last ten years.

The published works on the subject concerned themselves mainly with personal recommendations on 'how to do it' but no theory had been developed and no meaningful evaluation methods had been published. The general atmosphere was one of folklore and speculation.

Crawford and Hendrix made a first step in tackling the problem by setting up a research project to categorize the then published methods. They found that five categories covered the majority of cases, as follows:

(1) Attributes — Any idea which forces consideration of existing products from different points of view, e.g. dimensions, functions, benefits, stimulates productivity.

(2) Generic need assessment — A variation on the above is to look at the product user with a need to fulfil. Comparing the generic class of needs in products now available suggests avenues for development.

(3) Matrix analysis — The attribute analysis listed above forms into a matrix allowing an item by item comparison approach. Non-attribute factors may be introduced. Very simple to very complicated comparisons may be achieved.

(4) Scenario analysis — Both product and its usage are related to the environment; it is useful to forecast the environment and then deduce new product ideas from that. This concept has led to both static and dynamic analysis in several forms.

(5) Group creativity — This is the old idea that two heads are better than one. The categories above plus several created for group use have been tried. Most try to capitalize on the synergism of multiple minds and some try

to break away from logical patterns of thought – see Chapter 15, Creativity in R&D.

Some of the techniques are listed below as they might be applied to the manufacture of bicycles. (Where no reference is given, although the technique is mentioned in various places, no detailed description was found.)

Attributes

Attribute Analysis

Product dimensions, materials, fabrication methods and physical characteristics are listed and studied. Questions such as 'Why this way?' and 'How can it be changed?' are asked. Value analysis is the model. List all parts of a bicycle and then the attributes of each part (Crawford, 1950).

Function Analysis

Function analysis is similar to attribute analysis but uses functions of the product rather than attributes and characteristics. The listing and analysis is carried out in the same manner. A bicycle moves, holds, restrains, stops etc. (Lantis, 1970).

Benefit Analysis

All benefits associated with the product, both direct and indirect, are listed. Some overlap with functions but new aspects will emerge. A bicycle provides transportation, recreation, exercise, savings etc.

Attribute Extension

Attribute extension is applied to products which have changed over time. The past is plotted and the trend is extrapolated; the implications readily appear. The increasing number of gears, and the reduction in the size of tyres and seat are examples (Quinn, 1967).

Pseudo Product Test

The existing product is dis-branded and given to a group of users as a new product to be tested. Users are asked to list and describe (not evaluate) all attributes in detail (King, 1973a).

Idea Generation

Systems Analysis

The inputs and outputs of the physical system that involves the product area are listed and studied. Means of improving the efficiency of the system by developing new product ideas are sought. For example, viewing the bicycle as an energy transfer system suggests a search for a means of energy storage when coasting downhill to assist with ascent of the next hill (Bujake, 1969).

Repertory Grid

Users are shown three brands of the same type of product. They are asked to state in what way two are similar and the third is different. This approach will initially identify obvious differences such as absence of a cross-bar, number of gears etc., but eventually more subtle attributes will emerge (King, 1973b).

Generic Need Assessment

A list is made of user needs fulfilled or not fulfilled by a generic class of products. The unfulfilled needs suggest developments.

Composite Listing

All basic needs in the general product category are listed. These are rephrased in different ways, compared, contrasted etc. (Holt, 1976).

Problem Inventory

Attention is focused on currently un-met needs from the above list. Different product thinking may be triggered. It may be found that users have little identification with 'bicycles', creating a new starting point (King, 1973a).

Multi-dimensional scaling permits mapping of attributes of the product area constituting value to user, and positions of products are plotted in this space. Gaps are revealed representing opportunities for new products. The value points might turn out to be weight, durability and price, suggesting the need for a Volkswagen of bicycles (King, 1973a).

Differing Needs Assessment

Survey

Typical users in the product group are asked to identify their own needs and wants. A small sample may be adequate. This technique can be carried out by personal interview, by written questionnaire or by telephone. Caution! If the development will take over a year, most users cannot estimate what their needs will be.

Observation

Users are observed in their normal surroundings and in research facilities, buying and using the product type. This is most useful in identifying needs or wants that the customer is unwilling or unable to disclose. (This is a well-publicized concept but its application to new idea generation is not covered in the literature.)

Focus Group

A relatively small group of actual or potential users is assembled and, guided by an experienced leader, explores relevant topics. Six or eight cyclists meet with a leader. He starts discussions on 'Why did you buy the bike you have?', 'How often do you ride?' and 'Why don't you ride more?' (Conference Board, 1972).

Role Playing

The purchase of some products may involve emotions and interpersonal relationships which purchasers are unwilling to disclose. Idea seekers assume the role of the customer in an attempt to learn the nature of these (Stein, 1974).

Periodic Attitude Audit

Some product developers wish to include a temporal aspect. A regular audit allows small changes, which might otherwise be missed, to be collected. Users might be surveyed at different times of the year to observe purchase behaviour. The repetition adds to the usefulness of the data.

Matrix Analysis

Two-Dimensional Matrix

Every product or product utility situation is characterized by a number of key variables. These are features, product functions, benefits, processes in use etc. The variables are taken two at a time and their elements are listed along the axes of a two-dimensional matrix. The resulting cells are examined for leads. A matrix might be constructed for a bicycle using occupation of user and number of gears as axes. Each of the elements of the variables are then listed. A cell joining central city delivery to gears may be found. This might suggest a special bicycle for cities with many hills.

Multi-Dimensional Analysis

Matrix analysis can be extended by considering combinations of elements of three or more variables at a time. With a computer to handle the combinations, perspectives which a product designer would never have considered are suggested. A four-dimensional matrix whose axes are features, material, user and colour might yield a cell 'black rubber handlebars for older users'.

Morphological Research

Morphological research is an extreme form of matrix analysis. The combination of all elements of all variables is considered simultaneously. Such a large number of elements renders computer handling essential.

Scenario Analysis

A future environment is estimated and implications for the product category are studied.

Big Dream

The scenario may be approached by asking the following questions: 'What do we most want to happen?' 'If it came about, what would the conditions be like?' As an example suppose that all urban areas will be closed to motor traffic. What will the consequences be for cyclists? (Manufacturing Group, 1959).

214   Idea Generation

Seed Trends

Identify trends so important that they determine other trends and project them into the future. They may be synthesized into a picture relevant to the product studied. For bicycles such trends might be longer life span and increasing homogeneity of the world population (Marketing Insights, 1969).

Trend People

Some individuals have more influence than others in evolving or reflecting trends. They have also proved useful in generating scenarios. Identifying these individuals and the implications of their thoughts and behaviour are critical to this technique. The US President or an Olympic Champion might be a starting point.

Trend Areas

Just as some individuals repay study, some areas are more important than others for some subjects. The trend itself is not as important as the impact of the trend on other developments which may be useful in scenario analysis (see 'Big Dream').

New Products

Certain new products, such as televisions and motor-cars, have altered life-styles and institutions. Products which suggest future life-styles are CB radio, personal computers etc.

Newspaper

All events in a Sunday newspaper which could have far reaching effects are noted. All events are included, even if seemingly unrelated to the product being studied. Urban development, retirement, ageing of politicians might prompt some bicycle-relevant perception of the future.

Relevance Trees

A desired state is defined. It is placed at the base of a 'tree'. What must happen if the state is to be reached? A number of branches must be added to the tree to reach the state. Identify branches not currently feasible as starting points for new developments. This method formalizes 'Big Dream'. The disappearance of the corner shop and the growth of supermarkets outside towns suggest the need for a bicycle capable of carrying bags of groceries.

Group Techniques

Brainstorming

Brainstorming is the most discussed of idea-generating techniques. About six to eight people are assembled with an experienced leader and assigned a specific well-defined problem. The session is conducted in accordance with a set of rules designed to maximize productivity. These include deferring judgement of other people's ideas at the first stage. The initial ideas can be as far fetched as desired. No new idea must be lost initially; no bad idea must get through to the final stage (Osborn, 1963; Stein, 1974).

Phillips 66 Groups

A group of people are split into subgroups of six. Each subgroup brainstorms on the problem for six minutes. The main group is reassembled, divided into random groups of six again and the brainstorming is repeated.

Synectics

Synectics is an advanced form of brainstorming in which a trained leader chairs a carefully chosen group of participants over several months in elaborate surroundings. Any methods of creativity are used, synergism is critical and the brainstorming rules are adhered to (Gordon, 1961; Stein, 1974).

Think Tank

A group of highly skilled scientists are permanently withdrawn from diverse disciplines. They concentrate on a key product or a technological breakthrough. Pleasant surroundings and synergism are important. Bell Laboratories used this method in developing the transistor (Barrett, 1971).

Delphi

Delphi is unique in that members are not physically together. About fifteen leading authorities are sent a postal questionnaire asking specific

216   Idea Generation

questions. When the replies are received they are integrated and sent back to the members. The members are asked whether their views have changed now that they have seen the integrated replies to the questionnaire. The replies to this question are again integrated and recirculated. With fifteen members the answers tend to converge after a few rounds; with a smaller number convergence is not so certain. The method is useful in describing complex scenarios and new systems.

Inverse Brainstorming

Inverse brainstorming is the brainstorming approach but instead of being asked how a product can be improved the team is asked what is wrong with it or how it might fail (Haefele, 1962).

And-Also Technique

There are two participants, one of whom suggests an idea and the other adds to it, saying 'It is a good idea, and also can be improved by . . .'. The initiator then adds to the improved idea and the cycle proceeds. The technique can be used with two teams rather than individuals.

Trigger Words

Each member of the team prepares a list of trigger words, each relevant to the problem under discussion. The lists are read out, discussed and consolidated. If the problem were to design a faster bicycle the lists might contain words such as wheels, gears, momentum, safety, etc. (Stein, 1974).

Miscellaneous Techniques

Check Lists

A series of words, phrases or questions to act as stimuli to new idea creation are made into a list. They are read through item by item, and new ideas are recorded as they occur (Osborn and Small, 1959; Stein, 1974).

Creative Stimuli

Three steps are involved: (1) choose the idea subject; (2) specify the tangible goal; (3) consider a series of controlled, semi-abstract, symbolic, artificial stimuli one at a time. The stimuli, developed by Donald Cantin, are designed to prompt possible solutions (Cantin, 1972).

Systems or Weak Link

Products are often part of a system incorporating human being(s). Examine each system as a separate entity, searching for weak links. An improved product might benefit the system (Quinn, 1967).

International Plagiarism

Look around the world, particularly in remote areas, for products that have not yet appeared in your own market. Some idea of market conditions will be available and acceptability in your market can be deduced (King, 1973a).

Achilles Heel

Identify weaknesses in the current product that are serious enough to offer the competition an opportunity to cut the market share by (say) half.

Analogue

Two analogue situations can yield new ideas if aspects which are not held in common are studied. A kitchen table manufacturer studied machine feeding as an analogue to home feeding. The analogue is a major one deliberately sought as distinct from unexpected or hidden analogues (Gordon, 1961; Stein, 1974).

Induced Dissociation

Stare at the product while keeping the mind as blank as possible. The theory holds that the effort of denying actual sight will force the mind to substitute new images, a new way of looking at the product (Whiting, 1958).

In the same year, 1977, Souder and Zeigler then of the University of Pittsburgh published a similar paper with rather more detail on the techniques. They point out that, to achieve the best results, the techniques must be combined with organizational and administrative methods suitable for dealing with embryonic ideas. The reader is invited to re-read Chapter 10 and the section on Matrix Organization. They also state that there are no formulae for obtaining the right amounts of creativity under various conditions and circumstances. Chapter 15 on the catastrophe theory of creativity may be of some help here. Some of the descriptions of techniques are given below.

Brainstorming

The object is to generate, in a classroom setting, the greatest number of alternative ideas from uninhibited responses. Nothing is rejected or criticized. Any attempt to analyse, reject or evaluate ideas is prohibited during the brainstorming session. All ideas are written down for subsequent evaluation and development. Quantity, not quality, of ideas is the target and the technique appears to be most effective when employed by a group rather than an individual.

Problems that have only one correct solution or only a few possible alternatives do not lend themselves well to this technique. The following reasons are given (von Fange, 1959) for the effectiveness of group brainstorming: no-one stops to evaluate ideas presented; because of this no-one feels restricted or inhibited. Competition is evolved by the method; praise and encouragement stimulate achievement; idea generation takes place on the basis of what has gone before.

Some rather negative personalities may feel repressed despite having contributions to make. To deal with this problem cycled individual and group sessions have been developed and there is evidence that this technique is superior to either individual or group one-off settings in some cases.

Synectics

This technique was developed by Gordon (1961) and others. Creative solutions to a specific problem are sought through a two-stage process. In the first stage the order of ideas is reversed and 'makes the strange familiar' through analysis, generalization and model seeking. In the second stage an attempt is made to 'make the familiar strange' through personal, direct symbolic and fantasy analogies.

Participants stimulate each other with their offbeat approaches. There is intermittent involvement and detachment in dealing with the analogies. The final stage is a forced fit of the analogies to the original problem.

Gordon Method

The Gordon method is a technique for generating new viewpoints on which to hook ideas. It is used with a small group not initially made aware of the exact nature of the actual problem. The intent is to minimize preconceived ideas and preset patterns of thought in order to avoid that premature decisions are reached before there has been a full discussion of the general problem.

The discussion leader, who is the only one aware of the actual problem, gets the group to think aloud about a related subject. He then moves the subject nearer to the actual one and, eventually, on aspects very close to it. Finally the real problem is revealed to the group and the tape recordings of their discussions are analysed for possible idea hooks. Each idea hook is then brainstormed (or some other method is used) to develop a solution to the actual problem.

It is an advantage to have in the group some individuals whose skills are relevant to implementing the solution. An obvious limitation of the method is that all the creative thinking may be done by the leader; the choice of the leader is therefore important. He must be able to recognize a possibility when it arises.

Input–Output Technique

The input–output technique corresponds to the systems technique mentioned above. General Electric originated the method in 1953. It defines the problem in terms of system inputs, system outputs and limiting requirements. Then ways to bridge the gap between inputs and outputs are sought. A number of solutions for evaluation, test and development are found.

As an example, consider the problem of designing a device to shade a room automatically during bright sunlight. The input might be solar energy (heat and light). The output could be making the windows alternately opaque and transparent. The specifications could be the following: must be usable on various sizes of windows; must not admit more than 20ft-candles of illumination anywhere in the room; must not cost more than $100 per 40 square feet of window.

The input–output analysis would proceed as follows.

(1) What phenomena respond to the application of heat? Light?
(2) Can any of these phenomena be used directly to shade the window?
(3) What phenomena respond to step (1) outputs?
(4) Can any of these phenomena be used directly to shade the window?

(5) What phenomena respond to step (3) output? Would use of the phenomena be economical?

The technique concentrates on the job to be done. Thus it is best suited for discovering new or alternative ways to accomplish some desired end.

Morphological Analysis

Morphological analysis is a comprehensive way to list and examine all the possible combinations that might be useful in solving a given problem. These combinations may then be tested, verified, modified and developed. An example is presented in Table 16.1.

The problem was to develop a low cost, fully portable, high speed, 1000 line colour TV receiver. The four circuits (tuner, picture, sound and colour) could be achieved in three ways using all tubes, all integrated circuits (ICs) all large-scale integration (LSI). When this problem arose, however, it was felt that IC tuner and sound devices would not be ready for two years and that LSI tuner, picture and colour devices would not be ready for five years. As the analysis in the table shows, a compromise product had to be specified until these devices were available. The manufacturer entered the market with a sub-optimal product to be updated or replaced later.

It is noted that the method is that used in forecasting, to identify emerging technologies and to forecast technical needs.

Table 16.1 Morphological analysis

Function	Valve types	Time estimate	
		ICs	LSI
Tuner	Pentodes	2 years	5 years
Picture	Pentodes	Now	5 years
Sound	Pentodes	2 years	Now
Colour	Triodes	Now	2 years
Analyses			
Lowest cost	pentode tuner+IC picture+pentode sound+triode colour		
Lowest weight	All LSI (5 years future)		
Best validity	All LSI (5 years future)		
Compromise	pentode tuner+IC picture+LSI sound+IC colour		

Sequence–Attribute Modifications Matrix

The sequence–attribute modifications matrix (SAMM) approach is applicable to sequential situations where step by step activities can be listed logically, described briefly and explored for possible creative modifications. The illustration in Table 16.2 is of an actual hot steel slab rolling operation. The operating sequence listed on the left-hand side of the matrix is examined for possible modifications. The analyst has identified with an X several priority areas to look into. He has noted that the positioning and passing sequences can probably be combined and rearranged.

The method does not indicate how this is to be done; it simply identifies the areas. Other operational techniques can then be used to evaluate further. The method appears to be more effective in group work than in individual settings.

Kepner–Tregoe Method

The Kepner–Tregoe technique is suitable for defining the problem and then deciding what to do about it. A systematic outline describing the problem is made, together with a description of what lies outside the problem and what is closely related to it. An example is shown in Table 16.3. This outline reveals the possible causes of the problem and aids decision making. The technique is aimed at creative problem solving rather than at generating far-out ideas.

Table 16.2 SAMM technique

Sequence/attribute description	Item no.	A	B	C	D	E	F	G	H	I
Heat steel slag to pliable state	1								×	
Transfer from furnace	2									
Position rolls	3			×	×					
Pass slab through rolls (elongate)	4			×	×					
Check slag guage	5					×				
Shear slab to size	6	×								
Transfer sheared product	7								×	

A, eliminate; B, substitute; C, rearrange; D, combine; E, reverse; F, enlarge; G, reduce; H, modify; I separate.

222 Idea Generation

Table 16.3 Kepner–Tregoe method

WHAT	IS	IS NOT
Deviation	Carbon deposit	Blackening
Object	Filament from machine A	Other filaments
WHERE		
On object	On surface	In filament materials
Observed	On machine A	On other filaments
WHEN		
On object	After filament is formed	Before filament is formed
Observed	In trough at 3.50 p.m.	Before 3.50 p.m.
EXTENT		
How much	Heavy	Slight
How many	All machine A filaments	Machine B filaments

Managing Group Creativity

It seems to be true that some people are creative and some are not, and that this has no relation with level of education. Thus if a few creative people form a team to operate the appropriate technique the probability is that something will be achieved, and it will be more than any individual in the team would achieve alone. However, a team of non-creative people will achieve mainly frustration.

It should not be thought that any of the preceding techniques will reduce the work involved in creativity. It is always hard work. What the appropriate methods will do is to produce more and better ideas from the same starting data.

The training of scientists and engineers encourages them to follow logical patterns of thought and to dismiss ideas that appear irrational or far fetched. But it is this type of 'lateral thinking' that many of the techniques rely on for success. Scientists and engineers are thus often their own worst enemies in group working. It is not unusual for groups not to come to grips with the real problem. They spend much time on discussing the problem definition and criticizing ideas which are offered. Individuals leave the sessions feeling that they could have done better on their own and in some cases they would be correct. Yet there is evidence that group settings can provide essential stimuli to creativity.

Two members of a group are important for success. The group leader must be experienced in this type of work. He formulates the meeting and sets its tone. He provides corrective feedback if the group becomes too confrontational or too passive. The second is the problem 'owner'. He supplies knowledge of the application and existing technology and provides criteria for judging the 'goodness' of the ideas generated.

Review

In this chapter:
(1) Crawford and Hendrix (University of Michigan) classified the published methods of generating new products in five categories.
(2) Souder and Zeigler (University of Pittsburg) published a similar paper with rather more detail on the techniques involved.
(3) The problem of management of creative groups is discussed.

References

Barrett, F. 1971: Think Tanks, *Business Quarterly*, Summer.
Bujake, J. 1969: Programmed Innovation, *Res. Man.*, July.
Cantin, D. 1972: *Turn Your Ideas Into Money*. Hawthorne Books.
Conference Board, New York, 1972: Generating New Product Ideas.
Crawford, R. 1950: *How to Get Ideas*. University Associates.
Crawford, C. M. and Hendrix, E. P. 1977: Generating Ideas for New Products. Working Paper 154, University of Michigan.
von Fange, E. 1959: *Professional Creativity*. Prentice-Hall.
Gordon, W. 1961: *Synectics*. Harper and Row.
Haefele, J. 1962: *Creativity and Innovation*. Reinhold.
Holt, K. 1976: Need Assessment, *Res. Man.*, July.
King, S. 1973a: *Developing New Brands*. Halstead Press, Wiley.
King, S. 1973b: In Wills, G.: *Creating New Products*. Crosby, Lockwood Staples.
Lantis, T. 1970: How to Generate New Product Ideas, *J. Advertising Research*, 10 June.
Manufacturing Group 1959: *Individual Creativity and the Corporation*. Institute of Contemporary Art.
Marketing Insights 3 March 1969.
Osborn, A. 1963: *Applied Imagination*. Scribner.
Quinn, J. 1967: Technological Forecasting, *Harvard Business Rev.*, March–April.
Simberg, A. L. *Creativity at Work*. Farnsworth Publishing.
Souder, E. W. and Zeigler, W. Z. 1977: A Review of Creativity, *Res. Man.* no. 4, July.
Stein, M. 1974: *Stimulating Creativity*. Academic Press.
Whiting, C. 1958 *Creative Thinking*. Reinhold.

Further Reading

Crawford, C. M. 1987: *New Products Management*. Irwin.

17 Synthetic Case Study

The Pyro Instrument Company Limited

John Maxwell, Managing Director of the Pyro Instrument Co. Ltd, opened the meeting to which he had called his colleagues on the Board of Management.

'We are here today to discuss the progress of the second round of corporate planning for the next five-year period. The planning contributions and forecasts from your departments have been brought together by myself, Peter and Richard and the picture is none too good. We have more or less maintained our profit on an even keel for the last several years, but if we wish to maintain this level over the next five year period we have to find additional contributions rising to the level of £50 000 in two years' time.'

Maxwell's company was founded by his father and, in forty years of trading, had established a sound reputation for electrical temperature measuring devices for laboratory and industrial use. Some ten models of indicators, recorders and simple controllers based on thermocouples covering the range $-100\,°C$ to $+1200\,°C$, commanded about 60 per cent of the market for these devices in the plastic extrusion and moulding, dyeing, air conditioning, laboratory and industrial furnaces and boiler house equipment fields. The average life of these products in the market has been 5 or 6 years in recent times.

In the current year the company seemed likely to meet its turnover forecast at £6m, £1m due to merchandised equipment. The total strength of the company was slightly below 300, of which some 20 reported to Robert Tinker, the R&D Manager and a member of the board. Peter Booker, the Financial Controller, took up the story.

'Although our volume of production has fallen slightly in the last year, the price increases applied by marketing have maintained the turnover. Our problem is that the gross margin has shrunk, due largely to increases in general overheads and material costs. This must be a very general situation with our competitors and, in my view, we should increase selling prices to restore the gross margin to its previous level.'

'You may be right' rejoined the MD, 'but I would prefer to consider cost reduction possibilities before increasing prices. I suggest that we should do a Pareto analysis of the income from our products and carry out a value analysis exercise on those products which are shown to justify it. What order of cost reduction' – this to Richard Sellers – 'would be required to achieve the target profit increase?'

Richard did a few quick calculations and then said 'I make it about 16–17 per cent, and that seems to me to be a tall order. If we can achieve this order of reduction why have we not done it before now? I think what we need is a new and profitable product which will not compete with our existing range, and I think I have found one. We have never produced a radiation pyrometer. The market is about 10 per cent of the total industrial temperature measurement market and 80 per cent of the sales go to Tempo Ltd, with five or six smaller companies fighting for the remainder. Tempo have been in almost a monopoly situation for 10 years, something customers do not like, and are, in my view, vulnerable. The Physics Department of the University of Ardwick have come up with a new approach to dealing with the problem of changing emissivity which will give a performance advantage over the Tempo product. Robert and I saw it last week.'

Tinker nodded. 'Yes, it is technically interesting. The amount of radiation reaching the detector of a radiation pyrometer depends on the temperature of the radiating body and the nature of its surface compared with lamp black. This ratio is called the "emissivity" of the surface and can vary from 0.02 up to 1. Up to a temperature of 400 °C, and that covers 80 per cent of the total temperature measuring market, the improvement in accuracy is significant. I have only seen an experimental model so far, but the piece parts involved are similar to those that Hamish produces now and I guess it could be made for £120, which would make it our highest priced product. I can certainly say that the physics is sound and the performance improvement is real. Personally, I would prefer a less radical approach on a broader basis. Our current range of products has been designed piecemeal over the years and I believe we could realize significant economies if we were to standardize on a few subassemblies and major components over the whole range. By intelligent design we could use one thermocouple amplifier, one analogue display and one digital display instead of the seven or eight types of each that we have in production at the moment.'

'Would this reduce either the material or labour content of the redesigned products?' asked Sellars, turning to Hamish MacDuff, the Manufacturing Manager. 'Unless it does so I can't see how it helps, since the gross margin, and hence the trading profit, if selling expenses stay as they are, is related to the difference between the ex-works price and the average selling price.'

'No', said the Manufacturing Manager, 'it would reduce the variety but the material and labour costs would not be changed significantly'.

226 Synthetic Case Study

'In that case,' said Peter Booker, 'I agree with Richard.'

Richard continued. 'Another possibility that has struck me concerns our "Make or Buy" policy. Our merchandizing activity has increased substantially over the last five years and is showing a useful profit. Many of the items that we manufacture in-house could be obtained from subcontract sources which do not have our high overheads. Why don't we take advantage of this situation to reduce our material and labour costs? Would you consider that, Hamish?'

The Manufacturing Manager did not look too pleased. 'I don't like the idea of moving work out of the factory. It would be much more difficult to control technically. It could be done, but I would rather attempt to reduce our machine shop costs by investing in a new N/C sheet metal machine for producing our instrument cases. I believe we could halve the time for case manufacture over the whole range of our products for an investment of £60 000, which is about half the cost of developing a new product. We could have it installed in 3 months; a new product takes 2 years to get on to the market.'

'A good point' said Maxwell. 'Thank you all for your suggestions. We obviously can't implement all of them at once, even if I agreed with all your reasons, so some further thought is needed. My secretary will arrange another meeting in 10 days' time to give you a chance to evaluate the consequences of implementing these proposals.'

Exhibits in Pyro Instrument Co. Ltd case

The exhibits in this case are shown in Figures 17.1 and 17.2 and Tables 17.1 and 17.2.

Case Discussion

Which of the several options tabled at the meeting, if any, would you support? Maxwell is buying time. When he has to make a decision, what should he do? Before answering these questions you need to give thought to the following:

- Q1 Do the statements of the problem seem rational?
- Q2 Has the past pricing policy been sensible?
- Q3 Do you support the VA program?
- Q4 Would the proposed new product provide the additional profit required?
- Q5 Do you support Tinker's rationalization programme?
- Q6 Would subcontracting reduce costs?
- Q7 How would you evaluate the investment in new production equipment?

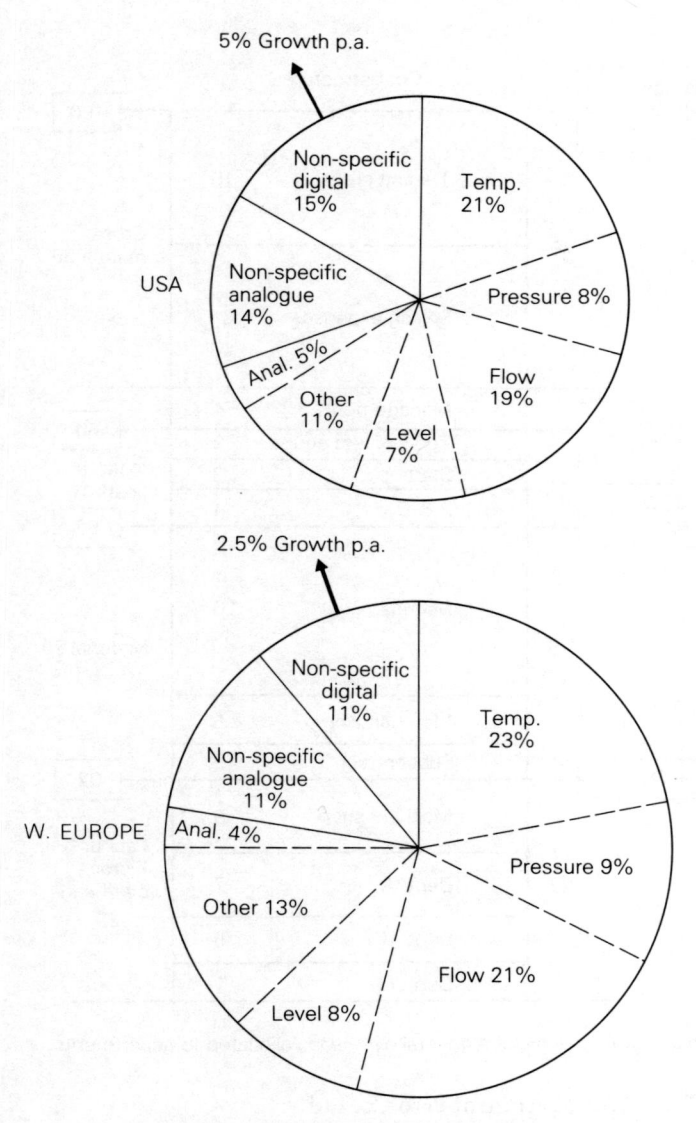

Figure 17.1 Process instrumentation markets

Cost structure

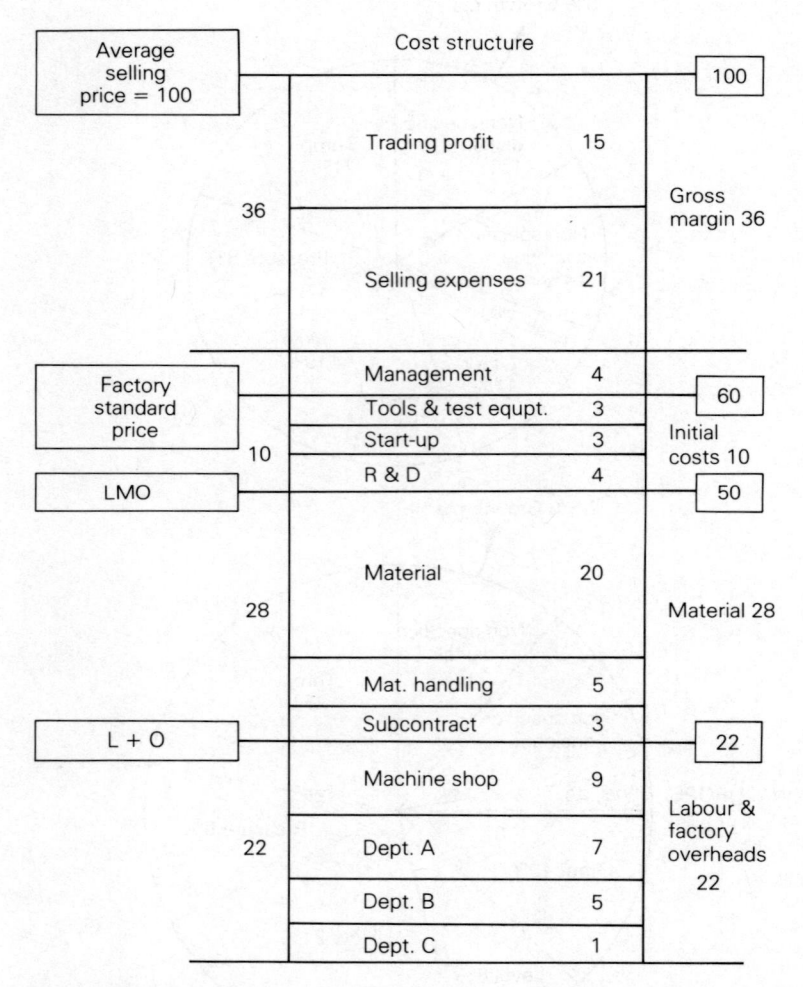

Average selling price = 100			100
	Trading profit	15	Gross margin 36
	36		
	Selling expenses	21	
Factory standard price	Management	4	60
	Tools & test equpt.	3	
	Start-up	3	Initial costs 10
	10		
LMO	R & D	4	50
	Material	20	
	28		Material 28
	Mat. handling	5	
L + O	Subcontract	3	22
	Machine shop	9	Labour & factory overheads 22
	22	Dept. A	7
	Dept. B	5	
	Dept. C	1	

Note: The above figures include general overheads allocated to departments.

Figure 17.2 Cost structure of Pyro Co. Ltd

Table 17.1 Investment in instrumentation (£m)

	UK		WG		France		USA	
	Plant	Instr.	Plant	Instr.	Plant	Instr.	Plant	Instr.
Food	169	3.04	245	4.41	417	7.51	667	12.01
Drinks	87	1.39	178	2.85	235	3.76	176	2.82
Tobacco	16	0.24	22	0.33	20	0.30	35	0.53
Textiles	122	1.95	168	2.69	266	4.26	408	6.53
Paper	72	2.52	137	4.80	131	4.59	563	19.71
Chemicals	391	21.51	760	41.80	851	46.81	1095	60.23
Petroleum and coal products	108	6.16	216	12.31	375	21.38	286	16.30
Rubber and plastics	85	5.44	195	12.48	90	5.76	390	24.96
Ceramics and glass	34	1.02	83	2.49	121	3.63	135	4.05
Iron and steel	241	7.47	531	16.46	483	14.97	648	20.09
Non-ferrous metals	78	2.57	122	4.03	64	2.11	243	8.02
Electricity, gas and water	619	11.14	1357	24.43	716	12.89	4000	72.00
Total	2023	64.5	4014	129.1	3769	128.0	8646	247.3
		3.2%		3.2%		3.4%		2.9%

Table 17.2 UK R&D expenditure

Period	Total industry sales £m	Total R&D £m	R&D as % of sales
	456	17.5	3.8
Last	521	20.2	3.9
six	566	21.5	3.8
years	548	20.8	3.8
	632	24.0	3.8
	738	28.0	3.8

Appendix 17.1 The Pyro Instrument Co. Ltd Case

When inspecting business plans or accounts top management is expert at detecting inconsistencies. They may know little about the product but will certainly, particularly in the case of parent company management looking at figures produced by a subsidiary, spot the anomalies since they have much practice in examining many cases of the same data presented in the same way. Any such weakness is the first thing to identify and remove.

230 Synthetic Case Study

Q1 Are the statements and data in the case self-consistent?

Maxwell says that the additional profit needed is £50k. Sellers says that the cost reduction needed is 16–17 per cent.

From the cost structure

Factory cost = 50% of TO = 2.5m
therefore 16 per cent of factory cost = £400k

current profit = 15% of TO (£6m–£1m) = £750k
but £50k = 7% on profit = 1% on selling price = chicken feed

Sellers figure is £400k which is 53 per cent on profit, and 5 per cent on SP. The figures are not self-consistent and must be analysed further. Maxwell's figure is most unlikely to be right and until further analysis has been done Seller's figure should be used as the more likely.

Q2 Has the pricing policy been sensible?

They should have maintained the gross margin unless the SP was forced down by the market. Since they are market leaders and have therefore a major influence on the market price there would normally be no problem in doing this. The competitors with smaller market shares would be likely to follow suit gladly. Pricing policy has probably not been good. It is often the sales department that are responsible for this if they are judged by sales volume rather than profit.

Q3 Do you support the proposed VA program?

A VA program is an investment in the hope of adding to profit by reducing costs and/or increasing sales. Unless it does the latter it does not increase revenue which is what supports overheads. Is there enough market life and volume to recover the investment? Could VA extend product life? Average revenue per product is only £500k for 5 years. On such low value, calculations of short-term return on investment would be difficult.

Q4 Would the proposed new product provide the extra profit?

At first glance this looks promising. According to Sellers:

Total EEC market = UK   64m
                    WG   129m
                    Fr   128m
              Total   321m for all industrial insts.
Temperature measurement = 23% = 74m
Radiation pyrometers = 10% of 74m = 7.4m

Synthetic Case Study

The additional £400k profit represents 2.7m additional TO, i.e. 36 per cent of the EEC market. As Pyro has 60 per cent of its home market in current products, this is just about possible if the new pyrometer is a potential market leader. Sellers thinks its performance improvement over Tempo justifies this. Do you?

Radiation pyrometers are used when (a) the temperature to be measured is too high for the much cheaper thermocouple, or (b) when contact with the workpiece is not possible.

The accuracy advantage of the new pyrometer, which is real, is only a consideration up to 400 °C. Thermocouples commonly go up to 1400 °C.

The real market for the new pyrometer is therefore only for non-contact applications below 400 °C, much less than 10 per cent. If it is 2 per cent, that is an additional TO of 1.48 m, a generous estimate. The additional profit would be 220k, about half the amount required. Seller's proposal is not viable.

Q5 Do you support Tinker's rationalization programme?

It has some merit. Reduction of variety in the factory reduces stock, handling, purchasing, training and servicing costs, in fact most overheads. But these savings are only realized if the resources now devoted to them — and this includes the people — are disposed of from the company or absorbed by increases in production volume. Could the latter be justified? Pyro has 60 per cent of a static market.

Q6 Would subcontracting production reduce costs?

Only if overheads and people are removed from the company or, as with Q5, if production volume is increased. (See discussion of Q5; see also Chapter 7 The Make or Buy Decision.)

Q7 What factors would you consider in evaluating the investment proposed by MacDuff?

    Percentage cost of case . . . function cost analysis.
    Percentage load on M/C shop affected by case.
    Cost of capital, say 12%, must be earned before benefit begins.
    Availability of capital.
    Running cost of M/C.

    M/C shop cost = 9% of revenue (from cost structure) = 450k.

If total load is cases (gross overestimate) saving is 225k which is not enough. If case load is 25% (possible) saving is only 45k and only then if resources allocated to existing methods are disposed of. Well intentioned, but a non-starter.

Q8 What would you do?

The price uplift required to provide the whole of the additional profit required is 8 per cent. The effect would be immediate and no investment is involved. The real uplift would be less than this by the inflation rate. To increase real profit the uplift must be more than the inflation rate.

As Pyro are market leaders the competition will almost certainly be pleased to follow the increase. There will be resistance from one quarter in all probability. Which one?

18 Project Management Game

TOWER-8 © S. A. Bergen 1984

This is a management game written for the BBC microcomputer. Its objective is to give players simulated exercise in engineering tasks, other than engineering technology, which are vital to profitable engineering projects.

These aspects include terms of contract, design specifications, design, estimating, costing, quotation and planning. The design content, while simulating the inter-relationship with labour and material costs, is simple and visual. Engineering calculations and specialist technical knowledge are not required.

Simulation

One of the problems of analysing project management is that the normal approach to systems analysis, that of making measured changes to parameters, preferably one at a time, then measuring the output of the system and testing for correlations between change and output – sensitivity analysis – is not feasible in real life. Projects take too long to produce this type of data for it to be relevant, even if top management would authorize the necessary changes. With a dynamic model of a system, working on a much compressed time scale, both of these objections are overcome. No company disasters can be caused and several runs with changed parameters can be made in the course of a day.

This is the first use of 'TOWER-8'. Such factors as the ratio between material and labour costs can be set at different levels and the effect on the design of the product and the consequent return on investment can be investigated. Eight parameters can be varied in this way including that of risk, providing hands-on simulation of decision making under uncertainty, a common industrial situation treated quantitatively in Chapter 5.

Competition

Whether concerned with selling R&D services commercially on a contract basis or selecting projects for internal investment, the element of competition is present. In the first case the contract has to be won against rival bids and in the second potential projects are competing with each other for selection. Both have the common themes of design, estimation and quotation and the package, while responding to the contract conditions or specification, must, if it is to succeed, be the most attractive offered. There must also be an adequate profit for the tenderer after taking into account all his costs. Hands-on simulation of these conditions is instructive and occasionally salutary, particularly for those companies whose background has been in 'cost plus' contracts in this field and who are now required to bid on a fixed price basis. Running the program as a competitive game between small syndicates makes a contribution to equipping engineers for their part in these activities.

The Project

The project is for the design and construction of a tower. The elevation of the tower is drawn on the VDU by selecting from a range of building block outlines and positioning them by entering X and Y coordinates. The coordinates define the location of the lower left-hand corner of the block in relation to the lower left-hand corner of the construction space. The space is defined by dotted lines.

The material and labour rates, together with a penalty rate and a risk index, are initial input parameters. The project consists of two phases, the planning phase and the construction phase. The costs incurred in each, both time and materials, are measured, summed and subtracted from the quotation price to give profit and ROI%. If the game is run competitively between small syndicates, the winning syndicate is that which achieves a predetermined ROI% with the lowest quotation price.

The initial parameters are part of the contract conditions:

SIZE 1 COST=
SIZE 2 COST=
SIZE 3 COST=
SIZE 4 COST=
RISK%=
PLANNING RATE=
LABOUR RATE=
PENALTY RATE=

When the last rate is entered the screen is cleared and a project name is requested for identification. The prompt 'PLANNING START' then appears. The 'Y' response starts timing the planning phase.

Planning phase

The contract data sheet is handed to the players enabling them to start design, planning, estimating and aids to planning and/or construction. The work study option, described later, is now prompted. All activities in this phase are timed and charged to the contract at the planning rate. Quotation price and delivery promise are entered as prompted. The question 'PLAN FINISHED?' follows. The 'Y' response stops the clock, displays the planning time and asks 'CONSTRUCTION START?'.

In case of error the planning phase can be restarted, at any time before the 'PLAN FINISHED' signal is entered, by pressing 'ESCAPE'. Costs incurred up to that point are charged to the contract. A 'Y' response to 'CONSTRUCTION START?' initiates the construction phase.

Construction phase

The tower elevation is constructed by selecting and positioning building blocks in response to the prompts:

CO-ORD X=
CO-ORD Y=
SIZE 1,2,3 OR 4?

A building block incorrectly selected or placed cannot be removed. The error is corrected by selecting and placing another block correctly, if necessary overlapping the first attempt. The costs of both blocks are charged to the contract.

At any time in the construction phase the screen can be cleared and the phase restarted. All costs incurred up to that point are charged to the contract.

When the designed elevation has been completed this is indicated by entering 999 instead of the next X coordinate. The display unit, and the printer if selected, will show the commercial results as follows:

TOWER-8
(c) S A Bergen 1984
PROJECT NAME
QUOTATION PRICE=
DELIVERY PROMISE=

PLANNING COST=
ACT DELIVERY=
MATERIAL COST=
RISK INCREASE %=
LABOUR COST=

TOTAL COST=
PENALTY=
PROFIT=
R O I%=
REPEAT? (Y/N)

If the response to the last question is 'Y' the screen is cleared and the planning phase is restarted with the same input parameters. If 'N' the program displays 'END'. Entering 'RUN' restarts the program by prompting new input parameters.

A Planning Aid – Work Study

There can be a factor of ×2 between the times different teams take to enter the same building blocks. Responding 'Y' to the prompt 'WORK STUDY?' produces the prompt 'GO?'. The response 'Y' starts the clock and presents the prompts 'CO-ORD X', 'CO-ORD Y' and 'SIZE?' as in the construction phase. When the size has been entered the clock stops and the prompt 'GO?' returns. The display shows (1) the number of block-laying cycles completed, (2) the aggregate time taken and (3) the mean time per block.

The blocks are not displayed as the purpose of the program is to simulate the action of laying blocks and provide a reliable average time to form a basis for estimating.

The team must decide whether the additional effort, which is charged to the contract at the planning rate, will benefit the overall project results. Responding 'N' to the 'WORK STUDY?' prompt bypasses this program.

A Planning Problem – Estimating under Uncertainty

All estimating in industry is carried out under conditions of some degree of uncertainty. This is simulated in TOWER-8 by applying a risk increase to each block cost as it is used. This takes the form of a random percentage between 1 per cent and the input 'RISK%' index parameter. Estimation of the actual cost can therefore be approached on a normal distribution basis. The estimate can be checked against the actual increase included in the cost of material as the latter is displayed in the commercial results.

These provisions help to reinforce the general message that profit is usually a small difference between two large numbers and that thoroughness in planning and estimating is often the difference between profit and loss.

TOWER-8 Program Listing

```
>LIST
   10 MODE 4
   20 PRINT
   30 PRINT "TOWER-8"
   40 PRINT
   50 PRINT "(c) S A Bergen 1984"
   60 PRINT
   70 PRINT "PRINTER? (Y/N)";
   80 IF GET$="Y" THEN GOTO 90 ELSE GOTO 110
   90 *FX3,0
  100 GOTO 120
  110 *FX3,4
  120 VDU2
  130 PRINT
  140 PRINT
  150 INPUT "SIZE 1 COST= "S1
  160 PRINT
  170 INPUT "SIZE 2 COST= "S2
  180 PRINT
  190 INPUT "SIZE 3 COST= "S3
  200 PRINT
  210 INPUT "SIZE 4 COST= "S4
  220 PRINT
  230 INPUT "RISK%= "RISK
  240 PRINT
  250 INPUT "PLANNING RATE= "PR
  260 PRINT
  270 INPUT "LABOUR RATE= "LR
  280 PRINT
  290 INPUT "PENALTY RATE= "PEN
  300 PRINT
  310 VDU3
  320 CLS
  330 INPUT "PROJECT NAME    "A$
  340 PRINT
  350 PRINT "PLANNING START? (Y/N)";
  360 PRINT
  370 IF GET$="Y" GOTO 380 ELSE GOTO 350
  380 LET T=TIME
  390 ON ERROR CLS: CLG: GOTO 410
  400 PRINT
  410 FOR N=1250 TO 850 STEP -25
  420 VDU24,845;20;1260;1000;
  430 PLOT 69,N,100:NEXT N
  440 FOR M=100 TO 850 STEP 25
  450 PLOT 69,850,M: NEXT M
  460 FOR O=80 TO 1250 STEP 25
```

```
470 PLOT 69,0,850: NEXT O
480 VDU28,0,30,25,0
490 PRINT "WORK STUDY? (Y/N)"
500 IF GET$="Y" GOTO 1650 ELSE GOTO 510
510 PRINT
520 PRINT
530 INPUT "QUOTATION PRICE= "QP
540 PRINT
550 INPUT "DELIVERY PROMISE= "DP
560 PRINT
570 PRINT "PLAN FINISHED? (Y/N)";
580 IF GET$="Y" THEN GOTO 590 ELSE GOTO570
590 @%=&20209
600 LET PT=INT((TIME-T)/6000):PRINT;PT
610 PRINT
620 PRINT
630 PRINT "CONSTRUCTION START? (Y/N)";
640 PRINT
650 IF GET$="Y" THEN GOTO 660 ELSE GOTO 630
660 VDU28,0,30,25,0
670 ON ERROR OFF
680 LET T2=TIME
690 LET C=0
700 LET CR=0
710 ON ERROR CLG :GOTO 720
720 PRINT
730 FOR N=1250 TO 850 STEP -25
740 VDU24,845;20;1260;1000;
750 PLOT 69,N,100: NEXT N
760 FOR M=100 TO 850 STEP 25
770 PLOT 69,850,M: NEXT M
780 FOR O=80 TO 1250 STEP 25
790 PLOT 69,0,850: NEXT O
800 VDU28,0,30,25,0
810 INPUT "CO-ORD X= "X: LET X=X+850
820 PRINT
830 IF X=1849 GOTO 1190
840 INPUT "CO-ORD Y= "Y: LET Y=Y+100
850 PRINT
860 INPUT "SIZE 1,2,3 or 4? "Z
870 MOVE X,Y
880 LET W=1+RND(RISK)/100
890 IF Z=1 THEN PROCSIZE1:LET C=C+S1:LET CR=CR+S1*W
900 IF Z=2 THEN PROCSIZE2:LET C=C+S2:LET CR=CR+S2*W
910 IF Z=3 THEN PROCSIZE3:LET C=C+S3:LET CR=CR+S3*W
920 IF Z=4 THEN PROCSIZE4:LET C=C+S4:LET CR=CR+S4*W
930 CLS: GOTO 810
940 END
950 DEF PROCSIZE1
960 PLOT 1,25,0
```

```
970 PLOT 1,0,25
980 PLOT 1,-25,0
990 PLOT 1,0,-25
1000 ENDPROC
1010 DEF PROCSIZE2
1020 PLOT 1,100,0
1030 PLOT 1,0,25
1040 PLOT 1,-100,0
1050 PLOT 1,0,-25
1060 ENDPROC
1070 DEF PROCSIZE3
1080 PLOT 1,250,0
1090 PLOT 1,0,25
1100 PLOT 1,-250,0
1110 PLOT 1,0,-25
1120 ENDPROC
1130 DEF PROCSIZE4
1140 PLOT 1,25,0
1150 PLOT 1,0,100
1160 PLOT 1,-25,0
1170 PLOT 1,0,-100
1180 ENDPROC
1190 LET DA=INT(TIME-T2)
1200 ON ERROR OFF
1210 VDU2
1220 PRINT
1230 PRINT "TOWER-8"
1240 PRINT
1250 PRINT "(c) S A Bergen 1984"
1260 PRINT
1270 PRINT "PROJECT NAME "A$
1280 PRINT
1290 PRINT "QUOTE PRICE= ";QP
1300 PRINT
1310 PRINT "DLY PROMISE= ";DP
1320 PRINT
1330 PRINT
1340 LET PC=PT*PR
1350 PRINT
1360 PRINT
1370 PRINT "PLANNING COST= ";PC
1380 PRINT
1390 PRINT "ACTUAL DLY= ";DA/100
1400 PRINT
1410 PRINT "MATERIAL COST= ";CR
1420 PRINT "Risk Increase%= ";(CR-C)*100/C
1430 PRINT
1440 LET L=DP-(DA/100)
1460 IF L=0 THEN LET P=0 ELSE LET P=ABS(L)
```

```
1480 PRINT "LABOUR COST= ";DA/100*LR
1490 PRINT
1500 LET R=CR+PC+(DA/100*LR)
1510 PRINT "TOTAL COST= ";R
1520 PRINT
1530 PRINT "PENALTY= ";P*PEN
1540 PRINT
1550 LET S=QP-R-(P*PEN)
1560 PRINT "PROFIT= ";S
1570 PRINT
1580 PRINT "R O I%= ";S*100/R
1590 PRINT "Repeat? (Y/N)"
1600 VDU1,12
1610 VDU3
1620 IF GET$="Y" THEN CLG:GOTO 320 ELSE GOTO 1630
1630 PRINT "END"
1640 END
1650 PRINT
1660 VDU28,0,30,25,0
1670 LET C=0
1680 LET SUM=0
1690 PRINT
1700 PRINT "GO? (Y/N)"
1710 IF GET$="Y" THEN GOTO 1720 ELSE GOTO 510
1720 LET T=TIME
1730 PRINT
1740 PRINT
1750 INPUT "CO-ORD X="X
1760 INPUT "CO-ORD Y="Y
1770 INPUT "SIZE 1,2,3 OR 4="Z
1780 LET D=(TIME-T)/100
1790 LET SUM=SUM+D
1800 LET C=C+1
1810 LET M=SUM/C
1820 CLS
1830 PRINT
1840 PRINT "N="C
1850 PRINT
1860 @%=&20209
1870 PRINT "SUM=    "SUM
1880 PRINT
1890 PRINT "MEAN=        "M
1900 PRINT
1910 PRINT
1920 @%=10
1930 GOTO 1700
```

Appendix 18.1 Contract Conditions

The tower shall be built in accordance with the specification below.
The input parameters shall be entered by the tutor.
The winner shall be the player(s) achieving an ROI of 10 per cent or better with the lowest quotation price. In the event of a tie the shortest actual delivery shall decide.

General Information

The construction space is 16 × 30 feet.
X coordinate 0 to 400, Y coordinate 0 to 750, from bottom left corner.
Planning phase timed in minutes representing hours.
Construction phase timed in seconds representing hours.
Rates in pounds per hour, costs in pounds.

		Y		X	
Size 1	block dimensions	1	×	1	feet
Size 2		1	×	4	
Size 3		1	×	10	
Size 4		4	×	1	

Specification

The tower shall be centrally positioned on the construction space X axis. It shall be 12 feet wide at the base and 30 feet high. It shall have a platform at least 2 feet wide with upper surface at 30 feet vertically. Vertical walls 2 feet or more wide are deemed self-supporting. Vertical walls less than 2 feet wide must be braced by horizontal members at maximum intervals of 3 feet. The width of the tower shall not decrease by more than 2 feet in any 1 vertical foot. Butt joints between blocks are deemed sound if two edges are coincident for at least 0.5 feet in either X or Y planes. Only butt joints are permissible.

Glossary

Addition principle	If events are mutually exclusive the probability of one or other happening is the sum of their individual probabilities of occurrence.
Attribute	Quality ascribed to anything.
Balance sheet	Statement in money terms of assets, liabilities and capital relating to company. Report on stewardship of management.
Bayes' postulate	When prior probability is unknown it should be assumed to be equal when events are mutually exclusive.
Bayes' theorem	Theorem which revises prior probabilities in the light of further information to give posterior probabilities.
Budget	Short term (1 year) statement in money terms of plan of action. Predicts but does not authorize expenditure.
Capital	Stock of wealth. All material objects and real assets forming means of production of goods and services.
Capital budgeting	Investment decision-making procedures of company.
Catastrophe theory	Theory developed by Professor Thom to describe discontinuous jumps in many branches of science.
CDF	Cumulative density function. Probability that a continuous variable is less than or equal to some stated value.
Cell production	In group technology, a group of workers and tools making a family of components arranged to facilitate work flow.
Classical theory of organization	Fayol, Urwick, Mooney, etc. Centres on division of labour, definition of tasks, relationships, checks and authority. Pioneered management as a subject for study.
Communication	Exchange of information and abstract ideas by means of symbols. Includes, but is not restricted to, language.
Conditional probability	Probability of occurrence of some event given the occurrence of some other event on which it is dependent.
Conflict	Divergence of interests between individuals and groups and requirements of the job. Creative and necessary when overt but destructive when covert.

Glossary

Consolidated accounts	Accounts reflecting the interests of central financial controlling body when several companies are under common control. Usually parent company accounts.
Contingency model	Leadership model due to Fiedler. Preferred type depends on circumstances of tasks.
Control charts	Method of examining and controlling quality or defectives in manufacturing process. Two sets of limits 'warning' and 'action'.
Cost of capital	Return on investment to break even on project.
Cost–benefit analysis	Long-term comprehensive assessment, including side-effects, of costs and benefits of investment. May use teams of specialists to cover some aspects.
Costing, marginal	Prime cost plus variable overheads.
Costing, standard	All overheads allocated to products.
Critical path method	A network planning method.
Culture	The sum of beliefs, knowledge, attitudes, customs and patterns of thought acquired in social conditioning.
DCF	Discounted cash flow.
DCF yield	Internal rate of return on DCF basis. Discount rate that makes net present value equal to zero.
Decision tree	Decision-making technique. Can utilize probability assessments and Bayesian theory.
Delegation	The transfer of a defined level of authority to subordinate group or individual. Responsibility for its use remains with superordinates.
Depreciation	Accounts procedure for providing for renewal of fixed assets and ensuring that their consumption is reflected in selling price of product.
Differentiations	Personal and other factors inhibiting communication.
DCF present value	PV of Po received n periods hence is $$\frac{Po}{(1+i)^n}$$ when i is rate of interest.
Economic batch size	Batch size and frequency of production to give lowest overall costs.
EV	Expected value. Average of payoffs from possible events multiplied by probabilities of events occurring.
Financial ratios	Relationships between company accounts figures giving some insight into company health.
Gantt chart	Bar chart showing planned activities on a time base and achieved activities as a line alongside the planned activities.
Gearing	Ratio of fixed interest debt to shareholders capital plus the debt. US term: leverage.
Group technology	Manufacture of parts in families rather than in small numbers of individual parts. Improves resource utilization. See cell production.

244 Glossary

Hawthorne effect	Informal social patterns in work groups are more influential than physical conditions (from studies at Western Electric Hawthorne plant).
Kendall τ	Statistical test for correlations between quantities not on an interval scale.
Law of large numbers	Large samples tend to represent parent population better than small ones. Sampling error is inversely proportional to square root of sample size.
Least squares method	Method of obtaining line of best fit through data points by minimizing sum of squares of differences.
Line and staff organization	Line managers have direct responsibility for achieving objectives of organization. Staff functions assist and advise them.
Line balancing	In assembly and flow work each station must complete its op(s) in same time. Achieved by allocating same work content to each station per period.
Management by exception	System in which management attention is drawn to factors not meeting objectives, typically discrepancies between budgeted and actual costs in standard costing system.
Management by objectives	System in which targets of performance are set for each worker in terms of results.
Market segmentation	Differentiation between buyers/users of identical product in terms of relevant marketing characteristics.
Marketing	Function of assessing and converting customer purchasing power into effective demand for product or service.
Merchandizing	In USA: point of sale promotional devices and displays. In UK: sale of complementary products made by third party.
Method study	Systematic recording and critical study of existing and proposed ways of doing jobs, leading to more effective methods. Creative aspect of work study.
Morphological research	Study of the form of plants and constructions.
Motivation	Process of initiating and directing behaviour.
Multiplication principle	If two outcomes are independent, the probability of both occurring is the product of individual probabilities.
Network analysis	General term for planning and control techniques such as CPM and PERT.
Objective	A goal specified in quantitative performance terms to be achieved in a stated time.
Operations research	Application of scientific method to problems of directing large systems of men, machines, materials and money in industry, government and forces.

Glossary 245

Operations	Management of systems for the provision of goods and services. Subsumes manufacturing and production management.
Overheads	Sum of all business costs that cannot be traced to specific items of output or where tracing would not be cost effective.
Pareto analysis	Histogram displaying a characteristic, e.g. income, by classes, e.g. product types. Usually 80 per cent of income is due to 20 per cent of types.
Payback period	Time needed for investment proceeds to recover cost.
Pearson r	Statistical test for correlations between quantities on an interval scale.
PERT	Project Evaluation and Review Technique. Network planning technique.
Posterior probability	Probability arrived at by modifying prior probability after additional information has become available.
Prior probability	Initial assessment of probability of a given event occurring.
Productivity index	Dimensionless figure indicating relative productivity.
Project Sappho	Project set up to investigate R&D projects by measuring times to complete small sections and treating the whole statistically.
PDF	Probability density function. Expresses probability that a continuous random variable takes any defined range of values.
Process chart	Graphical method of recording sequence of activities in a work process.
Producer's risk	Risk that a batch of satisfactory quality will be rejected by sampling plan.
Quality control	In mass production interchangeable items are not identical. The customer specifies limits and pricing is based on achievement.
RPD	Research planning diagram. Network planning system presenting probability of completion against time.
Rate of return	Net profit on investment divided by capital invested.
Redundant	In imperfect communication systems more information than theoretical minimum is needed to avoid ambiguity and detect errors in transmission.
Risk	Uncertainty to which a probability can be assigned.
Rollback	Decision tree analysis by starting from final choices and proceeding back to initial choice.
SAMM	Sequence-attribute-modifications matrix approach for step-by-step activity examination.
Structure	Formal patterns in organizations and channels of communication.
Standard deviation	Positive square root of variance. A measure of dispersion.

246   Glossary

Slip chart	Method of monitoring progress of project by continuous comparison of planned and elapsed time.
Synectics	Creative solution in two stages: stage 1, 'make the strange familiar' by analysis and model-seeking; stage 2, 'make the familiar strange' through personal and direct analogy.
TA	Transactional analysis. School of behavioural psychology due to Berne.
Time span of discretion	Time elapsed before manager can be sure subordinate has not been substandard in use of discretion.
Two factor model	Herzberg motivation theory involving 'hygiene factors' and 'motivators'.
Uncertainty	Condition when outcomes cannot be predicted.
Utility	Relative values of possible outcomes taking into account preferences of decision maker.
Value analysis/ engineering	Application of techniques of method study to product design.
Variable	Any quantity which varies in measurement.
Variate	A quantity which varies with a given frequency distribution.
Variance	Mean of sum of squares of all differences between values of a variate and the overall mean of all values.
Work study	Generic term for techniques such as method study used to improve productivity.

Index

account
   capital and revenue 39
   depreciation 32–3
   profit and loss 32
Achilles heel 217
adherence to programme 129–31
analogue 217
analysis
   attribute 210
   break-even 12–13
   cash flow 34
   financial 34
   gap 10–11
   investment 54–9
   market/product 14–20
   matrix 213
   morphological 220
   multi-dimensional 213
   ratio 35–8
   systems 211
and-also technique 216
ATLAS 194
attribute extension 210

benefit analysis 210
Berne, E. 186
bias factors 204
big dream scenario 213
bookkeeping
   exercise 46–9
   system 38
brainstorming 215, 218
budget
   cash flow 35
   project 42–3
   R&D 42, 44–5
butterfly catastrophe 203–4

case study, Pyro Co. Ltd 224–32
cash flow
   budget 35
   product 27–9
catastrophe model 200–2
chart
   Gantt 76–7, 180
   gozinto 90–1
   operation process 92
   process control 99–100
   slip 85–6
check lists 216
communication
   differentiations 170
   exercises 162–9
   feedback 173
   feedforward 174
   language, first 171
   structure 156–7, 164, 166
company capital 30–2
composite listing 211
computers in R&D 177–84
   notes 181
   planning systems 180–3
   reports 181
   shareware 182
   tracking 181
contracts
   conditions for 133
   definition, legal 134
   documentation 136
   drafting 137–8
   drawings 138
   form of 134
   incentives 138–9
   quotation 140
   specification 135
contribution
   engineer's 2
   to fixed overhead 40
   focus on 157
costing
   marginal 39–40
   standard 40–2
creative stimuli 216
creativity 199–208
   discontinuity 199–200
Critical Path Method 77, 78, 97
cusp catastrophe 200–2

248 Index

decision
  make or buy 101–4;
    examples 112–14
  tree 65–7, 70
delphi 215–16
differing needs assessment 212

Easy Project 182
EMI scanner 194–6
  market 195
  rise and fall 195–6

Fiedler, F. 192
focus group 212
function
  accounts 27, 29
  commercial 6
  company 4–8
  density, cumulative 64
  financial control 6
  interfaces 7
  manufacturing 7
  marketing 13
  R&D 6
function analysis 210

gap
  analysis 9–10
  post-development 88
generic need assessment 211
Gordon method 219
group creativity 222
group techniques 215–16

idea generation 209–23
induced dissociation 217
information
  additional 61
  cost of 67–70
input–output technique 219–20
interface
  functional 7–8
  R&D/production 88
international plagiarism 217
inverse brainstorming 216

Japan External Trade Organization
  (JETRO) 117

Kepner–Tregoe method 221–2

language, effect of first 171–2
learning curve 135

management
  definition 1
  by discipline 143
  and engineering 4
  feedback/forward 172
  functional 1
  matrix 144–7
  project 1
  by project 144
  relationships 154
meetings 23
morphological research 213
Morton's rule 75–6
motivation
  contingency model 192–3
  Hawthorne effect 185
  leadership styles 190–1
  TA 186–91
  two-factor theory 191

negative bias 204
network diagram 180
new products 214
newspaper events 214

objective
  definition 158
  setting 156–9
observation 212
operation management variables 116
operations variables 123

payback period 55
periodic attitude audit 212
PERT 80–2, 84–5, 87, 180, 181
Philips 66; groups 215
planning
  CPM 77; advantages 78; disadvantages 78; exercise 87
  engineering 74–5
  Gantt chart 76–7
  Gantt–CPM 79–80
  network dummies 78–9
  PERT 80–2; exercise 87;
    status 84–5
  project 72
  R&D resource 20–2
  RPD 82–4
  strategic 10–12
  systems 180
positive bias 204
probability
  Bayes postulate 63

Index

Bayes theorem 63
  combined 62
  posterior 6
  prior, assessment 60–1
problem inventory 211
product
  loop 72–4
  structure tree 89–90
productivity 126, 131
project
  checklist 51–2
  decision tree 65–7
  leader/manager 151–3
  leader self test 153–4
  leader styles 155–6
  leader test scores 160
  life cycle 142–3
  management variables 116, 118
  merit number 53–4
  organization 142
  profile 52
  ranking 50
  resource allocation 147–51
  selection 51
  technical success 127
  variables 124; correlations 126
project management game 233–41
  commercial results 235–6
  construction phase 235
  contract conditions 241
  estimating under uncertainty 236
  input parameters 234
  planning phase 235
  'TOWER-8' listing 237
  work study 236
pseudo product test 210

quality control
  frequency distribution 93
  limits: confidence 97; design 95
  mean 94
  process drift 99
  sample size 96
  sampling plan 98
  standard deviation 94
  statistical 92–100

relevance trees 214
repertory grid 211

risk, definition 60
role playing 212

scenario analysis 213–15
Science Policy Review Unit (SPRU) 194
screening, multidimensional 16–20
seed trends 214
sequence-attribute modifications matrix (SAMM) technique 221
shareware 182
smoothing factor 205–6
splitting factor 205–6
SPSS package 117
strategy
  market 17
  product 10, 17
structure
  communication 156–7, 164, 166
  development 166
  feedforward 165
  financial 30
  organizational 169
  product tree 89–90
survey 212
synectics 215, 218
systems 217

technology, maturity of 100–1
think tank 215
time, control of 22
time lags 197
trend areas 214
trend people 214
trigger words 216
two-dimensional matrix 213

uncertainty
  decisions under 63
  nature of 60

value engineering 104–11
variable correlations 125–9

weak links 217

X-ray tomography 194
X-ray Tomoscan 195